BEHIND BLUE EYES

A Life of Pete Townshend

Geoffrey Giuliano

Hodder & Stoughton

First published in Great Britain in 1996
by Hodder and Stoughton
A division of Hodder Headline PLC

British Library Cataloguing in Publication Data

Giuliano, Geoffrey
Behind blue eyes
1. Townshend, Pete, 1945– 2. Who (Group) 3. Rock musicians –
Great Britain – Biography 4. Rock groups – Great Britain
5. Guitarists – Great Britain – Biography
I. Title
782.4'2166'092

ISBN 0 340 63266 6

Typeset by Hewer Text Composition Services, Edinburgh.
Printed and bound in Great Britain by
Mackays of Chatham PLC, Chatham, Kent.

Hodder and Stoughton
A division of Hodder Headline PLC
338 Euston Road
London NW1 3BH

Dedication

To everyone's crazy mother. To several exceptional teachers. To B. H. Mangal Maharaj and A. C. Bhaktivedanta Swami for giving me something to do. To Deborah Lynn Black for her loyalty and hard work. To Pete for the passion and Donald for his friendship and guidance. To my mate Tony Secunda, who passed away while I was writing this book. An insightful, intelligent, and impossibly amusing man. We still got the magic, baby! I'll miss our crazy phone calls.

To all unpopular kids everywhere. Don't give up. You will win one day! To the untold millions of innocent farm animals who die each year for no good reason. You will be saved. The game's much bigger than you think. We are all forever.

Turn off the telly. Don't throw stones. Forgive yourself.

Space lotus flying
Chrome yellow sorrow
Unfolding prism flower
Nectarine rivers flowing
Everything at rest

Perimiter/85

Contents

Introduction

Blood and Stone

For all that was good and bad about that long-ago renaissance we remember now as the sixties, Pete Townshend easily leapfrogs both dualities, bringing a whisper of transcendence into the heady hurlyburly of our spent youth. Still, Townshend never claimed to be any sort of leader, rather just a gangly, musically inclined punk from Ealing who got lucky. Lucky enough to recognize that secret swirling river of soulforce that snakes invisibly through our lives and into the ocean of eternity. Lucky indeed.

'I sing my song to the infinite sea,' he has written. 'Let me get back to the ocean,' screams the terminally displaced antihero of the Who's *Quadrophenia*. The anguished, unanswered cry for release typifies Townshend's plaintive thematic ideal.

To view Townshend as any sort of top ten pop star is to miss the boat. For all his towering self-doubt, legendary delusion, human frailty, and innate bitchiness, Pete Townshend, like it or not, is a teacher. Not especially powerful or deep by guru standards, nor overly compassionate or exalted, but a teacher nonetheless. From the moment he prostrated himself at the feet of the Great Silent Incarnation Meher Baba back in 1967, the die was forever cast.

In the spring of 1989, during the Who's reunion tour, I asked him how his inner life was rolling along. 'It's on hold at the moment,' he answered quietly between thoughtful sips of white wine. As if even the Great Manic God of the Windmill could ever hope to ebb the crashing wall of ocean that even now thunders in the distance. Despite the soap opera drama of our day-to-day illusion, it's the same for us all. For the skeptical god incarnates in our lives as death and endless (and painful) rebirth. To the faithful a healing, compassionate power 'closer to us than our very breath'. Something Pete knows well. *Behind Blue Eyes* is the exasperating, unlikely tale of perhaps our last holy fool and a delicate power of music and light. Over and again his great faith and love overcame his mile-high pain. Over and again we respond to his brotherly spirit and tender, tangible emotion. Blood and stone are very definite. Much like Pete.

Here then is a tasty portion of Pete Townshend for those of you curious as to just how much rope it takes to forever hogtie oneself to the whipping post of superstardom. 'I want to drown in cold water,' the tortured multimillionaire composer screams through his musical alter ego, Roger Daltrey, on *Quadrophenia*. Buck up, mate, you're already halfway there. With deep affection . . .

Giuliano
Skyfield Manor
Western New York
1995

1

Lifehouse: *Childhood Trauma*

It seems there are always a thousand surviving, aching memories even from the cushioned emotions of the child fresh from the womb.

– Pete Townshend, *Horse's Neck*

There is in him something of Peter Pan and the Lost Boys. Peering into those haunted, penetrating blue eyes, it is easy to conjure up images of that motherless band of unlikely heroes surviving on their own primitive code of honor, battling villains with guile, invention, and sheer bravado.

For Pete Townshend, everything seems to lead back to those wondrous, torturous days of youth, when fears are wrapped in swagger, vulnerabilities carve deep and jagged edges, and the world is viewed in bold strokes of black and white. Even today his belief system seems to hold fast to the elemental good versus evil that winds its way allegorically across *Tommy*, *Quadrophenia*, and the children's fantasy *Iron Man*, forging a theme over three decades of hits from 'My Generation' to 'Give Blood.'

While most of his g-g-g-generation have now become settled, surveying their lives in ever deepening shades of gray, Townshend, now entering his fifties, is still driven by the rage, passion, and pain rooted deep in his youth. That he has retained the clarity of his childhood instincts, along with a brutal honesty and creative nobility, is a wonder. That he has rescued the mystery, magic, and innumerable contradictions of his youth too is a large part of his remarkable genius.

On a balmy May 19, 1945, Peter Dennis Blanford Townshend was born at Chiswick Hospital, West London, just ten days after the Nazi surrender in World War II. 'I was conceived in Wales,' Townshend said in 1988. 'This I learned from a profile, the author of which managed to ask my mother questions I'd had the decency to avoid. It was useful to find out where I'd been conceived; for years I've been wondering why I'd mentally narrate my autobiographical writing in a Dylan Thomas-esque Welsh accent. My recording studio of twelve years lies less than half a mile up the bank from Syon Park and the nearby riverside house in which I was born. My mother only revealed my exact birthplace last year. The house was a temporary annex to the West Middlesex Hospital just after the war. This Christmas I had my picture taken with the members of "Hospital Alert" and I was searching for an angle for the newspaper reporter. I forgot I was born there!'

Cliff and Betty Townshend's first child inherited a musical birthright on both sides of his family going back two generations. His father, Cliff, made his reputation as an alto saxophonist with the Royal Air Force's renowned dance band, the Squadronaires, while his mother, the former Betty Dennis, was a featured vocalist with the Sydney Torch and Les Douglas Orchestras. 'My dad's a great player,' he said in 1979. 'Not a cowboy but a really great player. My mom was a singer. She was a bit of a cowboy.' Pete's paternal grandfather, Horace, played piccolo and flute as a member of the Jack Shepard Concert Review. Betty's father was a noted vocalist for the Black and White Minstrels, and her mother an accomplished singer and comedienne.

Cliff and Betty met and married in a whirlwind. Betty, like Cliff, was a member of the RAF. 'I was working in London [when one day] somebody phoned and asked if I would help them out because a girl vocalist was sick. So I said yes, and then met Cliff. I knew him for seven weeks but only on Sundays. So I actually really only knew Cliff for seven days before we decided we'd get married.'

The young parents moved into a two-story brick home on Woodgrange Avenue, Ealing, West London, but hardly to settle down. Young Pete would know a splintered, uprooted, nomadic existence. During the first three years of his life, with Cliff and Betty constantly on the road playing military bases and clubs all over Europe, Townshend scarcely saw his parents. Instead, he was left in the care of Betty's family.

'I was to be alone often, and remember waiting, but I was always sure they would come,' he has written.

Pete's eccentric Granny Denny, as she was affectionately called, made an enormous impact on his early life. 'I was a postwar kid,' reflected Townshend in 1995. 'I grew up with parents who came out of the end of the war with a great resilience, excitement, and big ideas, and I got a bit left behind for a while. My parents split when I was very young, and I was sent to live with my grandmother, who had just been dumped by a very wealthy lover. She was in midlife crisis. She was my age today, and I identify very much with this woman who had to look after me. She ran naked in the streets and stuff like that. She was completely nuts. She was a very strict woman and I hated her. I wanted my mum and dad back. I had two years with her before my parents realized they'd left me with somebody that was insane.'

'This is such a bizarre story . . . They used a four-and-a-half-year-old boy to try to *fix* a woman who was going mad. It was an irresponsible act.'

Mrs Dennis frequently left Pete alone late at night, and he would awake crying only to find himself in an empty house. He was also subjected to his grandmother's bizarre treks in search of discarded handkerchiefs and other bits and pieces that she would then recycle at home. One time Pete discovered a pound note lying on the ground. To his amazement, Granny Denny seized it from him, exulting, 'I told you, I told you! I've found a pound! I'll boil it up and it'll be as good as new!'

These early experiences were so deeply embedded in Pete's subconscious that he only recently came to the realization his lauded rock opera *Tommy* was not the fictionalized sixties allegory he had believed. Instead, according to Townshend, it 'was completely autobiographical. All I knew was that I spent time with a grandmother whom I didn't like very much. "See me, feel me, touch me." Where did that come from? It came from that little four-and-a-half-year-old boy in a fucking unlocked bedroom in a house with a madwoman. That's where it came from. I suppose that was the revelation.'

This pronouncement belied the notion that for a quarter century Townshend had ostensibly drawn the inspiration for his masterwork from the classic 1922 Hermann Hesse novel *Siddhartha*, along with his interest in Persian and Sufi poetry, and his inscrutable spiritual guide, Meher Baba. No one, not even Townshend himself, realized that the tragic hero of his story, deaf, dumb, and blind Tommy Walker, was in fact based on young Pete himself, at the very age he passed through his own childhood trauma.

'I was so earnestly trying to avoid writing something autobiographical,' contends Townshend. 'All of the Who's first work was about their early audience; we felt rock should be reflective of its audience. That was what was unique about rock 'n' roll as an art form. I tended to write, if not my own biography, certainly an encapsulated biography assembled from bits of the audience. Yet *Tommy* felt to me – when I was writing it – to be the exception to that.'

It all came together late in 1991. Townshend had just broken his arm while bicycling and was recuperating at his mother's. She had just started work on her autobiography, and Pete asked her about the time frame between the ages of four and six, which, except for a few isolated incidents, was a mystifying blank. 'She told me what happened,' says Pete. 'It didn't contain the kind of trauma Tommy went through, seeing his mother's lover shot by his father, but it was pretty damn close.'

Still, Townshend wasn't able to make the connection fully until he began working with Des McAnuff, the director of the new Broadway production of *Tommy*. He discovered that McAnuff's father, like his own, had been production of *Tommy* in the air force. 'It was very strange to sit there with Des,' he said, 'and find out I hadn't written a fantasy at all; I'd written my own life story. It's a metaphor that tells a story of postwar life, and I was the child of a postwar couple. When I wrote, "See me, feel me, touch me," I thought I was talking to my master [Meher Baba]. But what makes it really poignant, so wonderful, and so sublime a fragment is that it came from that place. I had no control over it.'

McAnuff, accomplished director of Broadway hits *Big River* and *A Walk in the Woods*, remembers Townshend 'striding around the room, ranting about [his] childhood,' which became fodder for the Tony Award-winning production's darkly surreal setting.

Through this emotional bloodletting, Townshend found a significant tie between his parents' reunion all those years ago and a key element in the musical. 'Fortunately, they did reunite,' he says today. 'Many postwar marriages had trouble. But I am eternally grateful to them for getting back together. And there is the answer to the question I'd always carried . . . the father prevails over the lover.'

The most extended visits with his parents were summer vacations at seaside resorts like Clacton and the Isle of Man, where Cliff and Betty performed numbers by Benny Goodman, Glen Miller and the like for eager holiday makers. One such interlude in the coastal hamlet of Filey provided Townshend's earliest memory – at age two alone on the dunes watching his parents horseback riding on the beach. 'I knew what I waited for, what I missed, but they stayed only a minute and were galloping off again laughing and waving. Once when I talked about this to my mother in later life, trying to express the depth of my emotions as a child, she replied that I must be mistaken.'

This telling recollection, culled from his short-story collection, *Horse's Neck*, published by Faber and Faber, is one of the few accounts in the book that Townshend admits was strictly factual. 'It's very autobiographical,' claims one unnamed insider referred to here as Kathy Browning. 'The problem is if you don't know Pete, you don't know where the autobiographical bit stops and the fiction begins. It all has to do with his childhood, which he's never really properly dealt with.'

The collection, true to its title, is filled with horses, an animal that is clearly significant to Townshend on many levels, each in some way tied to his parents.* There is little doubt Townshend associates the animal with frequent separations from his parents and the resulting alienation. As he himself admits, 'The horse is tied up with my earliest memories of my mother and father. They couldn't actually ride up, tether the horses, and sit down with me. Neither could they carry me

* It was even a beloved equine who opened the door to literature to Pete. As a result of his unstable early life he didn't learn to read until the age of seven. 'It was my grandmother who taught me,' says Townshend. 'She read halfway through *Black Beauty* and stopped. She told me if I wanted to hear the rest, I'd have to learn to read. I simply learned to complete *Black Beauty*.'

on the animal. They always seemed to be arriving and going away.'

A review of *Horse's Neck* by Diane Hatz, which appeared in a 1985 issue the Who fanzine, *The Relay*, offers a fascinating theory on Townshend's symbolism. 'At first you close the book and wonder why all the references to horses make no sense. But then it becomes clear the horse isn't the actual theme; the theme is what Pete felt as a two-year-old the horses deprived him of. In the first story, "Thirteen," Pete waits for a kiss alone on the beach, and when his parents come over to him on the horses they stay only a minute and then gallop off. The whole book is actually Pete's search for that "kiss." He searches continuously but doesn't seem to realize it wasn't a physical kiss he desired; it is the kiss of love he so desperately needs.'

Townshend's early memories gave way to a romantic yet unrealistic view of his parents. He rarely saw them in everyday terms, but instead on duneswept beaches in exotic locales. 'They seemed to me all the more idealized, especially when I was a tiny baby. They were so unbelievably, stunningly glamorous, and that has become my object. I used to see my mother as this fantastically glamorous figure who kind of shot in and out in a different outfit. I'm in pursuit of glamour, of utter corny makeup beauty. I was very distracted by the idea that because beauty came to me, that somehow begged a question about me and my beauty. They seemed to me all the more idealized, especially when I was a tiny baby,' he affirmed.

A focal point in his development was Townshend's intense love for his free-spirited mother. The idyllic view of his parents as romantic lovers, though, was shaken early on. His father often went out on the road, and finding herself alone for long stretches, Betty pursued a series of torrid affairs. 'She was very, very seductive,' relates Townshend, 'a little click-up nose, long dark hair, deep gypsy eyes, sinewy calves in seamed stockings. Mum was always surrounded by crowds of men. She had plenty of money, was on her own a lot and I think that caused the split.'

According to Pete, his mother thought nothing of using her own young son as emotional bait to pursue her tawdry romantic encounters. Townshend remembers a tactic whereby he'd climb into a pedal car strategically placed at the bottom of a steep hill. Betty would then proceed to push him upward, playing the damsel in distress. Inevitably, a male passerby would come to the rescue.

'It would be into a coffee bar, he would see her again, and I would be drawn into this tremendous deceit. When I saw my father, I would feel guilty because I'd been in bed with my mother and her lover.'

Some critics have suggested Freudian ties in the repeated sexual references of *Horse's Neck*, linking cryptic equine and female images, but Townshend contends otherwise. 'It's not, "I want to make love to my mother" stuff, but rather the idea is the first woman any child falls in love with is their mother. You fall in love with your mother, in most cases when she's in a kind of prime after a great act of self-sacrifice to bring you into the world. For the lucky child it lasts a long time, into infancy and possibly beyond.'

For Townshend, though, it was a love he felt was not really reciprocated. 'As a child I had a very strange relationship with my mother. She was very beautiful and married a goodlooking man, then had this very ordinary kid. She was loving, but I could sense her confusion and disappointment. I somehow failed to interest her once I stopped being a baby.

'I felt I had to prove something to her. So in the end I decided that because I couldn't change the way I looked, I would become a millionaire.'

Those thirteen summers spent in vacation getaways shaped his youth in a manner unique among his contemporaries. Townshend was witness to the last age of true innocence, a bygone era strikingly depicted one rainy evening in the Palace Ballroom on the Isle of Man. 'It was decadent and splendid when I watched my father's band and the well-dressed dancers there as a child. I sometimes lost myself in the perfume of petticoats when tipsy girls found the sight of a little boy in a ballroom amusing and sat me between them as they gossiped, squabbled, and talked about the men they fancied.'

Another realization culled from observing these performances was Pete's stirring sense of purpose in music. 'The war went on as far as my parents were concerned. They stayed in uniform until I was five years old. Music to me was about the Air Force and men in uniform. There was definitely a function to my father's music for people who were separated from their loved ones, or who had actually lost loved ones in battle. So music for me has always been a lot more than just mere entertainment.'

This exposure also opened up a deep appreciation for the composers and styles that preceded his own restless generation.

'It's interesting to me because I loved the music my parents played. I loved that big band stuff, the writing of Cole Porter and Gershwin and the lyrics of Johnny Mercer. And I still love the craftsmanship.'

Back home in West London, Townshend enjoyed his first taste of the spotlight at an early age. 'My ambition was to be a journalist. I remember when I was seven, I had my photograph taken by a reporter on a very hot day. The photo came out the next morning in the paper, the *Acton Gazette*, with a caption, "Young Pete Townshend with his dog, Bruce," and a quote from me: "It was so hot we had to sit down and rest. Life is such hard work round here." It was my first glimpse of success.'

Many of Townshend's boyhood days were spent reading adventure classics like *Treasure Island* and *Gulliver's Travels*, leading to a lifelong love of literature. Another favorite pastime was haunting the streets of Ealing with neighborhood chum Graham 'Jimpy' Beard, who still lives close by in Syon Park, running a video-rental company. 'Jimpy and I haven't strayed far from our roots,' commented Pete in a 1988 article in the London *Observer*, 'because we were so happy as small boys. I was content to live in his shadow then; not only did he lead every gang in our neighborhood but he seemed to intuit I was destined to be famous. Jimpy was a natural star, but not destined to be an entertainer because he wasn't insecure enough. Once, working overtime, he said to me, "Pete, you are more intelligent than I am, but you've got no common sense." A man who at ten years old could be as right as that about another man obviously doesn't need the sound of applause. We still love each other even though we don't meet more than once every ten years.'

Curiously, Jimpy didn't perceive this eloquent account of their perennial closeness on quite the same level. Shortly after the article was published, Townshend family insider Kathy Browning met up with Beard at a barbecue. 'I didn't realize you were friends with Pete for so long,' she proclaimed. 'Neither did I!' quipped the astonished Beard. 'I never see Pete. Suddenly, out of the blue he's written this article about me and we're great friends again.'

According to Kathy, the episode highlights Townshend's often problematic perception of reality versus fantasy, a toll of his sudden early fame and turbulent upbringing. 'He's not someone who had a lot of friends when he was growing up,' she says. 'He spent more time with his parents' friends than he did with kids his own age. I think Pete is one of those people who's never really known who his real friends are. He doesn't know who to trust.'

As Townshend grew older, accompanying his parents on the road began to have new meaning. Sitting at the front of the bus, he would watch his father hastily pen arrangements and ready his instruments. 'I got into rock 'n' roll in the first place because it seemed my father was allowed to have loads of fun and get drunk while he was working. It was fabulous, fabulous, fabulous!' Townshend refers cryptically to these days in the song 'Stardom in Acton,' from his 1982 solo work *All the Best Cowboys Have Chinese Eyes*: 'Born in a trunk got my home, got my car, got serenity.'

'Everywhere we could possibly take Peter, we did,' recalls Betty Townshend. 'So Peter was there, in front of the stand watching the rehearsals and always trying to sneak in round the back when he should be in bed. Watching the band, jumping, playing the drums. Oh, he loved music right from the word go.'

'It was my first taste of show business,' notes Pete, 'seeing my father on stage and hearing my mother on record. [She] started as a singer with the Squadronaires. On stage, my father always used to smile this plastic smile. That's show business. My father went berserk if I touched his instruments, because clarinets and saxophones are very delicate.

'That was what life was for me,' he added, 'putting bottles in and out of the beer crate and making the trumpet player happy, looking out the front of the coach from show to show.'

Clearly these times, as romantic as they seem, were a source of deep confusion in Pete's later understanding of family life. In 1968 he reflected on the deep frustration he still felt. 'I can't get my family together, you see. They were essentially middle class, they were musicians. I spent a lot of time with them when other kids' parents were at work. And I spent a lot of time away from them when other kids had parents, you know.'

The loneliness and alienation of his childhood only escalated as Pete neared adolescence. Just as his mother quit the road, finally settling down to run an antique shop on Ealing Common, a dramatic turn of events rocked his world: the arrival of two brothers, Paul in 1958 and Simon in 1961. For the sensitive twelve-year-old, on the verge of discovering his own masculinity, the idea of his mother, especially this sparkling, talented woman he so worshiped, having babies was shocking in itself. More significant, at an age when he most needed guidance and attention, it was lavished instead on his infant siblings. For Pete, his brothers were beneficiaries of the love he only sporadically received, from the mother he jealously adored.

The way Betty tells it, however, her involvement in the rearing of the younger boys wasn't significantly greater. 'It wasn't really difficult because I was lucky enough to have my mother, who was separated from my father. And my mother did most of the raising. I wouldn't say so much the manners and the sort of real raising you do with a kid, but she was always there to change nappies, see the washing was done, change the beds, and see that they got a meal when they got back from school. I was lucky because I had my mother, and I had au pair girls from Germany and Spain. We always had somebody living in. I started an antique shop at the top of the street. I got so bored with my mother looking after the house I took over this little business.'

Family friend Kathy presents a rare inside glimpse into the family psyche: 'Pete didn't feel he got the attention and love he needed from his parents. You go into the sitting room and the only picture on the table is of Pete, and yet I'm sure he thinks Betty's giving too much attention to his brothers. It was the same with Cliff. When he died [of cancer in 1986], Pete was upset, but I think he was more worried that his dad paid greater attention to his brothers than him.

'Cliff was a nice enough guy, but he had a mean streak. It's on the Townshend side, not Betty's. They're a screwed-up family, very artistic and ultra sensitive. They've all got this jealous streak. It stems from insecurity, not from something horribly wicked. Pete never felt he was getting the love he should from his parents, and they didn't think they weren't giving it to him. It's all in the perception.'

The vast age difference between Townshend and his younger brothers made it difficult to relate to them. In actual fact, Pete would never really know his siblings until some two decades later. 'He wasn't around much,' recalls Simon. 'He moved out when I was three. One time he came into the house, he had a key to let himself in, and I was in the hall. I don't remember what I did wrong, but he spun me around and slapped my bum. Then he went out and slammed the front door. I was standing in the hall crying, and then he came back in ten minutes later and we cuddled. Pete says he had to follow me around pulling my fingers out of electrical sockets. I had a nickname, "Screw Loose." I used to get a screwdriver and undo all the handles.'

Something else was going on behind closed doors with the Townshends as well. All three brothers were witness to the frequent destructive rages of Cliff and Betty. 'Many a time have dinners gone flying across the kitchen through the window,' revealed Paul. 'If you're brought up in an environment where everything's getting smashed and there's arguments all the time, it rubs off on you.'

'Peter has got my temperament,' admitted Betty in a recent interview. 'When he used to smash his guitars on stage, I knew that part of his nature came from me, because his father was such a quiet man.'

Mrs Townshend in particular, alleges Kathy, was at one time 'a raving alcoholic' prone to making nasty scenes in public. Browning relates an incident while on tour with the Who in the eighties when she approached Pete to pay a compliment to his mother. 'He turned to me and screamed, "Yeah? What are *your* parents like!" I later learned that Betty had been drinking again and had just utterly embarrassed Pete.

'Pete and his mother are looking for the same thing,' suggests Kathy of this complex relationship. 'They're looking for it in each other, and I don't know if they'll ever find it.'

When Pete was younger, his parents would often throw parties for their musician friends, where no doubt the liquor flowed freely and, according to Browning, the couple would frequently go out club hopping, often leaving Pete home alone. If true, it isn't hard to imagine Townshend's feelings of rejection and guilt. How could he help but wonder where he stood in their priorities? Was there something so inferior about him that they couldn't stand to be around him?

Entwined in this daily turmoil, Townshend emerged from childhood a self-described 'carnival freak.' Looking in the mirror, the already insecure adolescent saw only a gangly changeling whose nose ballooned between his sad, luminous, choirboy eyes. 'When I was in school, the geezers that were snappy dressers and got chicks years before I ever even thought they existed would always talk about my nose,' says Pete. 'This seemed to be the biggest thing in my life: my fucking nose, man! Whenever my dad got drunk he'd come up and say, "Look, son, looks aren't everything" and shit like that. He's getting drunk and he's ashamed of me because I've got a huge nose and he's trying to make me feel good.'

Attempting to ease his son's self-consciousness, Cliff Townshend often pointed to Ronnie Aldrich, the leader of his band, who also sported an enormous proboscis. 'Look at Ronny!' he would say. 'He's the conductor of a famous orchestra; he's got a beautiful wife, a beautiful home, a lovely car. He makes music everyday; he's a very well-respected man. What more can you want out of life? He's got a huge nose as well, Peter.'

'My mother too was no help,' remembers Pete. 'She seemed to think that anybody who wasn't beautiful couldn't be any good. She was gorgeous, of course. My father was very good-looking too. How they spawned me, I'll never know.

'I know it's huge,' Townshend said of his nose at another point, 'and, of course, it became incredible and I became an enemy. I had to get over this thing.'

Although Townshend didn't quite know it, the way over the hurdle would stem from a most unexpected source. Over the summer of 1955, Pete and his chum Jimpy, accompanied by Cliff, attended a special Saturday preview of the film *Rock Around the Clock*, featuring the music of Bill Haley and the Comets. Already displaying his propensity for setting trends, Townshend cooked up a prepunk hairstyle for the occasion, using soap to create a nasty-looking center spike, dubbing the do 'The Tent.' 'Neither of us were surprised it took twenty years to catch on,' says Pete.

'Haley gave a very good show. We had seats in the gallery at the very back of the old Odeon Marble Arch, and the walls rumbled and the floor moved.

'I remember a chill ran up my spine as I heard the native rhythms,' recalls Townshend. 'I looked round at my father and I said: "What is this amazing music?" He said, "Hmm, not bad." And that was really all.'

But for young Pete – who went on to see the film four times in a single week – the experience was a revelation. 'My grounding in music was trad jazz and a bit of classical thrown in after listening to my dad's orchestra, and then suddenly the miracle of rock 'n' roll, in the shape of Bill Haley, Cliff, and Elvis. Rock 'n' roll got into my blood as a new form.'

After initially borrowing a homemade guitar from a schoolmate, Pete was elated to receive his first true axe, albeit a cheap Spanish model with wire strings, from Granny Denny on his twelfth Christmas.

'My father was going to buy me a guitar for Christmas, and he would have bought me a fabulous instrument. But what happened is that she bought it! She bought me one like you see on the wall of a Spanish restaurant, a phony guitar. I was excited for a while, standing in front of the mirror, but I realized very quickly that I was never going to be able to play anything on it. My father said, "Well, let's see what happens." So I struggled with this fucking instrument for two years.'

Even at this tender age, Townshend grasped the notion that his 'way out' went far beyond seeking the fame, fortune, and 'pulling birds' that propelled many of his contemporaries. His own motivation existed on a much more primal level, that of emotional survival. 'I realized the only way I was ever going to fit into society and have a role was via the guitar,' he recounted in 1974. 'I really did think this. I thought, I'll go and shut myself in my room and I'll learn the guitar. And when I come out they'll want me.'

True to his quest, Townshend secluded himself for some two years. Strangely, although he came from a musical family, the Townshend home had no instruments, not even a piano. 'Although Peter was in the choir,' says Betty, 'I never thought he was particularly talented musically. Otherwise I would have bought him a piano.'

Like most of his famous peers, Pete was largely self-taught, although Cliff did pitch in briefly, demonstrating a few basic chords and advising his son to learn theory. 'My father always used to tell me to read music, otherwise I wouldn't get anywhere. Of course, this was the tradition he'd been brought up in. You walked into a studio, a session, or a gig, and they'd throw the music in front of you and you're supposed to be able to play it. Things are different these days.'

Still, Townshend regrets not heeding his father's advice. 'I wish I'd have done a bit more work at learning to read,' he confessed recently. 'Now I'm doing slightly broader stuff, going off into other areas than rock, trying to do film scores. Or somebody says to me, "That's a nice song, but I sing in a slightly higher key than you. Could you transpose it up?" I just wish I was a bit more musically literate.'

Why the Townshends didn't actively encourage Pete remains unclear. It's ironic, though, that those very elements propelled Pete's unrelenting drive to follow in their footsteps. 'I must have made an early decision,' he remarked in 1985, 'that my parents were getting something out of the music business they weren't getting from me.'

This partly explains why he didn't idolize or pattern himself after rock pioneers like Elvis Presley, Chuck Berry, or Buddy Holly. Instead, he threw himself into his instrument in a much more private quest.

When Pete emerged from his self-imposed labors he was no guitar wizard, but he knew how to handle the rudimentary chords. That he made any progress at all was an achievement, since his old guitar was constantly falling apart and by the end was reduced to only three strings.

At age fourteen, he entered Acton County Grammar School. 'When I was just four years old,' he recounts, 'I went with Jimpy through the hole in his garden fence onto the playing field across the playground and into the then modern school. I remember dozens of blue-uniformed boys tumbling down the stairs and gathering round us. They were friendly, and I decided then I would attend that school. I was probably wearing my favorite infant-school outfit. I had a Fair Isle pullover, brown boots, gray short trousers, of course, and blond hair. I was absolutely, perfectly beautiful.'

There he met up with John Entwistle, a quiet, lanky trumpeter in two bands, one of which was an after-school jazz quartet called the Confederates. Entwistle held the lofty distinction of having formally studied piano and horn, even earning a position in London's prestigious Middlesex Youth Orchestra. As with Townshend, his parents were both accomplished musicians, but unlike Cliff and Betty, the Entwistles encouraged their son from an early age to seek a musical career.

Townshend's call to rock was temporarily detoured by Entwistle's surprise offer to join the Confederates. With the carefree Dixieland sound all the rage, Pete somewhat reluctantly made the required switch to banjo. 'When John asked me, I had to rush out and get a chord book,' says Pete. 'I'd been buggering about playing guitar for nearly two years and wasn't getting anywhere. They expected me to play and were fairly impressed, which I couldn't work out.

Perhaps they thought if you could play three chords, you could play the rest.'

Through his tenure in the band, Townshend began to foster a close relationship with Entwistle, whom he would eventually call his best friend. Together they would walk to school, pausing at the local music shop. They gazed longingly in the windows, dreaming of one day owning handsome new guitars and becoming pop stars.

Townshend also remembers Entwistle's first show of loyalty. One day Pete bragged to his mates that he had finally conquered the rapid strumming technique showcased by the banjoist in Acker Bilk's band. 'The drummer sneered, but John stood by me. "If Pete says he can do it today, he's lying, of course. But if we pretend to believe him, he'll be certain to be able to do it next week!"'

Joining the Confederates proved to be rich experience for Townshend, who played a repertoire that consisted of the traditional jazz of such luminaries as Acker Bilk and Kenny Ball as well as the high-powered skiffle of Lonnie Donnegan and rowdy military marches like 'When the Saints Go Marching In' and 'Farewell Blue.' Pete enjoyed Dixieland, later remembering it as 'reverberant guitar music played by original three-chord 'East Enders'. He went on to explain, 'Rock was unglamorous in its early days. The stars were homosexual or suspected of it. Jazz had respectability.'

The Confederates had another great advantage: a ready-made audience consisting of members of the Congo Club, a youth center run by the Acton Congregational Church. Being the house band provided public gigs for the group, the first of which is memorable for Townshend's one and only attack of stage fright. As he stood before a group of nubile young ladies, his insecurity about his physical appearance bubbled to the surface.

'All of a sudden I'd become aware there were little girls giggling and pointing at me nose. And I'd think, "Sod 'em, they're not gonna laugh at me!" I'd get angrier still. . . . Most pop singers were pretty, but I wanted people to look at my body and not bother looking at my head if they didn't like the look of it. So I used to think, "I'll bloody well show them. I'll push me huge hooter out at them from every newspaper in England. Then they won't laugh at me."' In fact, legend has it that he used to stand before the mirror trying to reduce the size of his nose 'by osmosis.'

The Congo Club broadened his horizons in another way as well.

It provided his first exposure to gang violence, highlighted by a nasty brawl with a young punk who mercilessly bottled him one day simply for saying 'hello.' Pete refers to this as one of many incidents in his 'bullied childhood.'

'The Congo wasn't just a place where we got together and entertained the troops, as it were,' he later revealed. 'There was a lot of violence, sex and stuff going on. It was when I came closest to being part of a gang. I started to live in the real world after that.'

Exposure to this violence would ultimately fuel the famous Townshend temper. John Entwistle abandoned the Confederates for a more promising band, and Pete soon found himself dealing with a continuous revolving door of musicians. Adding to this dissatisfaction was the fact that Pete's focus in music had been evolving. By now he was studying the stirring guitar work of Hank Marvin, Eddie Cochran, and the aggressive R&B riffs of Memphis sensation Steve Cropper. More and more the Confederates seemed hopelessly out of touch The final break came one day when blows were exchanged between Pete and drummer Chris Sherwin, culminating with Townshend striking Sherwin over the head with his school bag, giving the poor lad a nasty concussion. That one rash act marked the immediate and permanent end of the group.

The unhappy incident had disastrous consequences. To his largely conservative schoolmates at Acton Grammar, he became viewed as nothing more than a moronic thug. As he slunk through the hallways, dodging the jeers and derogatory whispers of his peers, he vowed silently that he would one day eclipse them all. 'Despicable creatures that we are when we're children,' he has commented, 'absolutely hateful, spiteful, nasty, and bloody-minded. If you're suspicious of anybody you ostracize them. And if you can, you hang them on a hook.'

For the better part of 1959, Townshend became a pariah. At school he was rejected and ridiculed; at home he felt isolated, superfluous, and unloved. His self-esteem, always precarious, now sunk perilously low. He himself termed it 'a very bleak period. . . . I went into a shell.'

Moreover, he wasn't even part of a band anymore. So once again he turned inward. Putting aside the banjo, Townshend acquired a Three-L acoustic Czechoslovakian guitar from his mother's shop and started practicing with a renewed sense of purpose.

On a personal level, music provided a vital escape for Townshend, a release from the mire of his predictable and dreary daily existence. 'That's what rock says to life,' he once said. 'It says, "You know I'm hip, I'm happy, forget your troubles and just enjoy!" The songs I like, of course, are like "Summertime Blues". Man, that's beautiful. It says everything: don't have the blues, it's summertime. You don't get the blues in summertime! There is no such thing. That's why there's no cure.'

At least he still had the company of John Entwistle. 'After school,' reveals Pete, 'John and I used to hike about four miles from his house in Acton to mine in Ealing just so we could plug into my amp together. We were about fourteen years old. . . . Rehearsal over, we would trek another three miles and back for fish, chips, and some ancillary items. John prepared his food methodically, always peeling two saveloys and cutting meat pies into bite-size pieces before beginning. I should have realized such a sensuous being would cause trouble in the end; watching his long fingers dismembering a sausage could have caused an earlier introduction of Nazi Clause 28.'

In an uncanny foreshadowing of events, Townshend's acquisition of an amplifier would also provoke another tantrum. He remembers, 'One day my grandmother ran into the room and said, "Turn that fucking row down!" I did a Keith Moon, long before I'd ever met him. You think that's a fucking row? Listen to this! And I got my guitar and smashed it over my amplifier. The first guitar I smashed was because of her. John was in the room with me.

'I'd smashed a perfectly good guitar, but I'd symbolically smashed the guitar my grandmother had given me and exorcised the whole thing. From that moment on, I found I could really forgive her.'

While Townshend was honing his electric guitar skills, John Entwistle was making a formative transition of his own to bass. Influenced by the snaky twang of Duane Eddy, Entwistle too abandoned the tired jazz craze. 'I never really liked trad, but it is the only thing you can play with a trumpet,' he recalls. Few know that John actually 'built' his first instrument atop his mother's dining-room table and became one of the first to explore and refine many new riffs and effects of the electric bass.

Shortly afterward, armed with a second bass – this one reportedly smuggled out of a guitar factory by a friend – Entwistle formed two groups in succession: the Aristocrats and the Scorpions. Finding himself in need of a rhythm guitarist, he once again called on his Acton school chum.

For Townshend, Entwistle's inclusion represented his redemption. Not only was it the end of his humiliating ostracism at school, it meant he could once more play his music. Indeed, his stint in the Scorpions unveiled Townshend's vast improvement as a guitarist. 'I was terribly happy with it, and people quite liked us,' Townshend recalls. 'It gave me new confidence. I hadn't made it very well with chicks, and when my mates started to get it together with chicks, I was getting into the guitar. It became quite an obsession.'

While the Scorpions – with colleagues Mike Brown and Pete Wilson – represented a giant musical leap from the amateurish Confederates, Pete and his band mates were still unable to break free from the confines of the Congo Club. They were definitely a far better band, but still going nowhere.

By 1960, however, things began to change rapidly. Approaching sixteen, Townshend was about to graduate from Acton Grammar and his future was filled with uncertainty. Although he breezed through his final exams, his test scores to enter university were less than adequate. This left him with three choices: music school, art school, or get out and pound the bricks for a job. 'It was probably the horrible noise I used to make on my first electric that made my father suggest I go to art school and concentrate on graphics rather than music.'

At this point Townshend viewed his situation at home with a detachment that belied a racing undercurrent of torrid emotions. 'They were always very respectable,' he spoke of his parents in 1968. 'Nobody ever stopped making me play the guitar and nobody ever stopped me smoking pot, although they advised me against it.

'They didn't stop me from doing anything I wanted. I had my first fuck in the drawing room of my mother's house. The incredible thing about my parents is that I just can't place their effect on me, yet I know it's there. I can't say how they affected me. When people find out my parents were musicians they ask how it affected me.

Fucked if I know; musically I can't place it and I can't place it in any other way.'

Townshend ultimately decided to move out of the house in 1960 at the modest age of fifteen to share a flat with some fellow students. 'I hadn't had rows with my parents or anything like that. It was just that I wanted to do what I liked, play records right through the night if I wanted to.'

This newfound freedom spawned a period of intense rebellion, where his illicit activities included several petty burglaries. 'There were no hard drugs then,' he says. 'It was just a way of making easy money, usually through crime.' Comparing it to the far more insidious teen drug problem of today he observes, 'As I look back on it, it all seems unbelievably healthy. Teenagers should never experiment with heroin; they should stick to the tried and tested pastimes of sex and housebreaking.'

Still, living away from home was lonely, and he was often filled with uncertainty and despair. In *Horse's Neck*, he harkens back to those 'sad streets' and 'rows and rows of little terraced working men's houses two up, two down.' At one point he paints this haunting description: 'Later the grey darkness I remembered descended on Acton. The streets took on their familiar negative glow. The pavements tried to hide, the street lamps tried to fade, the front doors of homes full of people shouted, "Nobody home! No one lives here!"'

Meanwhile, only a neighborhood away, a young man named Roger Daltrey also suffered the effects of a problematic childhood. His golden, cherubic looks and choirboy voice belied a brash street fighter from working-class Shepherd's Bush. Since his family had moved to the more middle-class Bedford Park in Acton when Daltrey turned twelve, he'd been unable to fit in with his new classmates, who jeered at his cockney accent and abrasive streetwise manner. As a result, he, a year ahead of Entwistle and Townshend, honed a reputation as a tough guy, joining a gang and acting out his rebellion in the halls of Acton Grammar. In fact, Daltrey would be dismissed from the school for several blatant acts of belligerence, including smoking and refusing to wear his school uniform.

In rock, Roger, like Pete Townshend, found himself. 'After I saw Lonnie Donnegan and Elvis Presley, I never wanted to be anything else,' he confided in 1982. 'Rock 'n' roll saved my life. A lot of my mates, the fellas I grew up with, ended up in jail. After I took my eleven-plus exams I was sent to Acton. But where I came from, I didn't know people like I met at Acton Grammar. I thought everybody talked like me until I got there. . . . I loved rock because they hated it.'

Unlike the self-absorbed Townshend, the tough-talking Daltrey was the envy of school – and the leader and guitarist of one of the best young bands in West London, the Detours. What's more they were actually playing weddings, graduations, and bar-mitzvahs. Soon Daltrey, seeking a stronger lineup, invited Entwistle to join. In turn John, realizing the shortcomings of Detours' guitarist Reg Bowen, persuaded Roger to drop him in favor of his longtime band mate.

Well aware of the gangly boy, Daltrey often referred to Townshend as 'a nose on a stick.' Still, secretly he sympathized with Pete. 'There was a group of about ten of us, the worst lot at school. I remember Townshend, and I know he used to have a hard time, but we never gave him a hard time. We were yobs, but we weren't bullies.'

Joining the band was a watershed for young Townshend. Daltrey's invitation made such a marked impression that Pete was able to recall the precise 'sacred spot' where it happened, the foot of the southeast staircase at Acton Grammar (the very same place where the uniformed students greeted him as a youngster a decade earlier). 'When Roger hit me with the question "Want to join my band?" he said it in such a way that if we had been from a different class he might have added, "It'll look good on your university entrance form." Even though it took me a year to accept his offer, it was the greatest moment in my life.'

Townshend fully realized he was about to cast his lot with a formidable, headstrong individual whose fiery temper would rival his own. 'If he had ever said, "Come out to the playground and I'll fight you," I would have been down in one punch. Music was the only way I could ever win. But I've despised him ever since.'

From this point on, Townshend's relationship with Entwistle would never be the same. Daltrey was a volatile wedge that left the pair distant bookends, straining the idyllic, uncompromising ties of adolescent camaraderie. As Pete recently observed, 'Our respective fingers were to move over respective guitar fingerboards, never more than thirty feet apart, for nearly thirty years. In the gap between us was to stand Roger Daltrey, whose guitar-playing fingers were bleeding the first night I played in Chiswick with his group.'

The tumultuous days of what would become a band famous for their savage infighting had begun.

2

Mirrored Sky: *The Detours*

Pete was the thing that made it happen for us. The day he joined there was a real difference. The whole thing of genius is that it's very close to madness, and it's the same with Pete.

– Roger Daltrey

At first the name Detours proved an all too fitting moniker for young Townshend's passionate goal of playing real live, blistering rock 'n' roll. Daltrey's boast of making 'good money' turned out to be a fairly hollow promise as the band listlessly churned out the colorless hits of the day for company picnics and kiddies' birthdays. Pete's role as rhythm guitarist in the tatty five-piece outfit was augmented by Daltrey on lead guitar, Entwistle on bass, sales representative Colin Dawson on vocals, and bricklayer-drummer Doug Sandom, the group's elder statesman.

For months they languished in relative obscurity. Their rawness was reflected in their constructing their own instruments in the tradition of Entwistle. '[Roger's] guitars were quite good except the necks kept folding up,' noted Townshend. 'He played one until about 1962. I cut a solid state out of a block of wood (which Roger helped me file down) to which we then added the neck of my Harmony guitar and some pickups.'

Theirs was the archetypal portrait of the expectationless back-street band, spending whatever meager income they'd earned hiring transport, looking to catch that one big break. 'It was a bit of a dreamland,' admits Pete. 'I remember going in for lots of things like Butlins' holiday camp auditions and failing.'

Enter Betty Townshend. Witnessing the unflagging determination of the boys – to the point of their sneaking into the Daltrey home to rehearse when Roger's parents were out – she decided to lend a hand, squiring the band around in her shop van over the objections of Cliff who, says Betty, 'didn't want to know.'

'I helped manage the band when they first started,' she remembers. 'I used to ride them around in a little yellow van and cart all their gear about. I helped as much as I could because I could see the potential. I used to hear them upstairs making all that noise. I told Cliff, "I'm going to try to help them because the only way of gettin' rid of them is to help them." Seeing that they don't live here forever.

'I didn't hang around and wait for them, though,' she admitted. 'Mainly I used to deliver the goods, come home, and then go back and pick them and the gear up. Very seldom did I want to stay with the noise.'

Betty also began to book gigs for them. 'I loved it,' she confessed. 'I got in touch with all the people I knew in the business, and practically all of them gave them jobs.'

Thanks to Betty's contacts, the Detours caught their first major break: an audition at the Oldfield Hotel, Greenford, for West London's top promoter, Bob Druce. Druce's Commercial Entertainment Limited supplied acts for pubs and dance halls throughout the city, but mainly across the sprawling Acton-Ealing-Greenford triangle.

The audition, however, was a daunting experience. Doug Sandom recalls that Townshend's face was 'white as a sheet,' and even the intrepid Roger Daltrey was nervous as hell. After completing four numbers during the interval at the Oldfield, the compere placed the band's fate in the hands of the audience. 'Are the Detours in or out?'

The crowd's exuberant cheers were enough for Druce. He immediately signed the band to an exclusive contract. He took 10 percent for management and an additional 10 percent agency commission, but left the band free to pursue their own work on weekends.

Actually, those weekend engagements initially proved most lucrative. 'We used to supplement our regular money from the Druce gigs by doing weddings and things,' reveals Townshend. 'At the end of the evening, you'd get some bloke come up pissed as a rat, determined to spend as much money as possible on his daughter's wedding. "You were great lads," he'd say. "Here's fifty quid."'

Another good word from Betty landed the boys an engagement at an American servicemen's club called Douglas House in London for a hefty seventy-five pounds. 'It was a USAF club,' says Townshend, 'and they would have country bands on. Because of my parents' connections, though, we got the date and eventually the band we replaced was my father's!'

That occasion served unequivocal notice to Cliff Townshend that not only was his son tenaciously determined to pursue his own musical career, but that it was now time for the torch to be passed. 'I remember the day my father handed over to me the function he felt he had been carrying out until the sixties,' says Pete. 'He said, "Things have changed, Pete, and now it's your turn." He knew that the war was finally over, and he never complained when rock 'n' roll usurped his audiences; few of the real musicians of the old big-band order complained.'

By all accounts, the early Druce gigs were a tough slog. Hauling gear was arduous, especially mounting Entwistle's vintage oversize Goodman amplifiers atop Betty's modest van. Then they had to endure the trips to and from gigs. One of the longest rides was to Broadstairs, a seaside resort for retirees with barely a dozen teens in residence. 'It used to be a bloody nightmare,' remembers Daltrey. 'John, Pete, and I used to go with Betty. Pete would sit in front with her, and we used to lay on top of the gear in the back of a five-hundred-weight van with the roof about three inches from our heads all the way to Broadstairs.'

For Townshend, though, those were essentially good days. 'The group was doing okay,' he remembered in 1974. 'We were doing five gigs a week in pubs and getting twelve quid a night split four or five ways. It would be blasphemous to say it was tough. We were young and enthusiastic. Actually, I think it's tougher now I'm a so-called millionaire. I find it troublesome leaping twenty feet across the stage getting housemaid's knees. No, I don't remember it being tough at all; I hated the long journeys, but one gets used to that.'

Eventually Druce broke down and shelled out forty quid for the band's own transport, an Austin van formerly used by the Post Office. The boys promptly turned the old rig into pop art in motion, painting bold strokes of red and maroon scattered with footprints. Daltrey's contribution was a welded black pipe designed to depict a chimney.

Townshend's inventive logo, however, was most striking. Alongside the white-lettered 'Detours' boldly painted on each side of the van, Townshend added a simple yet visually striking arrow. The idea, he joked, was that motorists would see the 'Detour' sign and blindly obey it, following the arrow around and around until it finally halted outside the band's destination.

At this point the Detours' repertoire was still very much a mixed bag: a bit of top ten, some country, instrumental covers of the Ventures and Tornadoes, even the occasional pop ballad made famous by middle of the road crooner Andy Williams. The group was generally billed as the Detours' Jazz Group on the strength of their well-known trad jazz medleys. Their wardrobe matched the conservative format with purple jackets, white shirts, and bow ties, designed by Townshend at Druce's request.

By the end of 1962, the band was working several popular night spots, notably the White Hart Hotel in Acton and the Goldhawk Road Social Club in Shepherd's Bush, which supported many of London's premier bands. Leading the pack were Screaming Lord Sutch and the Savages (whose lineup boasted future stars pianist Nicky Hopkins and guitarist Jimmy Page) and the Undertakers, who lived up to their outrageous billing with band members swooping in and out of makeshift coffins on cue.

John Entwistle noted that this bizarre atmosphere brought out the mischievous side of the Detours. On one occasion, for instance, the band shared the bill with a teen pop band called the Herd, which featured a baby-faced Peter Frampton. 'For a laugh,' Entwistle remembers, 'I tied Frampton to a radiator by his scarf and wouldn't let him go on stage.'

One of the foremost headliners of the day was Johnny Kidd and the Pirates. With frontman Kidd gamboling across the stage, leering from beneath his trademark eye patch, the band performed a ground-breaking brand of rock and rhythm and blues that instantly grabbed Townshend's attention. Pete was especially taken by their unique four-piece concept that eliminated the rhythm guitar player.

Pirates manager Tony Secunda remembers, 'Townshend always kept a close eye on the Pirates. It was my first band, and they were doing some pretty interesting things despite the obvious corniness of the pirate shtick. Mike Green, the guitarist, used to play lead and rhythm at the same time, probably because they were one member short, but it turned into this big revelation. For sure Townshend copped the idea for the Who. I used to know him to have a drink with, but he was a surly geezer and deeply jealous. When I managed the Move sometime later, there was incredible competition between them and the Who. People like the midget [Roger Daltrey] took it in their stride, but with Pete everything was always very personal, a real knife in the chest.'

Pete's attraction to the four-piece band, coupled with Roger's constant lobbying for a tougher, more earthy sound, brought about a key change. The Detours abandoned the traditional quintet format in favor of this bold new approach. In the process Daltrey handed over guitar duties to Townshend and promoted himself to vocalist.

This shift left singer Colin Dawson the odd man out. Pete, for one, wanted the Danish bacon representative immediately dropped. Dawson, with his lounge-lizard crooning, was hardly the figure to carry forward the emerging rock banner. According to Doug Sandom, 'Peter always used to say, "Look at him standin' there wigglin' his bum." He didn't like that. Peter would rather see somebody jump about or at least play guitar while singing. He had to go, he was fated to go.'

Although Townshend had now begun airing his views, Daltrey was still very much in charge. 'Roger was really the balls of the band and ran things the way he wanted,' says Pete. 'If you argued with him, you usually got a bunch of fives. It was good in a way because every band needs someone in that strong, pushy role.'

This had its negative side too, though. 'I used to respect Roger for his strength and as a leader,' Townshend commented in the mid-seventies. 'But he was still very much a thug in my eyes, not willing to listen to anyone else's opinion unless it fitted his own. He used to deal with opposition by saying, "If you say any more, I'll smash you!"'

With Dawson's departure came a change in the band's material. Daltrey's full-barreled vocals were hardly suited for the lightweight Detours catalog. No gentle balladeer or country warbler, Roger began introducing Motown and rock staples into the set. Interestingly, today, Daltrey readily admits he wasn't really up for his role as the band's front man. 'When the group started, I was a shit singer. They didn't need a singer in those days anyway, they needed somebody who could fight and that was me.'

This dynamic shift soon set them apart from the booming Merseybeat of Gerry and the Pacemakers, the Dakotas, and, most notably, the white-bread Beatles. There was no longer anything remotely tame about the Detours. Rather, something powerful and challenging was clearly in the works.

What added potency to the Detours' manic musical mix was their utilization of high-octane Marshall amplifiers, which Entwistle contends Townshend was the first to use in performance. The pair would frequent John Marshall's shop in nearby Hanwell, and at one point they asked him to custom-design their equipment. 'I said, "Make it bigger," ' recalls Townshend. 'John's eyes widened, and he said to the engineer sitting behind him in the shop, "Pete wants it bigger!" ' Townshend would later regret his words when the Who's distinction as 'World's Loudest Rock Band' would land them in the *Guinness Book of Records* and cause the musician permanent and painful hearing damage.

With Townshend taking over on guitar, Entwistle was free to indulge his desire to play a much more active bass, a role Jack Bruce would perfect three years later in Cream. 'The Who sound came from us playing as a three-piece band and trying to sound like more,' Entwistle stated in 1979. 'I certainly played standard bass, but I combined it with long runs where I took over lead while Pete bashed out the chords.'

As for Townshend, the musical environment around him was sadly lacking. He later dubbed it 'a pre-Beatles period when the Fabians and Neil Sedakas and that kind of empty artist were jumbled up and lumped in with the Everly Brothers and the Dions, making it very hard to see the forest for the trees.'

During the day Townshend attended the progressive, free-thinking Ealing Art School, where his contemporaries included Queen's Freddie Mercury, Roger Ruskin Spear of the Bonzo Dog Doo Dah Band, the Kinks' Ray Davies, and Ron Wood. Townshend pursued a four-year program of graphic design, with a specific interest in newspaper layout, but his first love was, predictably, still his music.

Pete's fortuitous meeting with American photography student Tom Wright was the beginning of a friendship that would endure for three decades. As it happened, Townshend was strumming on a borrowed guitar in the Ealing Art School common room when Wright, suitably impressed, offered to share his collection of blues records in exchange for a few lessons.

Townshend's frequent visits to Wright's spartan Sunnyside Road flat, right across from the college, provided an education itself in the form of Wright's gargantuan collection of jazz and R&B recordings. Pete, who'd never even owned a record player, was introduced to a whole new world.

'I heard everything for the first time, you know, the genuine article, the original version of "Rock Island Line" and stuff like that. Chuck Berry in large doses and Ray Charles. I discovered the blues, R&B, and suddenly realized I'd opened a treasure chest. People like John Lee Hooker had been recording since 1943. It was amazing to hear his first electric guitar recordings, which were some of the wildest you'd ever heard and done straight onto disk. It gives you a certain depth in your perception of the artist.'

Of all the music he was ingesting, it was the 1962 super hit 'Green Onions' by Booker T and the MGs, that Townshend dubbed his 'ultimate favorite,' because of Steve Cropper's economic, soulful guitar work. A few years later Pete, with a handful of hits of his own, finally realized the opportunity to introduce himself to his idol.

'I went up to Booker T and said, "Hey, I'm a big fan of yours, it's really good to meet you." He said, "Oh, thank you, what's your name?" and I said, "Pete Townshend." He made a very thoughtful face and said, "Oh, I must remember that," and just walked off. And I thought, "He will remember!" I laughed like a little teenybopper. I suddenly figured I was running around the guy like a child and he just treated me the way I treat teenybopper fans and yet I heard they never got that kind of treatment. They never had anyone run up to them and freak out, let alone a twenty-two-year-old man come up and start frothing all over them. Of course, he took it perfectly straight. He was soulful and very gentlemanly. He approached it sanely, steadily, coolly and politely.'

Apparently it was a lesson Townshend himself would not learn particularly well, as his own future hit-and-miss interactions with fans would show. It was these salt-of-the-earth artists, the pioneers, who drove and stretched the growing musician toward levels of heretofore unattainable perfection.

'When I was a kid of twelve or thirteen,' Townshend remembered, 'I could learn records in a couple of days, and I was playing the same licks as the guy on the LP. That gave me satisfaction for a little while, and then I thought, "Why am I bothering to copy this guy who can only really play as well as I can?" Then I started going beyond that.'

Pete soon found, though, that translating the shattering music of his idols wasn't so easy. 'I was getting to the point where I'd play and, I mean, I still can't play like I want to. When the Who first started, we were playing the blues, and I knew what I was supposed to be doing but I couldn't do it. I couldn't get it out. I knew what I had to play, it was in my head. I could hear the notes, but I just couldn't get them out on the guitar. I knew the music, I knew the feeling of the thing, the drive, the direction and everything. It used to frustrate me incredibly.'

As 1963 progressed, Pete experienced significant growth on many fronts. Ealing Art School, which Townshend confesses he entered 'with a blank mind,' was exploding with all sorts of new ideas. 'It was a great period,' he says today. 'I had a natural artistic bent, which was why I ended up at art school. I should have done something with writing, I suppose, but if I had I probably wouldn't have ended up so open-endedly creative as I later became.'

All told it was a time of great adventure and enlightenment for Townshend, who found himself thrown headlong into the emerging cultural movement of the sixties, a time when long-standing traditions in the arts were steadily breaking down. Pete dove into this new, rapidly evolving, avant-garde environment, soaking up lectures by playwright Dave Mercer and American pop artist Larry Rivers. 'There would be lessons where you listened to jazz or classical music or explored minimalism,' Townshend recalls. 'We had jazz musicians and film writers, playwrights; it was a clearinghouse, and music was something that was very much considered to be okay and not something you did only after hours. It was part of life. You could sit in a classroom with people painting and playing. I used to do it.'

At the heart of this renaissance swirled a new, holistic approach to art called cybernetics, which combined science with acting, sculpture, linguistics, and even automation. Townshend recalls taking on several abstract projects, one of which found him dispensing with the use of his legs for a trolley cart he pushed around for several weeks! Further, he chose to communicate via a self-invented phonetic alphabet.

Yet it was his role as campus dissident that would most strikingly shape his future. 'When I was at art school I became a sort of communist,' he admitted in 1966, even joining such leftist organizations as the Campaign for Nuclear Disarmament and the Young Communist League. 'I still stand by the Young Communist principles. If I was in Russia in some harsh five-year plan, if it was for the good of the country I wouldn't mind. I would get great joy out of seeing something done.'

Though he would later scale down his political philosophy to that of socialism, this lashing out against the rigid, centuries-old conventions of British society would figure prominently in future rock anthems like 'Baba O'Riley,' 'Won't Get Fooled Again,' and, later, 'Eminence Front.' Bucking the established institutions with their inequities and pompous mores was a theme he would repeat and refine over the years, applying it across a web of art forms with increasingly sophisticated results.

As an artist Townshend was only beginning to understand the implications of his unique historical position as a war baby. As he put it, 'All the old soldiers were coming back from war and screwing until they were blue in the face, and this was the result. Thousands and thousands of kids, too many kids, not enough teachers, not enough parents, not enough pills to go round.'

Pete was enjoying a growing personal confidence as well. 'I soon decided I was going to get nowhere as an introvert and that I'd become an extrovert and that's what I did.' His newfound self-assurance got a boost from the outgoing ladies on the Ealing campus. 'Incredibly beautiful women would talk to you without needing to see your credentials. I took such a step forward, discovering that women actually talked to me. Discovering that women were actually approachable human beings. Having been to a boys' school it took me about a year to get over that.'

In this first heady rush of acceptance, Townshend nearly bottomed out for good. 'I fell in love with a girl,' he related in 1986. 'This was a couple of girlfriends before I met my wife. I realized this girl (who I'd really put on a pedestal) was interested in me. I told her an enormous amount of lies, created a fantasy. I said that the group was very popular. This was when we were still playing in pubs and stuff. I said we played jazz because she was a jazz fan when we were really just a rock 'n' roll band doing a few R&B songs on the side. It was really quite pathetic. Anyway, one day it became clear she was very, very interested in me. The penny dropped one afternoon when we were sitting in some park. I was faced with the fact that this girl was interested in me and I didn't really know how to take it. Obviously, at that point I couldn't tell her the truth. I don't know how it would have made any difference, she probably knew anyway. I lucked out, though, when she went off with another guy, dropped him a couple of weeks later, and then went back with her boyfriend, who really was a jazz player.

'I remember thinking how lucky I was I hadn't gotten into an adolescent affair on the rebound with this girl. Because if she'd dropped me the way she dropped him I would have killed myself. There's absolutely no question about it, I would not have been able to stand it. A couple of later incidents showed me I wasn't strong in that way, my ego was so fragile. I used to get suicidal about broken relationships with people I didn't even like.'

Interestingly, Townshend would make the same mistake two decades later, an infatuation recalled in the passionate 'Somebody Saved Me' from *Chinese Eyes*: 'You would have thought I had learned/Twenty years ago or more/A beautiful girl raised her mouth and yearned/But I didn't know what lips were for.'

'I wrote it after I made a complete fool of myself,' confesses the self-described 'sentimentalist.' 'All of a sudden, without actually realizing it, I fell in love with somebody I'd never even met! Really falling to the extent that I was feeling tremendous physical pain at the separation from this person. It happened in America and suddenly when I got back to London I realized I'd been very, very lucky I hadn't been able to reach this person. It reminded me of what happened when I was at art school.'

Townshend's misfortunes with women were in stark contrast to Daltrey's reputation as a ladies' man, which was to long remain a sore spot for Pete. This had been apparent from the very beginning. 'In 1961,' Townshend recalls, 'on the way to my first rehearsal I saw a beautiful blonde girl running toward me. She was weeping, and my adolescent heart went out to her. For a second I faltered because I realized she was approaching me. "Are you going to Roger Daltrey's house?" she demanded. I proudly confirmed her suspicions. "Well then," she sputtered, "you can tell him it's either me or that guitar of his!" She then burst into tears again and flounced off into the night. As far as I could project, it was quite clear the Detours were finished, and I popped along to Roger's to let him know I didn't mind and would probably be quite happy back at Sea Scouts. But Roger chose his guitar, and the first rehearsal went well, with no mention of the pretty girl, whom I never saw again.'

There would, of course, be endless lines of pretty girls parked at Daltrey's doorstep, which only served to highlight Pete's still painful memories of adolescence, where the 'geezers who got the chicks' would rub in their conquests by teasing Townshend about his nose. 'Roger's a great-looking guy who could probably seduce any woman he wanted to. But with me it's different,' he lamented.

Roger boasted, 'I was the original pop star, knocking off as many birds as you could get in one night. Pete's got a bit of a chip because I used to get all the girls.'

Townshend found some retaliation in dating Daltrey's younger sister for a time during art school, but his main weapon was always his guitar. John Mendelsohn of *Rolling Stone* suggested that any bid of Daltrey's to be promoted as a sex star in the mode of Mick Jagger was blocked by Townshend's determination to draw attention to himself with his instrument. Even in those early days, Mendelsohn noted, 'No sooner would one focus on Daltrey than Townshend just to his left would go slashing at his guitar so ferociously that it could have been God himself up there strutting in Daltrey's place and one still would have *had* to watch Townshend.'

Pete figured it was his only way to draw a girl's attention away from his hooter. 'I figured that one day someone would fall in love with me because I was a genius guitar player.'

This jealousy became the source of a deep rift that began to surface between the two band mates. On an even more basic level, the wedge stemmed from the unmovable British class system. To the rough-cut Roger, Pete was decidedly middle class, the son of two prominent artists, the soft, privileged student who'd never done a lick of hard labor in his life. Although Townshend was supplementing his income with stints as a milkman and later a butcher's boy (Entwistle worked as a tax clerk for the Inland Revenue), that could hardly compare with Daltrey's grinding day job as a sheet metal worker making cabinets for scientific instruments. 'He's never known what kids really have to do,' insisted Roger. 'He did rough it a bit in art school, if you call that roughing it.'

Countered Pete some years later, 'I used to take it on the chin when Roger would do an interview and say: "I'm working class, but Townshend isn't."'

With their personal tensions, Daltrey wasn't even sure he wanted to keep Pete in the band, as evidenced by the following telling incident. The Detours auditioned for a residency at a pub in Willesden, and afterward, while Pete was in the hall packing away the instruments, the promoter motioned John, Doug, and Roger into the bar for a drink. 'You're a good group, fellas, but there's a problem.' He nodded in Townshend's direction. 'Your mate, the guitarist. You drop him, find someone else, and I'll sign you right now.'

Daltrey's ears perked up. 'Well, we'd have to think about it, but maybe it could be arranged,' he ventured cautiously.

With that the older and wiser Sandom got a quick handle on the situation. 'Fuck off!' he barked to the astounded promoter. 'Either you take us as we are or you can get stuffed.'

A new element in Townshend's life would alienate not only Daltrey but the rest of the group as well: Pete's introduction to dope by his American flatmate, Tom Wright. Still largely unknown among the budding rock community, marijuana had long been the drug of choice for jazz musicians across Greater London. For Townshend, it was just another taste in the exploding sensations of his liberating new lifestyle.

'When I first got into pot, there was a newness about art college, having beautiful girls around me for the first time, having all that music around me for the first time. It was such a great period. It was very exciting, but although dope was important it wasn't the biggest thing. The biggest thing was the fact that pot helped to make already incredible things even more incredible.'

For Wright, however, things weren't so rosy. He was caught with the naughty weed and was unceremoniously booted out of school. In the wake of his dismissal, Townshend, along with fellow student Richard Barnes, took over the flat.

Townshend would remember these days in the song 'Somebody Saved Me.' 'So I left my folks in the mud and rain, it always rains in Sunnyside Row. I lived hippie jokes getting stoned insane till the rain looked just like snow.'

The scene at Sunnyside with Pete and his middle-class mates lazing about in the lounge passing around joints while listening to Jimmy Reed and discussing Jackson Pollock was a world totally foreign to the blue-collar Daltrey, who was more at home in pubs swilling beer and chatting up the local talent. Clearly, these were two very different personalities, the sensitive, budding intellectual pitted against the streetwise, though talented, working stiff.

This was the inauspicious beginnings of a nearly thirty-year power struggle very much in the same vein as John Lennon and Paul McCartney, and Mick Jagger and Keith Richards. At least they started out as best friends, but for Townshend and Daltrey, it was a long, bitter struggle. In fact, it wasn't until thirty years later that Townshend even acknowledged Daltrey's considerable attributes. 'Good old Rog. Good lad he is. Woke me up bright and early to get me to the gigs in the old days. Such a pothead I was back then in 1962 that without his driving, tin-plate, cutter-uppers force I would still be languishing in the garret of the visual artist I was training to be.'

While Daltrey sparred with his fists, Townshend's acerbic tongue was an equally intimidating weapon. 'You couldn't help but like him,' recalls Doug Sandom, 'but Peter could be a pig, a real pig of a man. He had a very nasty thing about him; he could be so sarcastic it was unbelievable. He could do things that you'd think "God, Peter, what are you doing?"'

According to Sandom, Daltrey and Townshend regularly duked it out, especially during rehearsals, when musical disagreements sent tempers flaring. 'Roger used to have a go at Peter. You couldn't argue with Pete, and that was why Roger was always punchin' him out. I've never seen Pete throw a punch, and yet he'd have a bleedin' nose.'

Townshend, however, vehemently denies these stories, insisting the pair never actually came to blows until well over a decade later. 'We do get on badly,' Pete told the *Music Echo* at the time. 'He causes a lot of trouble because he is never satisfied with the sound and is the only one who will speak up about it. Roger is not a very good singer at all, in my opinion. He's got a good act, but I think he expects a backing group more than a truly integrated unit. I don't think he will ever understand that he will *never* get a backing group.'

For his part, the long-suffering John Entwistle offered this assessment of Pete toward the end of the Who's turbulent years together:

35

'No one understands him very well. [He's] a moody person. One day you'll say something and he'll jump down your throat, and the next he's extremely amiable. He's quick tempered and believes in saying what he thinks, whoever he's with.'

On another occasion the bassist said, 'The things I hate about Pete [are] his temper, which is over in five minutes, his drive for perfection, which can be maddening, and his depression when things don't go well.'

Meanwhile, by mid-1963 a multitude of influences were blitzing the impressionable young artist. As his hectic schedule often prevented him from seeing many other bands, much of his creative style was shaped by secondhand accounts. When close friend Richard Barnes hurried up one evening to rave about the innovative Yardbirds with their freewheeling improvisations of rock classics, Townshend began searching for ways in which the Detours too could redesign their material and stamp it with their own identity.

Townshend's real brilliance may well be his penchant for taking the merest slip of an idea and propelling it into a full-fledged force. As he said in the mid-seventies, 'I was trained in graphic design to be an ideas man, to think up something new and different.'

He began to experiment by positioning his amplifier at the same height as his guitar. With Entwistle's knowledge of amplifiers, it didn't take long to hit on the idea of stacking their Marshalls, thus creating a wailing wall of feedback. Pete was eager to introduce this gimmick in performance, and when he did the Goldhawk crowd went wild. 'He'd sing about four high notes and then go back to the amp and twiddle the knobs,' noted one onlooker. 'The only time you would see a guitarist at the amps in those days was between numbers, and then the singer'd be looking at 'em like, c'mon, man! But with the Who it was a regular part of the show.' According to Roger, Pete's innovative use of this technique wasn't the refined artistry later mastered by super axe men Jimi Hendrix and Jeff Beck, but rather a crude maneuver owing far more to showmanship than music. 'He'd just bang it,' reported Roger matter-of-factly.

Just who originated performance feedback remains a controversy to this day. 'In the mid-sixties, Dave Davies and I used to have hilarious arguments about who was the first,' says Townshend. 'I used to pull Dave's leg by saying we both supported the Beatles in Blackpool and you weren't doing it then . . . "I bet you nicked it off me when you saw me doing it." And Dave would scream he was doing it long before that. Then one day I read this incredible story about Jeff Beck in which he said, "Yeah, Townshend came down to see the Tridents rehearsing and saw me using feedback and copied it." Well, I never *ever* saw the Tridents and the man is pathetic. Obviously Beck may feel deeply enough that he invented feedback, but who really gives a shit? Why even comment on it? It doesn't fucking matter – it's just a funny noise made by a guitar.'

One band Townshend did see – and a major influence on him over the years – was the Rolling Stones. At this early stage, though, his attention was arrested by a trick of showmanship that would become his trademark. Pete first became aware of the band when they were jamming with Alexis Korner's Blues Incorporated. 'They started in Ealing and Richmond,' says Pete, 'and I used to go to Richmond and hang about by the river at weekends and played there. In fact, one of their first gigs was a seedy little club near Ealing Broadway Station. I think that was the first place Mick, Keith, and Charlie ever played together with Alexis. And I was there that night lurking about in the back.'

The Detours, by this point backing such up-and-coming artists as Manfred Mann and the Hollies, were booked to open for the Stones at St. Mary's Ballroom in Putney on December 22, 1963. They were well aware of the band's reputation, and long before the Detours took the stage the hall was full of the Stones' boisterous supporters, gathered together in tight knots of rabid devotion. 'It was a revelation,' recalls Pete. 'I was amazed . . . they were so scruffy, so organic, and yet they were stars.' His amazement was further compounded when he dropped by the Stones' dressing room after the show. 'Jagger was very polite and so was Brian, who was extremely complimentary about the Detours. . . . It was like God touching me on the head.'

In these days a curtain was still used. It was a hold-over from an earlier era, but many bands were making good use of it as a dramatic device. This particular evening, Townshend stood at the side of the stage watching Keith Richards. 'He swung his arm up in a swirling motion before the curtain, [then] as the curtain opened he sort of brushed it away and they went into "Come On" [the band's recently released debut single].' This gesture, latter dubbed the windmill, was born that moment. Indeed, later, one night at the Glenlyn Ballroom, a girl approached following the show and fired, 'You're just copying Keith Richards, you know.'

'I thought I was copying Keith as well,' confesses Pete. 'I was sure it was something he did every day. So when we did a gig with the Stones later, I didn't dare do it all night.

'Somebody I know mentioned it to him, "You know, Townshend stole that arm-swinging thing you do."

'"What arm thing?" Richards retorted. "I don't swing my fuckin' arm!"

'He must have got into it as a warm-up thing that night,' reasoned Pete. 'He couldn't even remember doing it.'

At this point Townshend and Co were commanding the teen stages of West London. Their sets offered extended variations of scorching rhythm and blues blasting from towering double stacks of Marshalls. Townshend himself was fast becoming a major draw, highlighting his extraordinary stage movements as a substitute for what he was convinced was a profound lack of musicianship.

'I used to try to make up visually for what I couldn't play,' he says. 'I'd get into very incredible visual things where in order to make one chord more dramatic, I'd make it a really lethal-looking thing, whereas really it's just going to be picked normally. . . . This got bigger and bigger until eventually I was setting myself incredible tasks.

'In fact, I soon forgot all about the guitar because my visual thing was more my music than the actual guitar. I got to jumping about so much the guitar became unimportant. I banged it and I let it feed back, scraped it, rubbed it against the microphone, it wasn't even part of my act. It didn't deserve any credit or respect.'

In their transition to a more bluesy vein, Daltrey had taken up harmonica à la Mick Jagger as well as adopting a raspy, low-pitched vocal style. Everywhere volume was becoming a factor, and the Detours cranked it up louder than any band around. Although the change was initially met with resistance by the group's followers, within a few months the gritty new sound was packing them in threefold. Thus began the boys' deep, enduring connection with their fans, a hallmark that would distinguish the Who above all others.

It was a true interaction as well, ranging from Townshend and Entwistle giving a budding guitarist a few lessons to allowing the game individual to jump on stage and blow some harp with Daltrey. During intervals Pete and the boys would have a drink and mingle with the crowd. To the music-loving youth of the Shepherd's Bush neighborhood the Detours were very much their own. 'Those people I used to play to in the pubs still come up to me in the street and tell me to get my act together,' says Townshand. 'They hung on somehow with the band even today. I still meet them and study what has happened to their lives. They all seem to be incredibly eccentric characters.'

He continues, 'Being a West Londoner meant two things to me: you were brought up to live with the sound of airplanes, and you were also aware of the Irish community around Shepherd's Bush, how volatile and artistic they were as people. They might have been hod-carrying, hole-in-the-road diggers, but they were still reading James Joyce. A lot of the important mod figures who congregated at the Goldhawk were of Irish origin.'

Leading the brigade was 'Irish' Jack Lyons, a short, skinny, nondescript teen from across the Irish Sea who spotted Townshend in one of his earliest appearances at a Shepherd's Bush dance hall called Bosleys. 'The band were dressed in black stage suits, white shirts with black ties, and the almost mandatory white cardboard handkerchiefs. They did numbers like "Apache," some country and western, and "Telstar" by the Tornadoes. After a while I found I couldn't take my eyes off this guy with the nose who played rhythm guitar, chords really, in a jazz style. To me he looked fuckin' incredible. Just studying him from where I stood was a revelation.

'I thought Townshend's nose looked classical, like Rembrandt's beret. A secret trademark only the owner knew the secret of. It was a moment of decision for me because seeing Townshend's face for the first time was actually encountering one of my all-time fantasy faces. . . . I thought, "If I had a face like that, it would be a weapon and I wouldn't give a fuck how I spoke because I knew everybody would be too busy staring at my nose."'

In Townshend, Lyons recognized a voice for all the downtrodden, misplaced Irish Jacks of the world. The band's very first superfan, Lyons followed them all across London, leading the frenzied mob of zealots at the Goldhawk, where Townshend's transcendent guitar temporarily lifted them above the dead-end blight of Shepherd's Bush.

The Goldhawk Road Social Club was a pretty rough venue, with nightly brawls among patrons 'just out of nick,' as Irish Jack put it. Roger Daltrey was in his element here, raising a pint with mates with names like Choppy, Claky, Scuffer, and another very suspect pair called the Parrish Boys, 'keen on cheerful violence,' as Townshend put it.

All during this period Pete was rounding out his musical education. One significant influence was Andy 'Thunderclap' Newman, a bearded, bespectacled jazz pianist who more resembled a college professor than a musician. From out of nowhere Newman dropped in on campus one lunchtime to deliver a spontaneous piano and kazoo concert in very unconventional time signatures, mystifying Townshend, who was immediately taken with this eccentric musical beatnik. Eventually Newman turned up at the Sunnyside flat, speaking eloquently on such topics as the twenties jazz legend Bix Beiderbecke, a coronet player and composer with the Wolverine Orchestra, whose uncanny, innate harmonic sense made him years ahead of his time.

Newman's influence, however, didn't stop there. Perhaps even more important was his early experimentation with multitrack recording. In an age when the Beatles and their savvy producer, George Martin, were still working on a two-track machine (Martin wouldn't seriously experiment with multitracks until 1966), the progressive Newman was setting up two single-track tape recorders in his bedroom and creating multiple sound effects and orchestrations, some featuring over twenty instruments.

'If I had ever learned to read music,' reasons Townshend, 'I don't know whether I would have gotten as hung up on recording, and if I wasn't as hung up on tape recording as I was, I don't think I would have learned to write.'*

Like just about every musician at the time, Pete was also strongly influenced by Bob Dylan. A female friend at school turned Pete on to the introspective midwestern folksinger, whose first two albums, his self-titled debut and the follow-up, *The Freewheelin' Bob Dylan*, Townshend immediately devoured. Initially, he admitted, he didn't pay much attention to the lyrics, concentrating instead on Dylan's demanding chord work. Not until Dylan's fourth release, 1964's

---

* Pete would later launch Thunderclap to brief stardom by producing his 1969 classic 'Something in the Air,' with drummer Speedy Keen (who wrote 'Armenia City in the Sky' for the Who in 1967) and the diminutive Jimmy McCullough, the talented, short-lived guitarist with Paul McCartney and Wings. Pete also produced the group's follow-up 1970 LP *Hollywood Dream*. Because of its haunting, affecting piano work, Townshend hailed 'Something in the Air' as 'a work of art.'

Another Side of Bob Dylan, did Townshend realize what power lyrics could have on listeners.

'Dylan opened the door for rock to say bigger and better things,' said Townshend in 1974. 'I think rock became more idealistic. It became the music of the adolescent and a vehicle for the denunciation of whatever we didn't believe in. If there was something a bit dodgy, we knew that pretty soon there'd be a song about it, and through the music we'd know what we felt to be right and what we felt to be wrong. It was an affirmation.'

Unlike artists such as David Crosby and Roger McGuinn of the Byrds and John Lennon, who unashamedly adopted Dylan's style by exploring alienation on a deeply personal level, Townshend would focus on the bigger picture and write anthems for the masses.

This was in the future, though. For the moment Pete was still making his first feeble attempts at composing. Nonetheless, it was a song that Townshend wrote at the age of sixteen, called 'It Was You', that was responsible for the Detours' first recording.

This time it was not Betty but Cliff who lent a hand. Through his friendship with Barry Gray, musical director of the popular children's program *Thunderbirds*, Cliff arranged the Detours' first session, which took place in Gray's basement studio with Barry acting as engineer. Although the record didn't go anywhere, it's pleasant Merseybeat style was ideal for a Brian Epstein act, the Fourmost, who later recorded the song as a B side. If nothing else, the tune displayed Townshend's aptitude for composing.

As 1964 began, Townshend and Barnes found themselves living in a van, having been ousted from the Sunnyside flat for various transgressions. After a few weeks they moved in with Cliff and Betty. Pete called this experience 'a very safe independence, a phony rebellion until I moved to Belgravia in 1965.' To his parents' dismay, Pete and Richard proceeded to install a recording studio upstairs, complete with a thick layer of concrete on the floor for soundproofing. 'They had egg boxes everywhere on the walls,' remembers brother Paul, 'and they knocked a hole in one wall to put in a window [but] they didn't get round to that. Then the cement made the ceiling start to bow in downstairs. There was a blazing row, and my mom and dad kicked them out.'

Before this happened, Pete made good use of the homemade facility. Here he laid down his earliest demos, among them the trivial

'Call me Lightning' and 'You Don't Have to Jerk.' Recorded over the winter of 1964 on Townshend's 2 X Vortexion Mono recorders and released as an improbable single in 1968, 'Lightning' might be called 'sixties California sound meets fifties doo-wop.' It does, however, feature some limber guitar runs, showing Townshend's continuing musical improvement.

For the band, a huge stepping-stone was a real manager, in the unlikely figure of Helmut Gorden, a doorknob factory magnate and Brian Epstein wanna-be. Recruited to a Detours gig at the White Hart by Doug Sandom's sister, who worked at Gorden's foundry, the businessman caught one whiff of the frenzy and sensed this could be his cash cow. For Pete and his mates, here was the financial backing they'd longed for. Gorden agreed to manage them, allowing Bob Druce to keep them on his circuit. Gorden splurged for a posh new wardrobe of leather waistcoats and Beatle boots, plus badly needed equipment and, wonder of wonders, an updated van.

The new manager quickly proved his worth by securing the band a coveted Tuesday night residency at the Railway Tavern, with Richard Barnes in charge of booking. The crowd at the Railway was younger, hipper, and Barnes managed to pack a thousand raving teens into a pub that comfortably held just 180. Many of these newfound fans began to flock to the Goldhawk to catch the group's weekend gigs. The Shepherd's Bush club was fast becoming an electrifying scene of ever evolving fashion trends like sneakers with buckles, dogtooth trousers, and French crew cuts. Dances were in one week, out the next; face and body posturing spoke of 'attitude' decades before the term was popular.

Townshend remembers, 'I used to say to the band, "Listen, we should look right, we should have an image, we should walk in a particular way, talk in a particular way. We should look different from other people. And after a concert is over, if we talk to people we should maintain the facade."'

A change of the band's name was also in order, although it would be only temporary at first. Heading into the new year of 1964, the group discarded another name. The original alternative monikers ranged from 'No One' to 'Group' to even 'British European Airways.' Pete, in a moment of pot-fogged inspiration, came up with 'the Hair.' Hair was on everyone's mind during the controversy regarding the Beatles' mop tops and the Stones' so-called unkempt locks, which would soon brand them the 'Great Unwashed.' Finally, it was Barnes who suggested 'the Who.' 'It made people think twice, and it worked well on posters because it was so short and therefore would print up big,' he reasoned.

After subsequent arguments over the two finalists, the Hair and the Who, the decision was ultimately hammered down, predictably by Daltrey. One Saturday morning, upon coming to collect his mates to pick up equipment at Marshall's, he simply grunted in his no-nonsense manner, 'It's the Who, isn't it?'

Impressionistic, ambiguous, and coolly abstract. A perfect name for a new generation that would gleefully break all the rules and cross every line. The age of the mod was upon Britain, and Townshend, an emotionally isolated, insecure entry-level musician and composer, was about to be crowned its moody king.

3

Jagged Glory: *Mod World*

Being angry at the adult world is not all of us. It's not me and it's not John. It's only half Roger but completely Pete.

– Keith Moon

Pete Townshend didn't find mod. It found him. That he was not an original member of this trendy youth rebellion was somehow fitting. As an outsider he was better able to grasp all the angles, like a prism absorbing and then reflecting light, enabling him to project his own variation on the theme.

'We weren't mods,' he admitted, 'but we became mods . . . I was at art college, had long hair, was smoking pot and going with girls with long red hair and all that. Painting farty pictures and carrying my portfolio around. I had to *learn* to be a mod.'

Enter Pete Meaden, a beautifully dressed, fast-talking freelance publicist and record promoter looking to launch a new pop sensation. Having worked with Rolling Stones mentor Andrew Loog Oldham, Meaden reportedly got a little too loaded at a Stones reception one evening and was summarily dismissed from the organization.

When Meaden got wind – through manager Helmut Gorden's barber – of new group causing a stir at the Railway, he decided to turn up one night and catch their act. He instantly liked what he saw. The Who, with their inventive blues approach, weren't quite like anyone on the scene: far removed from both the Beatles' bright, chirpy sound and the raspy, sullen Stones. There was also something uniquely stirring about the guitarist, something telling in those renegade steely blue eyes.

Meaden had been searching for a band which would embody all that he himself held dear, the still-secret world of the mod. For Meaden the subculture was a full-blown obsession, heightened by the notorious Clacton Riot of March 26, 1964, when several hundred mods battled their arch foes – the rockers.

The craze had actually begun five years earlier with the advent of a slender paperback called *Absolute Beginners*, written by fifty-five-year-old Colin MacInnes. The racy cult novel catered to, as Daltrey put it, 'the first generation after the war to have a lot of money.' For the first time youth not only had spare cash but a growing realization that they could wield a sociopolitical influence, if even in the most superficial terms of music and dress. They wanted to buck the establishment, with its crumbling mores and tired values. Theirs was a frontal assault on, as Townshend put it, 'good taste, discipline, and rules, which as I far as I was concerned added up to nothing.'

Keith Altham, a former Who publicist, described the growing trend this way: 'Mods were a fashionable elite with style, swagger, and pointed boots, with tab collar shirts, who rode nifty Lambretta scooters decked out with masses of wing mirrors, chrome, and the obligatory fake raccoon tail streaming out behind from their preposterously tall radio aerials. They were as English as they could get and in direct opposition to their hated rocker rivals, who based their image on early Brando and the music of Elvis, Gene Vincent, and Chuck Berry.'

The pairing of Meaden – voluble, intense, incredibly knowledge-able, and indisputably ace – with Gorden – shrewd, intelligent, and wealthy – seemed perfect. Certainly Townshend thought so. In fact, he and Daltrey slyly suggested that Gorden pull back a little and let Meaden take over the band's management while acting as a silent backer, coming up with the cash that would make Meaden's dreams a reality.

Initially Gorden resisted. After all, they were his 'little diamonds.' To emphasize his claim, he began to assert his authority in two significant ways. First, in the spring of 1964, he set up an audition with respected record producer Chris Parmeinter at the bamboo-lined Zanzibar Club on London's Edgware Road.

As the band performed the three-song set that Townshend and Daltrey decided was most suitable for the occasion, they could not help but notice the increasingly irritated glances Parmeinter was shooting at Doug Sandom. Following the audition, Parmeinter admitted he liked the band, but soon after told Townshend, 'If you ever wanna make a record, you'd better get the drumming sorted out.'

Within the shocked silence of the room Townshend turned on Sandom and erupted, 'Are you ever gonna get your act together? What the fuck is wrong with you anyway? If you can't get it together you're out of the group!' His face purple with rage, the apoplectic Townshend stalked off.

In truth, trouble had been brewing for some time. Sandom's age and conventional marital status didn't fit with the young rebel image Meaden sought to convey. Moreover, the drummer had always considered his place in the band a part-time vocation, something to bring in a few extra pounds. Now not only was the Who getting serious, but they were going mod with a raunchy blues style he simply could not relate to. To his credit, Sandom bowed out gracefully. 'I've been thinking of quitting for a while now,' he told his band mates. 'I think it would be best if I dropped out. I'm only holding you back.'

Several years later, Townshend had this to say about the incident: 'We always saw ourselves as the New Young Ideal, and he was a bricklayer, about thirty years old. A very good drummer, but he didn't fit in. My first taste of ruthlessness was the day we came to throw him out. The group wouldn't do it, so I turned round and said, "Listen, if you've got to go, you've got to go." I don't think he's spoken a word to me since.'

For a month the group carried on with various interim personnel, including someone called Dave, the drummer for the harmonic Fourmost. He played well, but to Gorden 'looked wrong.' Gorden even suggested he undergo plastic surgery. Mitch Mitchell, who would later win acclaim in the Jimi Hendrix Experience, also enjoyed a brief stint.

Then one April evening in 1964, materializing out of nowhere at the Oldfield Hotel in Greenford, appeared an elfin 'apparition,' as Daltrey termed it, with dyed ginger hair and a flaming crimson suit. Roger explains: 'Word had gotten round to all the local groups that we were looking for a new drummer, and this guy with great big brown eyes out in the audience said, "I play the drums a bit, can I have a go?" So he got on the drums, played two songs, and by the end the whole kit was in pieces. This drummer who was filling in for us was in tears. It was like, "He's gotta be our drummer." He was phenomenal.'

Keith Moon was then a seventeen-year-old, puppy-eyed imp from Wembley, fresh from the Beachcombers, a so-called surf group proliferating tunes highly derivative of the Beach Boys. The way Moon saw it, his talent was tailor-made to the loud, raucous sound of the Who.

'When I heard their drummer had left,' he said, 'I laid plans to insinuate myself into the group. They were playing at a pub near me, the Oldfield. I went down there, and they had a session drummer sitting in with them. I got up and said, "Well, I can do better than him." They said go ahead, and I got behind this other guy's drums and did one song: "Roadrunner." I'd had several drinks to get me courage up, and when I got on stage I went *arrrgggghhhhhhh* on the drums, broke the pedal on the bass, two skins, and got off. I was scared to death.'

The over-the-top gingerman was immediately presented with a desultory left-handed job offer from Messrs Townshend and Daltrey. 'You'll have to give up work,' they informed him. 'There's a gig on Monday. If you want to come we'll pick you up in the van.'

As Moon noted, 'Nobody ever said, "You're in." They just said, "What are you doing Monday?"'

Just like that, the apprentice electrician (a scary thought by any standards, considering his future penchant for high-voltage destruction) became the missing piece in the Who jigsaw. To Pete, essentially a rhythm guitarist, his hyperkinetic thrash-and-burn style, the twirling and tossing of drumsticks, was a revelation.

'Keith had an inner metronome which clicked away,' recalls Townshend. 'But he was also capable of playing with somebody else's metronome. From the time we found him, it was a complete turning point. He was so assertive and confident. Before that we had just been fooling around.' Engineer Glyn Johns noted, 'He wasn't the greatest drummer in the world, but he was the only drummer for the Who.'

Moon himself wasn't so sure at first. He once confessed that he temporarily left the band a scant three weeks after he joined, after tussling with, of all people, the usually taciturn John Entwistle. Here was the ultimate study in contrasts. Whereas the conventional Sandom had been a rock-steady timekeeper, setting down a calm, even highway for Entwistle to navigate his bass lines, Moon's over-the-top fills and solo runs made for inevitable collisions.

According to Entwistle, 'Keith must be the hardest drummer in the world to play with, mainly because he tries to hit nearly every drum at once. And if you try to fit in with one of his beats, you have to play like him, hippity-bippity, all over the place. It's really difficult.'

Guitarist Danny Kortchmar, who played on Moon's 1975 solo album, *Two Sides of the Moon*, agreed. 'He plays full out as soon as he starts: eighth notes on bass drums and fills all over the place, intense.'

Rock journalist Peter Goddard, though, took a larger view of the maniacal percussionist. 'Musicologists can be brought in to determine when the Stones went from being a white rhythm and blues band to a rock band or the precise moment the Beatles' own style took over from what they were borrowing. But the Who had the chance to become the Who the moment Keith Moon snapped off the bass drum pedal at the pub that night. All it needed was Pete Townshend to take them there.'

With the final lineup in place, Meaden set his sights on their material, infusing a bold new twist into their fairly traditional R&B approach. 'This is New Wave rhythm and blues, got it? Motown, funk, everything fast, tight, and sharp!' he cried. Material was selected from soft R&B artists like the Miracles, the Impressions, and Tony Clarke. These tunes were certainly more up-tempo, but still far removed from the primordial, sizzling brew Townshend would soon concoct.

Next to be addressed was wardrobe, the ultimate identifying imprint of the mod. Meaden came up with the idea that Daltrey, as front man, would logically be the Face, the hip captain in this mod regiment. As such, Roger was outfitted in a white seersucker jacket with black trousers, black knit tie, and black-and-white two-toned shoes. Townshend sported an Ivy League jacket while Entwistle and Moon donned jeans, t-shirts, and black boxing boots. As the four tramped down to get their hair snipped in the French crew cut favored by Meaden, only John balked at the makeover, grumbling, 'I don't want to dress like a little ticket.'

Townshend, however, regarded the proceedings with an almost mystical reverence. 'Pete Meaden taught me that mod wasn't just a fad; it could be something sublime or even celestial. I spent the next two years mixing and matching things I noticed in our audience with an exaggerated pop look I thought might suit the color magazines of the day.'

Finally, the group underwent yet another name change. In his quest for commercialism, Meaden rejected 'the Who' as being too obscure and chose the 'High Numbers,' a name alluding to the top of the charts as well as the digits mods often wore on their T-shirts. The moniker also bore an obvious link to the inevitable leapers, or uppers, they consumed.

In June 1964, the retooling complete, the group returned to the studio once again under the guidance of Chris Parmeinter. The session featured two snappy compositions by Meaden, 'I'm the Face' and 'Zoot Suit.' Both essentially shackled the band's talents while singing the praises of the mod lifestyle. 'I'm the Face,' emulating Slim Harpo's 'Got Love if You Want it,' featured the trite lyrics 'I'm the big wheel baby/Won't you roll with me.' 'Zoot Suit' offered much of the same: 'The main thing is unless you're a fool/You know, you gotta know you gotta be cool.' Both songs were redeemable only for Townshend's nifty guitar work: a brief jazz break in 'Face' and an even better, faster single-string jazz picking on 'Zoot Suit.'

'It was our first record,' says Townshend. 'The first time we'd ever been in a recording studio together. We were very excited. It was very self-consciously mod. It talked about fashion, faces, and tickets. That record was a clear indication of how the mod movement as a fashion was really self-contained . . . We brought out that very self-conscious record "I'm the Face" – you know, I wear white buckskin shoes and side jackets with five-inch vents. The kids out in the streets didn't need that kind of leader. They knew that information before you even thought of the lyric.'

Predictably, the single, released on July 3, 1964, proved a stellar flop, although it did make a significant impact on what had become mod central, the Scene Club in Ham Yard, Soho. As Meaden put it, 'If they could turn these kids on, they could turn on the world.'

In this dingy basement catacomb of padded walls and floors

littered with pillows, Townshend became fully immersed in the movement. 'The Scene was really where it was at, but there were only about fifteen people down there every night. It was a focal point for the mod movement. I don't think anyone who was a mod outside Soho realized the fashions and dances all began there. We were lucky enough to be involved in the movement at that particular time.'

If the Goldhawk was a magnet for burly drinkers, the Scene was the cloistered underworld of mod fired by the ever present purple hearts, a moniker for Drynamil, a potent amphetamine that was the nectar of the mod gods. Another specialty was French blues, an upper purchased for a shilling right on the premises. A steady dose enabled the mods to maintain their dual lifestyle, Clark Kent office boys by day, Supermen at night, dancing, partying, or simply posing in doorways until dawn.

Within this highly charged atmosphere, Townshend, always a quick study, assimilated the action, watching the ace faces with their chicks, trying to perfect the mod way of walking, the casual saunter that by its very understatement, demanded attention. He took in the dances, the block and the bang – mod terms for getting high. He even excelled at the necessary art of standing around doing nothing but acting cool. Eventually the band landed a series of return engagements, an enormous coup since mods were notoriously critical of live music.

During his continual evolution Townshend came to the conclusion that art school was no longer a productive or rewarding endeavor. 'I deserted school for music,' he says. 'I gave it up. I thought, This is ridiculous, trying to screw around making a buck out of painting signs and cigar commercials, music is so much more vital.'

Surprisingly a teacher, Roy Ascot, hastened his decision. 'You play guitar in a group; how much do you earn?' he asked one afternoon.

'About thirty quid a week.'

'Thirty quid a week! For God's sake, leave! That's more than I earn here after twenty years!'

In Brighton over the summer, Townshend would experience how it felt to be a true believer. 'I know what it's like to be a mod among two million mods. It's like being the only white man at the Apollo. Someone comes up and touches you, and suddenly you become black. It's like that incredible feeling of being part of something much bigger than race – it was impetus. It covered everybody. Everybody looked the same, acted the same, and wanted to be the same. It was the first move I have ever seen in the history of youth toward unity: unity of thought, unity of drive, and unity of motive. It was the closest to pure patriotism I've ever felt.'

For Townshend, a philosophy that had been sequestered within the safe quarters of college was now applied to the real world. 'You see, as individuals these people were nothing. Not only were they young, they were lower-class young. They had to submit to the middle class's way of dressing, speaking, and acting in order to get the jobs that kept them alive. They had to do everything in terms of what already existed around them. That made their way of getting something across that much more effective. The fact that they were hip and yet still, as far as Grandad was concerned, exactly the same. It made the whole gesture so much more vital. It was incredible. As a force, they were unbelievable. That was England's real Battle of the Bulge.'

Pete's allusion to fighting was more than just figurative. As Townshend would recall in *Quadrophenia*, the mods had arch rivals who despised all they stood for, the rockers. The rocker movement grew initially out of the Teddy Boy craze of the late fifties with the birth of skiffle, led by Lonnie Donnegan. By the sixties they'd evolved into scruffy, beer-guzzling, motorcycle-cruising renegades; many were members of gangs from rural towns. The surly rockers disdained all the London mods stood for: their smart preppie clothing, neatly cropped hair, and interminably cool attitudes. When mods descended on their territory – mostly seaside resorts – violent and bloody turf wars broke out.

This was the case in Brighton that summer. Townshend remembers one night in particular. 'I saw about two thousand mod kids, and there were three rockers up against a wall,' he says. 'They'd obviously come into it thinking they were going to a party and they were really scared as hell and the mods were throwing bottles at them.

'The people who were kicking rockers out in front would come in and listen to our music. I knew then I had a certain kind of power. There were all the tough guys looking at me, waiting to hear what I was about to say.'

The Who's status as leaders in the movement, however, would

not be enough to propel them to the next level. For this they needed stronger management.

One sweltering July night, the High Numbers were playing in the packed and steamy Railway. In the audience was, in Richard Barnes's words, 'this posh-looking guy in a dark gray suit.' Scouting the clubs in search of a band to be the subject of a film project, the stranger was ultimately directed to Pete Meaden. Meaden was keen to sell his young charges to this upper-crust gentleman. In retrospect, it was the arch mod's undoing. 'I hard-selled myself right out of a band,' he later lamented.

In truth, this dapper Oxford-educated elitist, Christopher 'Kit' Lambert, needed little convincing. 'The atmosphere was fantastic,' he told journalist George Tremlett. 'The room was black and steaming hot. The audience seemed hypnotized by the wild music, with the feedback Townshend was already producing from his amp.'

Lambert had no doubt he'd found his subjects. The following night he dragged his partner, Chris Stamp, to the Watford Trade Hall to catch the act. Stamp recalls, 'I'd never seen anything like it. The Who have a hypnotic effect on an audience. It was like a black mass. Even then Pete was doing all the electronic-feedback stuff. Keith was going wild on the drums. The audience were in a trance. They just sat there watching, or shuffling round the dance floor, awestruck. "This is it," Kit said to me, and we both knew that it was.'

The pair had met on a movie set at London's Shepperton Studios, working as assistant directors on such projects as *Of Human Bondage*, *The L-Shaped Room*, and the Judy Garland vehicle *I Could Go On Singing*. As individuals they were polar opposites: Lambert, the son of a lauded composer-conductor was flashy, over the top, and energetic, while Stamp, the East End son of a tugboat captain, was calm, anchored, and steely. Together, however, they shared a single-minded goal: to set the entertainment business on its ear in the mode of the Beatles' Brian Epstein. In mod they saw an opportunity to match Richard Lester's success with the Beatles' offbeat film *A Hard Day's Night*.

The follow-up audition for the band that next Sunday was a mere formality. Lambert and Stamp decided to abandon their movie plans temporarily to become the group's managers. Helmut Gorden was disposed of in short order; his contract, signed by the group when they were still legally minors, declared null and void. Meaden too had no binding claim, since he was only Gorden's hired gun. The pill-pumped, frazzled manager was bought off by the sharp-talking duo for a mere 450 pounds.

The new contract guaranteed the boys a wage of a thousand pounds per year along with 15 percent of the group's earnings. One aspect of the deal, however, took 'a percentage of all personal writing,' and here Cliff Townshend slammed his foot down. 'I said, "Not that, no!" What Pete did when he was twenty-one was his own business. But before that I crossed it off.' By doing so, Cliff effectively derailed any attempt to sign away his son's composing rights, potentially saving Pete millions and the future extended litigation that has notoriously plagued other artists.

With Lambert and Stamp in charge, the High Numbers began backing the likes of Dusty Springfield, Tom Jones, and Marianne Faithfull. They were soon escaping London for weekend junkets to Leicester, Oxford, even Glasgow, playing support to the wide-eyed Lulu. At Blackpool's Opera House, they shared the bill with none other than the Fab Four, although Townshend quipped, 'The Beatles are no more mod than Elvis Presley. They were already riding high on their second record. Kit Lambert and Andrew Oldham plus Robert Stigwood and Brian Epstein were going to form this big management monopoly. So we used to have lots of wonderful dinners up at Eppy's.'

The High Numbers continued their residency at the Railway Tavern, churning out the sizzling extended covers that had become their trademark: 'Heat Wave,' 'Smokestack Lightning,' and a Townshend favorite, Robert Parker's catchy 'Barefootin'.' 'That was a popular track they used to play in the clubs in 1963 and '64 when black R&B was just hitting this country, which had such an influence on writers of my generation,' remembers Pete. '"Covered" is a very polite way of putting it. A lot of people felt it was stolen. What made it okay for the British is a subtle difference. If Jan and Dean had taken an old R&B song, it would have been considered outright theft. Elvis got away with it, but only just. For the British it was different, because we were so far removed. . . . We really identified with the blues as the music of the minority.'

That fall a stage extension at the Railway elevated the band, especially Townshend, a lean sixfooter, perilously close to the ceiling. One night during a dramatic exercise in feedback, the guitarist flung his instrument into the rafters, where it bonged and vibrated to the delight of the audience. During the band's second set some front-row enthusiasts, mostly Townshend's art school chums, encouraged an encore of the amazing feat.

This time, however, as he launched his twelve-string Richenbacher upward, the guitar snapped, and the neck dangled from the ceiling. 'It kind of shocked me,' admits Townshend, 'because I wasn't ready for it. I was expecting everybody to go, "Wow, he's broken his guitar," but nobody did anything, which made me determined to get this precious event noticed by the audience. I proceeded to make a big thing of breaking the guitar. I pounced all over the stage with it, threw bits to the crowd, and picked up my spare guitar and carried on as though I really meant to do it.'

Word soon got around, and the following week a packed Railway crowd eagerly anticipated a repeat of the spectacle. Although admonished by Daltrey, Entwistle, and Lambert (he ruling it was too expensive), Townshend refused to comply. This time Moon took up the gauntlet and smashed his kit in the finale. The antics quickly captured the attention of the press, and when Lambert learned that photographers were showing up at gigs, the wily manager not only approved the destruction but encouraged it. From the wings he shouted, 'Smash your guitar! The *Daily Mail*'s here! We can afford it!'

Within three weeks, Townshend had latched onto the concept as an art form in the philosophic vein encapsulated by his esteemed Ealing Art School lecturer Gustav Metzke. 'To me it wasn't violence, it wasn't random destruction,' insists Pete. 'At the time I considered it to be art. The German movement of autodestructive art. They used to build sculptures which would collapse. They would paint pictures with acid so they autodestructed. They built buildings that would explode. So I used to go out on stage thinking this was high art.'

What Townshend sought to elevate to an esoteric plane, the irascible Keith Moon brought thundering down to earth. 'When Pete smashed his guitar, it was because he was pissed off. When I smashed me drums, it was because I was pissed off. We were frustrated. You're working as hard as you can to get that fucking song across, to grab that audience by the balls, to make it an event. When you've done all that, when you've worked your balls off and given the audience everything you can give and they don't give anything back, that's when the fucking instruments go.

'That's one way things got smashed. Another was if a member of the group was too fuckin' stoned to give it their best. Then he was letting down the other three. In a lot of cases it was me, drinking too much. Then Pete, Roger, or John says, "You cunt! You've fucking let us down! You fucking bastard, if you want to get pissed, why don't you wait until after the bloody show!"'

Daltrey, in turn, says the mayhem erupted simply as a release from their boring twelve-bar blues repertoire: 'Muddy Waters, Slim Harpo, Jimmy Reed, nice harmonica solos, but it gets monotonous. You get frustrated. You can't get enough out of it. That's when it started getting more aggressive. That's when the feedback started coming in. You draw out the solo and make it off the wall. We were in a very small club one night, and the ceiling was quite low. Pete put his guitar up to play a chord, broke the neck off, and got absolutely no reaction. To break a four hundred pound guitar in those days was a hell of a lot of money. So he proceeded to break up the thing completely, which got a reaction. Being in a group in those days was all about getting a reaction out of the audience.'

For Pete, this simple yet wildly dramatic act proved a major ego boost. The instant approval generated a still more aggressive attack, a pivotal stepping-stone in his surging confidence. While insecurities may have still plagued him off stage, once he stepped into the floodlights he was transformed into an uninhibited exhibitionist, a jittery persona whose acts he often didn't even recall afterward.

'I don't really feel the showmanship side of my contribution to the Who's stage show is fundamentally part of my personality. It's something that automatically happens and I forget who I am. It stems from the early days when we had to learn to sell ourselves to the public; otherwise nobody would have taken a blind bit of notice of us.'

Their rapidly improving act earned them a coveted regular Tuesday night gig at the popular Marquee at 90 Wardour Street, Soho. Lambert seized on the idea of marketing the band with the slogan 'The Who: Maximum R & B.' In a nugget of true PR brilliance, the old Detours' logo was revived for a poster blitz to get the word out. Townshend's original art school design featuring the white arrow was used, only this time rising from the 'O' at the end of the band's name, resembling the medical symbol for the male. The top left-hand corner of the poster depicted Townshend in his dramatic 'birdman' stance, his arm raised to strike his guitar. Two thousand stark black-and-white placards were plastered all across London. So potent was the image that it has been revived in a number of mod reincarnations over the past thirty years.

During these supercharged performances Townshend honed and polished his moves, pogoing about the stage, leaping and sliding dramatically to his knees. The flurry of instrument smashing became the obligatory climax of every concert. However Townshend's playing was increasingly authoritative and inventive, although still not as much as he would have liked.

'What I like about the way I play is what everyone else likes. I get a particular sound nobody else gets, and I play rhythm like nobody else; it's a cutting style, sorta Captain Power-chords! I do like to have a bash every now and then at a wailing guitar solo, but halfway through I usually fall off the end of the fretboard. But I've resigned myself to the fact that I haven't got what it takes to be a guitar hero.'

This hardly mattered to one of the group's many early admirers, Elton John. 'I used to go see them when they were the High Numbers at the Railway Tavern near where I grew up. They were astounding when they started out, they were so loud. . . . Nobody knew what was going to happen. That wasn't the point; it was just sheer excitement.'

Townshend's own view of the band's spontaneity was more tempered. 'I'm very suspicious of all this talk. I've got a feeling that the group were probably one of the most calculated merchants apart from Kiss. . . . A lot of the spontaneous outbursts on the stage were far from spontaneous. We did have that open door; it was expected that anything that could happen with the Who was likely to happen.'

Lambert and Stamp's campaign eagerly pushed those boundaries, selling Townshend on the concept. 'Never let the music get in the way of the act.' What set the duo apart from other managers was their background in film – they operated from a visual perspective, in which the music was secondary to the spectacle. The band, for instance, was the first to carry their own theatrical lighting rig and wear stage makeup. A 16mm promotional film was shot in and around the Railway to sell to booking agents and record company execs, and was finally sold to a television program.

They also employed countless publicity stunts, like hiring professional groupies – dubbed the 100 Faces – to follow the band to every appearance. Lambert and Stamp barraged the media, encouraging the group to make outrageous statements to the press about how much money they spent on their clothes, luxury items, and hobbies. Their clients were packaged more like the latest Hollywood discovery than a local pop band.

Expenditures in this full-blown campaign were staggering. Between the nightly instrument and equipment destruction, publicity and wardrobe, the band was laying out an astonishing amount per gig. This sort of money the budding impresarios did not have. Beneath their flash Carnaby Street suits, Lambert and Stamp were in fact mere paupers who would unabashedly work every scam available to achieve their lofty goal. Their posh Belgravia address gave them access to a chain of bank accounts and credit cards, leaving a trail of high-flying checks all across London. In desperate times Lambert even gambled at the Casanova Club to try and secure a few hundred pounds while Townshend once nicked a guitar off the wall of a music shop.

Pete's relationship with Kit, much like Tom Wright and Pete Meaden before him, was deepened over a four-month period when he shared a Belgravia flat with Lambert while Stamp was traveling on a movie assignment. Evenings would be spent discussing art and literature, as well as listening to baroque music, one of Lambert's passions. Lambert's influence would show up later in Townshend's 'The Kids Are Alright' off the band's first LP, with its creative use of suspended baroque chords.

Lambert even introduced the beer-guzzling Townshend to the virtues of fine wine. He taught Pete the subtler points of appreciating wine, beginning with the firm injunction, 'You taste it. You do not pour it down your throat. You are not filling a car.'

For all his highbrow tutoring, Lambert was always quick to embrace the most brazen commercial schemes. 'The importance of people like Kit is what he said to me from day one,' said Townshend. 'He said all great art is crap, and I've found that out. We read that Mozart was doing commissions on numbered motifs and selling his copyrights. "Oh, the bloody Prince of Denmark wants another piece of music and I'm busy. Give him fifteen of number twenty-two, six of number four, none of number fifty-eight. . . ." It was very much like computer music. And, of course, Bach was a mathematician. These people have all been elevated to some kind of artistic gods.

'Kit used to be extraordinarily funny on the subject. He said, "You've got to be pretentious, you've got to go for the gold, you've got to be over the top!" So as an agitator he was wonderful, because instead of devastating the whole thing, he was actually making it more real.'

Kit Lambert's homosexuality, which he desperately tried to keep under wraps, did create some tension. 'Apart from anything else, he was worried because he was lying to me about his sexuality,' remembers Pete. 'He was bringing boys back and stuff, and the next day he'd introduce them at the breakfast table saying, "This unfortunate fellow had a terrible accident last night and hurt his foot, and I had to put him up for the night."

Irish Jack, though, had his own views on the manager. He met him on the dance floor of the Hammersmith Palais, dancing the dog in a Harrington jacket and college scarf 'like he was fuckin' mod incarnate,' remembers Lyons. 'Inevitably, because of his sexuality he came in for some stick from the hard boys of the Goldhawk, but Kit could cut anyone down to size simply by opening his mouth. I've seen him being quite unmercifully cruel with his acerbic wit. I think Pete picked up a lot of his sixties sarcasm from listening to Kit. He was a much deeper person [than Chris] and totally taken up with pop art ideas. Every word spoken was gilt-edged with a quality of Oxford-uttered truth about it. A hard act to follow.'

Lambert's greatest contribution was encouraging Townshend to compose. He generously provided two Vortexion tape recorders which were soon replaced by state-of-the-art Revox models. Once Pete began experimenting, there was no turning back. Lambert, with his schooling and knowledge of classical music, coupled with a flair for reading the current pop scene, created a perfect sounding board for Townshend's burgeoning ideas. 'Kit actually had something, a language, you know,' recalls Pete. 'He had a great grasp of musical terms and was able to make an intelligent critique. He used to throw in a lot of ideas that seemed completely inappropriate, but whenever I tried them, they used to work.'

Townshend's plunge into songwriting was spurred on by a sense of urgency. After a failed audition with EMI in October 1964, just months after the summer debacle of Meaden's two tunes, Pete realized the importance of playing original compositions. The days of R&B covers had run their course, and now all the top acts – the Rolling Stones, the Kinks, the Beatles – were making their stamp by writing their own material.

'I knew deep down that the only way I was really going to be confident was to become something everybody could respect. So I labored at the guitar, trying my best to be incredible within a few weeks. And when it didn't happen, it destroyed me. It was only later I realized I actually did have talent. As soon as I started to write, everything really came together in one piece for the first time. Even in the early years of the Who, I suffered that frustration of searching for my niche. That's why my first songs were so screwed up and indecisive.'

Townshend's indecision was apparent on his first demo, 'I Can't Explain.' 'It can't be beat for straightforward Kinks copying. . . . It came out of the top of my head when I was eighteen and a half. It seems to be about the frustrations of a young person who is so incoherent and uneducated he can't state his case to the bourgeois intellectual blah blah blah. Or, of course, it might be about drugs.'

Interestingly, Pete had another view by 1974, explaining the tune this way: 'I thought it was about a boy who can't explain to a girl that he's falling in love with her. But two weeks later I looked at the lyrics, and they meant something completely different. I began to see just what an outpouring the song really was. . . . I was two people: someone who sat down and wrote a song for some particular purpose, and then somebody who looked at it and saw something totally different. Then I realized, of course, that's why Bob Dylan doesn't know what to say when people ask him about his songs, because he doesn't fucking *know* what it's all about.'

Whatever it means, 'I Can't Explain' had an immediate impact. When it was brought to the attention of Kinks' producer Shel Talmy, he proclaimed the sound 'loud, raw, funky, and superballsy.' Talmy instantly signed the group, procuring a deal with Decca. The band tramped into Pye Studios and recorded the song in a scant two hours. Though Townshend says that the band was 'manipulated' – with the use of a backing vocal group, the Ivy Leagues, and gunslinger Jimmy Page on rhythm guitar – he acknowledges that the track still stands out today for its 'Louie Louie' guitar riff, Daltrey's slurred vocals, and Moon's brilliant, galloping drum work as a lead instrument. Five years later he deemed it an absolute favorite. 'It still turns me on.'

The resulting feedback from the street impressed the artist as well. 'When "I Can't Explain" emerged, a bunch of kids from the Goldhawk came up and stuttered at me, "Th-th-is is our song. You've said what it is we've been trying to say." And I said, "Well, what's that?"

'They said, "You've said that we can't explain how we feel." So I said, "What I've actually said is that *you* can't explain how you feel." They said, "Well, that's it and we want you to write some more straightaway."

'Then I wrote "Anyway, Anyhow, Anywhere" and "My Generation," and I think that's where I found that voice.'

The single 'I Can't Explain' was released on January 15, 1965, and shot up the charts to the number eight position, selling 104,000 copies. In anybody's book this was a real breakthrough. The success of the song secured an appearance in late February on *Ready Steady Go!*, the trendy pop TV show that was Britain's answer to *American Bandstand*.

'RSG was what was really going on,' says Townshend. 'They actually used to send people out to clubs in the provinces and pick out potential trend-setters. Fights used to start in the studio. People would appear on screen with sawed-off shotguns. They were so careful in picking people that were the faces they often got too close to the mark. They got people who really cared about their image.'

Meanwhile, the Who quickly found themselves on a treadmill of having to release a new song about every three months. The second Townshend composition, 'Anyway, Anyhow, Anywhere,' which was released on May 21, was a rare effort on which Roger Daltrey contributed lyrically.

'I dreamed that up listening to a Charlie Parker record,' remembers Townshend. 'I just thought, This is so free, so loose. He's playing this series of notes, but from him it's just . . . "anyhow, anyway, anywhere." The freedom suggested by the title became restricted by the aggression of our tightly defined image when I came to the words. In fact, Roger was really a hard nut then and changed quite a few words to toughen up the song to suit his temperament. It's the most excitingly pigheaded of our songs. It's blatant, proud, and, dare I say it, sassy.'

After laying down the basic track, Townshend set up his monolithic speaker stack and then reproduced the effects of a live performance including feedback, the clash of drumsticks against microphones, and the trashing of instruments. For this reason the record was erroneously perceived by Decca U.S. as a cacophony of technical faults and blatantly rejected.

In Britain, however, the single became the thundering theme-song of *Ready Steady Go!* and its throng of ardent mod disciples. Yet ironically, as mod achieved mass exposure, its original adherents had long since moved on. In fact, Marc Bolan, the flamboyant lead singer for the early seventies glam rock band T-Rex, boldly denounced the Who as imposters, stating that the craze had died before they'd even taken up the cause.

'It really wasn't the same anymore,' Townshend conceded, 'because in the real mod scene nobody'd tell you. It wasn't just fashion detail [but] more of a hint of how they felt. There's something in the way the real mod kids look at life today that has a mod stamp on it. They were poetic for working-class kids, always job flitting. It was incestuous, secretive, and difficult to be a real, up-to-the-minute mod 'cause no cunt'd tell you where to get the clothes. It wasn't something you decided to be, you just were.'

Irish Jack claimed that once the Who raised mod out of its cult status, it became a different entity. 'The mods of the sixties were not a movement; they were a fashion. Apart from the rockers, mods were the only youth culture in evidence from the end of '63 to at least '66. So a market in clothes and records which we helped create and was counterproductive in helping to sustain us was born. The Who were of that market, and Pete Townshend hit the nail on the head when he said of the Who, "We led by being led." If you can suss the sentiment of that classic statement, you will understand the period.'

In any case, Townshend was already moving in another direction. 'I dreamed up the idea of pop art music, which Kit then jumped on. I explained it to him, and he thought that whatever I'd explained to him didn't necessarily make sense, but it was good enough.'

Pop, largely an American movement, found its art in everyday life, from newspaper articles, billboards, and commercial advertisements epitomized in Andy Warhol's now legendary silkscreened soup cans. As with mod, Townshend wanted to make a statement with his rig: 'I designed the Union Jack jacket [mid-1965] and took the pattern to Savile Row – I got the idea for the target T-shirt from Jasper Johns and borrowed the chevrons motif from Bridget Riley. The Who were fops whereas the audience was pure mod, so the debate is nonsensical. We reflected an image, but we used a distorting mirror.'

Much more than fashion however was evolving for Townshend. Into his song writing, for the first time, entered the potent idea of protest. No longer was he concerned about mods and rockers. He wanted to voice the rising anger of youth against the establishment.

'"My Generation" was born out of a single incident. After our first two hits I got an American car [a 1963 Lincoln Continental], the first big car I'd ever bought. I was driving it down Beauchamp Place with the window open. I was about twenty-two. [Actually, he was nineteen.] And there was some woman driving the other way in an open car wearing a string of pearls, blonde hair, very beautiful, about thirty-five. We stopped and looked at one another and she said: "Driving Mummy's car, are we?" and drove off without giving me a chance to reply.

'What I found so offensive was that I'd been denied the right to even appear to have earned any money, even if I'd spent it unwisely. And I lived in Belgravia [with Kit Lambert] at the time.'

'I actually felt slightly ashamed of my people. What made me write "My Generation" was that this woman reminded me a bit of my mum. A bit stuck-up and sneering. Not only are you not rich enough to have a car like that, you're not pretty enough. The line "Hope I die before I get old" is about everything I felt she represented.'

In 1989, however, the composer placed an entirely different spin on the tale. In this scenario Townshend tells of parking his car (this time, a Packard hearse) outside his Belgravia flat only to find it missing the next morning. Hysterical, he phoned the police only to be informed that it had been towed away. Pete picks up the tale: 'It turned out the Queen Mother had it removed. She drove past each day from Clarence House to Buckingham Palace, and she'd seen the car and said, "Have it removed!" I was outraged.

My first car and I couldn't afford to get it back. That was the world I lived in, the world of imperious landlords. You do things their way, people like the Queen Mother who, with a flick of her finger, can have the first car you've ever bought removed from the face of the earth. That's where "My Generation" came from: I'd rather die than be like you people! I never want to become like you old fuckers. That's what I was saying.'

With Chris Stamp accurately predicting a huge success, Lambert hounded Townshend to rework and polish the tune, adding his own suggestions. At his prodding, Pete delivered the many upwardly progressive key changes, in the vein of the Kinks.

Daltrey's signature stutter too came about quite by accident. Many stories have circulated over the years from Daltrey doing it off-the-cuff to a tongue-in-cheek tale that he was cold in the studio and shivered as he recorded his vocal. The real lowdown, however, came from Keith Moon. 'Pete had written out the words and gave them to Roger in the studio. He'd never seen them before, so when he read them the first time he stuttered. Kit was producing us then, and when Roger stuttered, Kit said, "Leave in the stuttering." When we realized what had happened, it knocked us all sideways. And it happened simply because Roger couldn't read the words.'

Townshend, though, implied at the time that it was fully contrived, offering still another scenario for the song's unusual content. '[It's] about someone trying to object to today's poor educational system, but can't get it out because he stammers. I suppose it will be called protest, but I hope not because I think protest songs are a load of rubbish.'

Released on November 5, 1965, the three-minute anthem catapulted to the number-two position in the charts despite a temporary ban by the BBC. The stammering, suggests critic Goddard, held 'the mere possibility of naughty words.'

In 'My Generation' Townshend first released the anger and frustration he would never outgrow. 'All right, you motherfuckers,' proclaims Pete. 'I am going to have you! I'm going to be bigger, richer, and I'm going to move into your neighborhood. I'm going to buy that house next you, Lord So-and-so.'

Riding high on the song's enormous impact, Townshend was carried away on waves of elated bravado. 'Rock 'n' roll is enormous,' he hailed at the time. 'It's one of the biggest events in history.

It's equal to classical music. It's transcending slowly but surely, because of the impetus, the sheer weight of the feeling. It's like saying, "Get all the pop music, put it into a cartridge, put the cap on it, and fire the gun." You don't care whether those ten or fifteen numbers sound roughly the same. You don't care what periods they were written in, what they mean, what they're all about. It's the bloody explosion they create when you let the gun off. It's the event. That's what rock 'n' roll is. That's why rock is so powerful.'

Here Townshend was beginning to articulate more fully his 'us versus them' philosophy, a concept that had festered for centuries in a society sharply divided between bluebloods and commoners. 'What I couldn't understand was not that polarization of the class system, but the idea that you could never ever move or grow if somebody saw you in a particular way. That's not something the working classes have ever carried. I think there's a generosity in the working class which says, "Good on you, mate, if you can pull yourself up by the bootstraps." There's never been that generosity on the other side.'

To members of the music press, forced to write about the powder-puff drivel of Gerry and the Pacemakers, Herman's Hermits, and soppy Peter and Gordon, the Who, with its raucous sound and outspoken guitarist, made for stirring copy. *Melody Maker* hailed their sound as 'vicious'. This is a note-perfect showbiz group singing in harmony and playing clean guitar runs. There's sadism in their characters and their music. . . . They could well become tomorrow's big stars.'

'When I get the feedback noise,' Townshend commented in 1965, 'it sounds like a bomber. Then Moon can bang the drums, and the audience thinks of guns and smashing people up. They envy our music. They would love to get hold of a two-thousand-pound guitar and wallop it. They would like to jump on the stage and yell about why can't kids have pills and why the young are being put down by people of forty who want to be twenty. We're catering to their suppressed aggression.'

Added Daltrey, 'We've always been about letting people's frustrations out. We have always done it. That's the secret of the Who. We had this knack of writing what everyone was feeling and we could communicate. That's what we've always really done well.'

The critics agreed with this assessment. Upon release of the band's first LP, *The Who Sings My Generation*, compiling their early singles, Greg Shaw wrote: 'Each song is basically about one thing: finding self-image through the release of frustration born of tension. Tension and its release was the whole essence of the Who, both thematically and musically.'

Inevitably, the audience at Who concerts provided the litmus test. Guitarist Brian May of Queen revisits those wild early performances: 'They were the most outrageously adventurous thing I'd ever seen. They were just hooligans. But amidst all the hooliganism there was this wonderful breadth of sound and the great brain of Pete Townshend. . . . I remember they played at one of the colleges in London, and they were an hour and a half late. No one was sure if they were gonna show up, and the place was seething with about a thousand kids. When they finally came on, they didn't give a shit. Townshend waved his arms and started making airplane noises for about twenty minutes before they even played a song. They didn't have any regard for anything, and it was wonderful and real.'

Behind the scenes, Kit Lambert was steadily egging them on. Even while he tutored the band in highbrow culture, masterminding their smart Carnaby look, even disdaining pot smoking as 'playacting decadence,' he was simultaneously instructing them to 'be scruffy and shoot your mouth off.' Lambert further instructed the group to step up their already loud, irreverent stage show.

'If there was one major obstacle I confronted in my life,' Pete has said, 'it was the physical ugliness that was thrown in the Who's face in the early days. People used to come see us and say, "Jesus Christ, they're ugly!" I, in some way, took that as a value judgment.'

For the defensive and fiery Townshend such negative reaction was an open invitation for retaliation. 'My guitar is like a machine gun,' he said. 'When I play it, it's like grenades going off. It silences the audience. It makes them hear me.

'We were leading a revolt against the old values and order of music,' he later explained. 'Everybody was full of resentment. It was also a means of intimidation: This is all there is. If you're in this room with us, all you get is us.'

Their stage act, always explosive, now featured an apocalyptic climax: Townshend would ramrod his guitar into the amplifiers, piercing the cabinets and bludgeoning the speakers while simultaneously splitting his instrument into fragments, continuing the assault until it lay in tiny pieces all over the stage.

Meanwhile, Moon would topple his drum kit, kicking the pieces as they rolled across the floor. Daltrey would launch his microphone into the cymbals. For the grand finale, Roger booted out the floodlights one by one while Moon tossed buckets of water over the frenzied audience. The entire room would be cast in an acrid yellow haze from the smoke bombs hurled from the wings by Kit and Chris.

The destruction was fueled as well by the fact that the boys often played when they were high. 'We used to play up north and dash back in the furniture van to play Tottenham,' reveals Entwistle. 'We were complete pill heads, and we'd often still be playing when the other group went on. Then we got to playing drunk, and I'd often forget I'd done a gig. Moon would pass out before a gig, sober up just before we went on, play like a maniac, and go back on the bottle as soon as we finished.'

For Townshend, the abuse proved even more invasive. 'When the band started in 1964–65, I really thought we were gonna explode. I thought I was gonna die . . . I never ate. It was all dope, dope, dope, and horrible vibes of aggression and bitterness. Out of that we were saying, "We are the mirror for the desperation, bitterness, frustration, and misery of the misunderstood adolescents, of people in the vacuum.'

Added to this was the unnerving experience of finding himself a celebrity while still in his teens. As Betty Townshend remembers, 'It was in the local newspapers that the group were Ealing- and Acton- based . . . You could imagine what it was like here. There were people walking up and down saying, "I bet that's the house. Go ring the doorbell and see if that's it." Peter just loathes being hounded. He thinks it's disgusting when people turn up at the door; he thinks it's really bad form.'

Townshend insider Kathy notes that Pete didn't handle his sudden fame with great grace. 'He was a nothing who joined a band at seventeen, and it became the hippest group in England. People would kiss his ass. Pete would throw up into his glass and rather than someone saying, "You're a disgusting pig," they'd throw up in their glass too. So he would think it's all right. He's grown up not understanding what's right and wrong.'

At his attic flat on Wardour Street, Soho, in 1966, Townshend would flaunt his newfound success belittling his old mates. Richard Barnes recalls a particular evening when some art school friends gathered and they were out of refreshments. Barnes offered to replenish the supply, fully aware that Pete knew he was on a tight budget. Yet Townshend, grabbing a five-pound note, took the opportunity to degrade his old room-mate.

'You can afford it,' egged Pete, waving the note teasingly before him. 'Sure you don't want this?' Townshend cruelly milked the moment. 'Are you certain you don't want it?' then he proceeded to slowly tear up the bill.

Townshend's relationship with Daltrey, always rocky, was now at the point of disintegration. Roger complained that his vocals couldn't be heard above the din, and vehemently opposed the group's new grittier sound. 'Pete wanted to record his stuff, of course,' reveals Stamp, 'but he couldn't push it, so it was down to me and Kit. The only block was Roger. The group was moving out of his grasp, and he wanted to do this heavy R&B thing so that songs like "I Can't Explain" and later "Substitute" were like pop to him.'

Moreover, Daltrey disliked and mistrusted the group's managers. It didn't help that Chris Stamp was openly campaigning for Pete's 'more interesting' voice over Roger's. It was even rumored that Roger's replacement would be Boz of Boz's People. Daltrey was also resentful of Lambert taking over the sessions for the group's first LP, even to the point of coaching his vocals.

While Townshend was living the good life, now newly ensconced in ritzy Belgravia, Daltrey had taken up residence in his van because he was having problems with his pregnant wife, Jackie, whom he had married secretly earlier that year. Their tenuous relationship was undermined by Lambert's directive to Daltrey: 'Leave your wife and get your own bloody flat.'

Now that Townshend's songwriting was quickly leading the group toward stardom, the takeover of Daltrey's old band was all but complete.

Townshend and Daltrey were now even discussing their problems with the press. 'Arguments? Sure, we have 'em all the time,' Roger ventured. 'It kind of sharpens us up. We've all got explosive temperaments, and it's like waitin' for a bomb to go off. . . . We're not mates at all.'

'Ours is a group with built-in hate,' commented Pete. 'If we liked each other, we probably wouldn't exist. Once we took a few days off to go away and hate each other, and when we came back we played twenty times better.'

Daltrey's profound alienation from the rest of the group emanated partly from his rejection of the uppers the other three were swallowing hand over fist. The resulting tensions culminated during the group's first Scandinavian tour, when Daltrey tossed Moon's stash down the toilet and punctuated his fury by landing a knockout punch. As Keith explained, 'I was taking a lot of speed. Roger wasn't because it used to fuck his voice up. Roger was drinking and we were all speeding. One time in Sweden Roger blew up: "You're all fucking junkies! The group's finished as far as I'm concerned." And he took a swing at me.'

Not surprisingly, Daltrey was unceremoniously booted from the group. His exile, however, was brief, only a week later he returned. 'I was a bastard, a real cunt. I thought if I lost the band, I was dead. I realized the Who was the reason I was successful. I didn't fight anymore . . . for a couple of years anyway.'

'The first two years of the Who were absolutely horrible,' Townshend confided. 'The music is lighthearted and funny, but underneath it was agonizingly sad, no real friendships, honesty, or trust. We weren't very nice people. I wouldn't go through that again for anything.'

At another point he reflected: 'If there was ever a period when the Who might have split, it would have been in the days of "My Generation". We had an image of no time for anybody, and mod arrogance in a period when we were actually a very ordinary group. We hadn't really done anything good. We didn't have any self-respect as a group, but we knew we were capable so we managed over a period to get it together.'

As the new year dawned the Who discarded their mod skin for a more mainstream look. Pete's writing too was taking on a new maturity. 'Substitute' rode all the way to the top of the *New Musical Express* charts. And it had a nice touch of wit and irony: 'Substitute you for my mom/At least I'll get my washing done.'

Townshend has said that the song was actually a takeoff of the Stones' 'Nineteenth Nervous Breakdown.' 'On the demo I sang with an affected Jagger-like accent which Kit obviously liked, as he suggested the song as a follow-up to "My Generation." The lyric has come to be the most quoted Who lyric ever. It somehow goes to show that the "art, not the artist" tag that people put on Dylan's silence about his work could be a good idea . . . "Substitute" makes me recall writing a song to fit a clever and rhythmic-sounding title. A play on words. Again it could mean a lot more to me now than it did when I wrote it. If I told you what it meant to me now, you'd think I take myself too seriously.

'The stock, downbeat riff used in the verses I pinched from a record played to me in "Blind Date," a feature in *Melody Maker*. It was by a group who later wrote to thank me for saying nice things about their record in the feature. The article is set up so that pop stars hear other people's records without knowing who they are by. They say terrible things about their best mates' latest and it only makes the pop scene snottier and more competitive. The record I said nice things about wasn't a hit, despite an electrifying riff. I pinched it, we did it and you bought it.'

Townshend's writing was truly taking shape. 'I'm a Boy,' 'Pictures of Lily,' 'A Legal Matter,' and 'Happy Jack' are all vignettes sculpted from a deeply personal perspective. Adolescent themes, however, still abounded. 'Pictures of Lily,' Townshend's 'ditty about masturbation,' was allegedly based on his parents catching him in the act and lamenting aloud, 'Why can't he go out with girls like other boys?' Another time he stated that the song was inspired by a twenties poster of vaudevillian star Lily Bayliss. Peter told *New Musical Express* that 'it's just a look back to that period in every boy's life when he has pinups.'

The greater significance of these tunes is Townshend's shift from rabble-rouser to a more thoughtful, scaled-down approach tailored from real-life experience. 'Happy Jack,' 'a nonsense song' set on the Isle of Man, is a lyrical tale about a reclusive simpleton teased by youngsters on holiday that clearly evokes his own awkward youth.

While Townshend dismissed the song as yet another throwaway, Lambert adroitly saw otherwise. 'I think "Happy Jack" should be your next single,' he told Pete.

'Are you kidding? Never in a million years will it be a hit for the Who.'

When the offbeat number eventually scored in the United States, Townshend conceded, saying that he had learned 'a hard ego lesson. The public are the people who will decide, not you.'

What was not in doubt was the preeminence Townshend was gaining in the band. These songs were all his. In fact, his meticulous process of recording material before the group even heard it is one that set Townshend apart from his contemporaries. While the home demos of most artists are ragged first draft, Pete's are as precise as scripts passed out to actors. According to *Melody Maker's* Chris Charlesworth, 'At home in his private studios, Townshend painstakingly overdubs everything until he has produced a solo single of his own. This he duplicates and sends out to the other three so they may learn their parts and improve on them before the actual group recording.'

'What happens,' Pete said in 1968, 'is I will suggest the bass riff on the demonstration record; John takes it and goes from there. But the bass line I would suggest on the demo would be very simple. It would be economical, tasteful, and just a vehicle for the song. And if I use the piano or drum, it's as simple and effective as possible in putting the piece across to the group.'

Yet in the same breath he maintained that it's not a mere skeleton he presents to the members but a complete product. 'What I've got to do is get the rest of the band to dig my number. If I've got a number I dig, I know I've got to present it to them in the best light. That's why I make my own recordings, so when they first hear it, it's not me stoned out of my mind plunking away on a guitar trying to get my latest number across. It's a finished work that might take me all night to get together, but nevertheless it's gonna win them over.'

According to Charlesworth, the latter is closer to the truth. 'In hushed corridors it's said by those who have heard Townshend demos that they frequently rival the finished product.'

Keith Moon once confirmed that there was precious little leeway for change. 'When Pete writes something, it sounds like the Who. The drum phrases are my phrases, even though it's Pete playing. He's playing the way I play. He's playing my flourishes. The same thing for the bass part, and the guitar, of course, is his own. Only the vocals change some.'

With a string of hits behind them, by 1966 the Who were now

soaring in popularity. They had become a major attraction on their European tours and at jazz festivals, clearly having outgrown pubs for theaters and ballrooms. They were commanding three to five hundred pounds per appearance plus a generous piece of the gate.

Yet the Who weren't the only attraction, and Townshend was jealous of anyone who seemed to outshine him. He first encountered an upcoming young gun named Eric Clapton at an Ealing bus stop on his way to a gig in 1964. 'He looked extremely smart and modish,' Pete recalled. 'He'd shaved all his hair off. We hardly spoke. Two weeks later, I saw him at a clothes shop, Austin's in Shaftesbury Avenue. . . . I went up to him and said, "I've heard your band, the Yardbirds, is great." What I meant was, "I've heard they're a load of rubbish, but you're quite good."'

Clapton, however, politely snubbed him. As a traditional blues player, he didn't harbor much respect for the lightweight Tamla sound the Who were pumping out under Pete Meaden. In turn, Townshend brushed off the rival guitarist despite, at that point, never having seen Clapton play. 'To me, a London white performer trying to play blues was a joke. I felt that what the Who had at least done was turn into slightly more of our own urban form of music that depended very much on the lyrics. How could a young white boy from Surrey really play the blues?'

Admitted Townshend, 'Musically he felt superior, and I know I certainly did.'

They were beginning to forge a tenuous friendship when an upstart young American rocketed onto the scene. Jimi Hendrix came to see Townshend on his first day in London at IBC Studios to ask where to buy equipment. 'I was very unimpressed with Jimi that day,' Pete remembered. 'He was wearing a beat-up US Marines jacket, and he looked scruffy, jet-lagged, and pockmarked. I thought, "Ugh." Two days later, though, I saw him play at Blazes and it was devastating.'

Even so, Townshend was put off by Clapton's instant case of idol worship. 'Eric was quicker to accept him than I was. He used to tell me, "I stand on stage now and pretend I am Jimi, and I play better." I couldn't play anyway, so there was no chance of me entering that kind of guitar world.

'It was tough for me and Eric because we'd appropriated

this black American blues and imported it for the fourteen- to twenty-year-olds in London. Now here's Hendrix saying, "I'm taking it back. You've finished with it. I'll show you where it goes next."'

Still, he was absolutely determined to outplay every other act. 'I remember once saying to Eric, just after Jimi had first appeared on the scene and both of us were enamored with him. I said, "One day I'll play him off stage." 'He just said, "Fuck off." "No, I will," I said.

'I later realized I had to say that. I had to believe it even though I felt there was no way I could.' This was proven months later, at Brian Epstein's Saville Theatre. Although the warm-up band to the Who, Hendrix completely upstaged them. 'I'm not ashamed to say he blew us away,' Townshend admitted, looking back.

Meanwhile, the band's nasty internal warfare had once again escalated. 'The Who,' Pete observed, 'were a group who were chopping away at their own legs. We were autodestructive, out to destroy ourselves.'

As John Entwistle pointed out, 'I was always breaking up fights, pulling Roger off somebody, usually Pete. Keith and I were fed up with all the punching and with Townshend being so big-headed, thinking he was a fucking musical genius.'

The four went at one another with fists, bottles, and even knives, Moon happily displayed his scars to prove it. '[We] smashed glasses, bottles . . . it was incredibly violent for a time. It was common knowledge in England because there were a lot of people coming to see our shows and we came on with sticking plasters, bleeding. There were even fistfights on stage. Every five minutes somebody was quitting the group.'

At one critically explosive point it was Moon against everyone. On May 20, 1966, playing the Ricky Tick Club in Newbury, Moon knocked over a drum and a cymbal that struck Townshend on the leg. Pete abruptly swung his guitar around and caught Moon on the head, leaving him badly bruised and requiring three stitches. This was the final straw. Keith announced he had quit the group, refusing to answer the door and accept Townshend's apology. Although he soon recanted and rejoined his mates the following week, the tension was still ominous.

'In the beginning I just couldn't get through to Peter,' Moon explained. 'We really have absolutely nothing in common what-soever apart from the music.'

As 1967 approached, John and Keith were more than ready to pack it in for good. 'Keith and I decided we'd go off and form a band with Richard Cole, who used to be our chauffeur,' says Entwistle. 'A big band making much more money than the Who could ever make. I was gonna call the band Led Zeppelin, and I'd designed a cover of an R/101 Zeppelin going down in flames. I was gonna do it in black and white, very subtle. I was always better at naming groups and designing album covers.'

Chauffeur Cole, meanwhile, went to work for Jimmy Page just two weeks later, taking with him the soon-to-be-famous name and artwork.

A critical reason for the band's internal fighting was their over-the-top spending. They were in desperate straits, a half-million-dollar hole that would take five years to climb out of. Furthermore, the band's new deal with Polydor was costing them dearly. Shel Talmy had proven a dictatorial force in the studio, allowing the band little creative freedom. He was also allegedly creaming off too much of the profits. Wrangling out of it, especially when Talmy's resistance was spearheaded by negotiator Allen Klein, became a vicious battle that finally extricated the boys, but only after a brutal financial bloodletting.

By 1967, Townshend and the Who found themselves at an impasse. *Ready Steady Go!*, boosted by its mod following, had reached the end of its run. Now that mod was dead, the band was left without an identity. Their fee dropped to a mere fifty pounds per gig. They were too big for the pubs, yet ballrooms were hardly their venue. Like all bands, they had to change with the times or be buried. Their only way out was to head overseas.

In order to make real money all British bands had to export their product. This meant America, and for the Who this meant dealing with their seemingly disinterested company, Decca. But none of that deterred Townshend. He was predictably excited, cocky, and bullishly single-minded. It was time to show these American upstarts what the real British invasion was all about.

Even as he made plans to cross the Atlantic, something bigger was brewing in his mind. The Who couldn't remain a singles band forever, and Townshend already had an idea of how he was going to change all that. It would mean tearing up the very foundations of contemporary music. Pete Townshend was about to build a brand-new house of rock in which an entire generation would take up residence.

4

Titans: *The Who*

The Who are an enormous business machine, surrounded by all kinds
of controversy, and I suppose a great amount of media power. A lot of
that comes from the success of things that are happening around the
band. The *Tommy* film is a case in point: an average, entertaining film,
blown all out of proportion. It's really got very little to do with frontline
rock 'n' roll, but it does affect the way people see the band.

– Pete Townshend

For Pete Townshend, coming to America was like coming home.
He had always regarded it a sacrilege that the Who and other
British groups recycled and then exported America's black heritage
stateside. Now he was about to truly experience the music in which
he'd been baptized and ordained: the blues.

'I felt a kind of spiritual buzz from the surviving Soul Stirrers,' he
once said. 'Rock comes from R&B, R&B from gospel with a swing,
and swing from the Soul Stirrers. There's no reason hymns shouldn't
swing. No reason God shouldn't be sexy. America created rock 'n'
roll, but it's become a symbol of the liberation of its people. . . . It
all began with freedom from slavery and the kind of Christianity
the Church was imposing on its slaves.'

Top American deejay Murray the K first brought over the Who

for his annual rock show, slated for March 25 through April 2, at New York's RKO Theater. On the bill were five other acts, including blues rockers Cream, whom Townshend once termed 'a fucking ripoff.' Upon their arrival the Who found themselves in a frenetic weeklong schedule of five shows daily at fourteen minutes per.

'One and a half minutes of "My Generation," ' remembered Keith, 'one and a half of "Substitute," then smash your fuckin' instruments, and rush off.'

'I spent more time as a carpenter gluing guitars together than a musician,' Pete later quipped.

Off stage Townshend and Cream members Eric Clapton, Jack Bruce, and Ginger Baker hurled obscenities at one another good-naturedly. 'I wasn't very impressed with Pete's playing,' recalls drummer Baker, who incidentally penned the Who B-side instrumental 'Ode for a Pig' when the band was short a tune for a 1966 single.

'All show and no substance,' agrees bassist Bruce. 'I can't stand Pete's stuff. It's all twee and twaddle. We all know there are three chords, and it's up to the rest of us to use them more effectively than he does!'

Eric Clapton, though, tossed in the final good-natured insult. 'We had these fourteen-pound bags of flour and eggs we were going to use on stage, but Murray somehow heard about it and said we wouldn't get paid if we did. So we spread them around the dressing rooms. Townshend ended up swimming fully clothed in a foot of water when his shower overflowed!'

American audiences took immediate notice of the Who's gangly guitarist, who viciously assaulted his equipment on a regular basis. His notoriety was further cemented by the band's controversial television appearance on the popular *Smothers Brothers Comedy Hour*. 'When it came to the actual show,' remembers Pete, 'the drum exploded so fiercely my hair was singed and Keith crawled from the wreckage covered with blood. Bette Davis and Mickey Rooney, who were also on the show, were having heart attacks. They had to be stopped from rushing on to help us!' In fact, the usually feisty Ms Davis actually fainted in the diminutive Rooney's arms.

'Americans were amused by our performances, but to their credit they listened to us play,' recalls Townshend. 'That was kind of a novelty for us. They were genuinely interested in the music.'

Whereas back home the often stodgy British establishment

frowned on the utter mindlessness of pummeling a perfectly good guitar, the Yanks lined up to provide a steady stream of free instruments for the purpose of destruction. Townshend, by the way, was now regularly smashing top-flight customized Gibsons.

It was the beginning of a twenty-year mutual love affair with the Yanks that was in part based on the band being appreciated as musicians, not the mere stylists they were dubbed in Britain. 'The vibrations you pick up are incredible,' Townshend said of his adopted fans. 'They really want to hear what you are playing.' Later he would proudly submit, 'America bought my house, my car and carpeted my floor.'

Off stage the band took full advantage of the open invitation to rave it up during their American tour. 'We like smashing hotels,' Pete proclaimed. He himself generally confined his pranks to trashing furniture and tossing the odd cherry bomb at unsuspecting guests. Keith Moon, however, did virtually anything to get attention. 'If he thought it would get a laugh, he'd pour petrol over himself and set himself on fire,' Pete once cracked, only half joking.

'I feel the same way toward hotels our audience feels toward us: I'm grateful they exist, but I hate the prices they charge. . . . It does 'em good to know there's still a few ripe bastards left in the world.'

Still, Townshend did have a penchant for getting into trouble in his newly adopted country. One time when the band was playing the legendary Fillmore East in New York, a fire broke out in an adjacent building, launching a cadre of police to evacuate the theater. In the melee a plain-clothes officer leaped on stage yelling, 'Fire!' Townshend, along with Daltrey, jumped him, sending both directly to jail. Pete was subsequently charged with assault and fined. 'We mistook him for some kind of heckler,' Pete explained to the press. 'We very much regret the whole thing.'

Another incident occurred at Memphis airport when Townshend, having just boarded a flight to Atlanta, made an offhand remark to a passenger regarding the success of their new album in the States. 'It's not really doing very well here, but it's "going a bomb" in New York.'

A stewardess, overhearing the quip, misunderstood, and within minutes all fifty passengers were shunted off the plane. Townshend too was immediately escorted off by the FBI. 'I tried to explain it was just a phrase [meaning "doing well"], but they wouldn't listen,' he recalls. 'I've learned one thing: Never mention bombs on planes.'

His waywardness continued when he returned back home. The guitarist was introduced to the latest cult drug, LSD. Painter Michael English, who occasionally did graphics for the group, recalls tripping with Townshend at a house near Victoria. 'He had a bad trip the first time. Somebody spiked his food, a terrible time. I remember saying to him, "You can really learn something wonderful if you take it in the right environment, are ready for it, and have an experienced guide." So I got some acid and we all took it: Pete, myself, and some close friends. He was able to have a deep experience. I think it made his music a lot richer and his lyrics certainly more meaningful. Not that one could actually compose whilst on a trip. You can't, it's the memory of what you've learned that's valuable.'

Townshend delved further into the psychedelic experience, often tripping at London's trendy UFO Club, where his longtime girlfriend, Karen Astley, worked as a waitress. He tagged the illicit drug's attraction as 'sinister, feline, sexual, and inherently female.' 'There's a spiritual process going on in every person's head that's overwhelmingly complex and beautifully balanced. Acid feeds on the distortion of that balance. People find pleasure in distorting the balance. The human being is such a beautifully equipped piece of machinery, it's very spiritually disturbing to topple it and think that it's good.'

It didn't take long, however, for Townshend to reject the trendy hallucinogen as all flash and no real substance. 'If you know you're throwing yourself out of balance, like when you're drunk, you hate yourself, so that's all right. But when you trip, you love yourself. You don't realize you were better equipped as you were. The trips are just a side street, and before you know it you're back where you were. Each trip is more disturbing than the one that follows until eventually the side street becomes a dead end. Not only spiritually (which is the most important), but it can actually stop you thinking.'

On a minitour of the States in June 1967, at a sound check for the eagerly anticipated Monterey Pop Festival, Townshend was given a particularly potent hit from the hands of notorious Berkeley chemist Augustus Owsley III. 'He was introducing like version seven of his acid,' says Pete. 'You never knew exactly what you were getting when you took it. I did some in San Francisco and never touched a drug again for eighteen years. It was incredibly powerful. Owsley must have had the most extraordinary liver.'

Their historic performance at Monterey on June 18 was, ironically, also the U.S. debut of the Jimi Hendrix Experience. Jimi was scheduled to precede the Who, making Townshend very apprehensive. Jimi had already upstaged the band on a number of occasions, freely copying Pete's windmill and even setting his guitar on fire at the Saville Theatre.

John Entwistle, for one, wasn't impressed. 'Certainly he can play, but what he plays is an amalgam of every other guitarist he has seen.'

'Yeah,' agreed Townshend, 'he definitely took something from everywhere. It took me a long time to get used to it. He was unabashedly doing it. He came to London, saw a couple of Who shows because he was on our label, and immediately started doing guitar pyrotechnic routines. Have you ever noticed how few guitarists swing their arms? Jimi would do what the fuck he liked. He thought, "Sure, they do it, but when I do it, it looks better!" He was that confident.'

Word soon got around backstage that Hendrix had decided to 'sacrifice' his instrument by bludgeoning it to smithereens and then setting it ablaze – a galling move that threatened to defuse the Who's entire act. Seething, Pete stormed into Jimi's dressing room. 'I had it out with him,' recalls Townshend. 'I said, "You're not going to go out and smash your guitar, are you?" He got very nasty about it and started to get very flashy. He varied between being very nice to rather arrogant.'

In the end, adulation, if not awe, overcame Pete's indignation. 'He was a fucking genius. He could have stolen my wife and I would have been happy about it. I had a very reverential attitude toward him. He could make you *see* what he was playing without acid. He was a cosmic player. . . . Compared to Hendrix [I'm] a complete nonentity.'

As it turned out, the Who's performance was a thundering success. They became instant heroes with the Love Generation crowd. Townshend remarked on the irony of being hailed by flower-power hippies. 'It was a funny time because we were all aware of the caricatures we represented. Roger, with his plastered-down psychedelic hairdo, me with my boiler suit, and

Moon with his "must-nip-back-to-the-hotel-as-I-forgot-to-throw-the-television-out-the-window" and Entwistle's complete inability to hold on to a dollar bill for more than fifteen seconds.'

Returning from San Francisco, Townshend made the mistake of popping a tab someone gave him, not realizing it was the potentially deadly mind-altering chemical STP. 'I had a couple of astral visions, heard voices, and seemed to be able to leave my body and look at myself. I felt that if I had cut off my own head, the horrible feeling would go on for eternity because I wasn't in my body. The effects lasted seven days, and when it finally finished I felt so devastated I resolved never to use drugs again.'

But Townshend found it wasn't so easy. Although he swore off psychedelics for good, over the next year he continued to smoke pot and even indulged in a short-lived flirtation with cocaine. He was able to quit only after a period of hard self-reflection when he realized how much he had credited to his drug use: his success, personality, even composing, admitting most of the band's early singles were written 'as a pill head mod.' 'I used to think it was what made me tick, the only way I could write, sing, or enjoy life. I felt I could only appreciate good music or a sunset if I was high.

'When I found out life was not the same, if not *better*, I realized they had been wasted years. That time did a lot to my psyche. I lost a lot of drive and ambition.'

Back to the business of music making, in mid-1967 Townshend hit on a novel idea for the band's third album, *The Who Sell Out*. The result was Pete's self-dubbed pop art music: absurd, crass, blandly commercial, the musical answer to Andy Warhol's soup cans. Complete with corny jingles, phony commercials, obnoxious deejays, and silly sound effects, it paid tribute to the band's early success. At the same time it was also a satire on the popular advertising scene: loud, trivial, for the moment. 'We wanted to make fun of ourselves to a degree,' recalls Townshend, 'and take some of the gravity which seems to be weighing the group down in America.'

While the album encompassed elements of the Beatles' *Sgt. Pepper*, the Beach Boys' innovative *Pet Sounds* and Dylan's magnificent *Blonde on Blonde*, injected with Townshend's quirky humor, ultimately it was a brilliant idea that never fully blossomed. Too ambitious, scattered in too many directions, devoid of any real continuity, it ended up an uneven jumble of scrambled musical images. Interspersed with jingles about deodorant and a long-winded commentary about acne medication, the material runs helter-skelter all over the board. 'Tattoo,' another Townshend tale of adolescent sexual repression, is followed by the intensely romantic 'Our Love Is.' The absurd 'Cobwebs and Strange' later became a commercial ad for Heinz baked beans.

One reason for this often muddled, at times brilliant, mess can be found in the project's inspiration, a song called 'Jaguar,' which Pete had written in a similar musical vein to the *Batman* television theme. It was a case of the composer not being true to his own vision, but rather bowing to his band mates' desires. Pete termed it 'a very clear example of how difficult it was for me to reconcile what I took to be Roger's need for macho chauvinistic lyrics and Keith Moon's appetite for surf music and fantasy sports car love affairs.'

Nik Cohn of *Queen* magazine called the record a 'failure. What this album really should have been is a total ad explosion, incredibly fast, loud, rash and vulgar, a holocaust, an utter wipe-out, a monster rotor whirl of everything that pop advertising really is.'

Even its December 1967 release date was out of kilter. It was an offbeat petal of pop art out of season in the full bloom of the psychedelic era.

Fortunately, the album spawned the sublime 'I Can See For Miles,' a genuine Townshend masterpiece as well as mentor Kit Lambert's production tour de force. Lambert's choice to record in Gold Star Studios, with its state-of-the-art echo chamber, greatly enhanced the track, drawing out Daltrey's demanding vocals and Moon's drumroll flourishes. 'One of the best songs I've ever written,' Townshend later remembered. 'Quite a fiery Wagnerian piece. I spent a lot of time working on the vocal harmonies and structuring it.

'It was [originally] written about jealousy but actually turned out to be about the immense power of aspiration. You often see what it is you want to reach, and know you can't get at it and say, "I'm gonna try." Those words start to move you in a direction, as long as you say, "I can see what I want, but there's no way I can get it."'

Though the song was embraced in the States, it inexplicably flopped in England. 'It didn't sell a single copy. I was humiliated. I thought, "What are the Who going to do? What am *I* gonna do?"'

In the wake of the song's commercial failure Townshend put out several 'strange records,' like 'Dogs' and the spirited, though lyrically inane, 'Magic Bus.' 'My writing had gone ape shit,' he later remembered. 'I was definitely coming out with some really weird stuff.'

In fairness, though, it was a time of transition for the young composer. Townshend left his bachelor days behind when, on May 20, 1968, he married art school steady Karen Astley at Didcot Registry Office, Berkshire. A former model and entry-level dress designer studying to be a teacher, the tall, often moody redhead was the daughter of film composer Edwin Astley, among whose credits was *The Mouse That Roared*.

'I remember the first time I saw her back,' remembers Townshend. 'It was in 1963. She sat in the booth behind me in Sid's Cafe by Ealing Art School. I thought she was a much younger girl because she hunched her shoulders up and from behind seemed so small. When she stood up and walked out, I realized she was actually very tall and graceful, her face stunningly beautiful.'

Their unlikely courtship unfolded a study of opposites: the working-class rocker and the aristocratic lady. Underlying the throes of passion, however, simmered hints of problems later to surface: Townshend's deep-seated sense of unworthiness; his keen outspokenness pitted against Karen's resolute desire for privacy; his obsession with the Who while she shunned it. Pete's drinking was also a problem. The bane of many a musician's life, Townshend's consumption greatly increased while on tour, especially filling those boring hours on buses in the States with endless rounds of beer and scotch.

Following their wedding, the Townshends moved into a three-bedroom, 1745 Georgian town house in Twickenham, Middlesex, overlooking the Thames, which he purchased for £16,500. Fatherhood followed with the birth of daughters Emma on March 28, 1969, and Aminta on April 24, 1971. On the surface Pete appeared to have his ideal life. And while he publicly proclaimed the union 'a marriage made in heaven,' it would be severely tested time and again over the next three decades.

Pete contended that being married changed at least one aspect of his life dramatically: his writing. 'When I wrote the first five or six songs for the Who, I was completely and totally alone. I had no girlfriend, no friends, nothing. It was me alone addressing the world.'

With Townshend's writing in a state of transition, the halt of the Who singles bullet train was in hindsight a blessing. 'I don't find [forty-fives] fulfilling because I'm not sure what I'm trying to get across is actually coming across. I've always been upset that the allegories beneath songs like "I'm a Boy," "Pictures of Lily," and "I Can See for Miles" might only appear when I sit down and write my autobiography.'

Much as the short story is to a novel, a mere single couldn't hold his increasingly expansive, highly original ideas. Evidence of his talent for larger compositions had already surfaced. 'A Quick One While He's Away,' a nine-minute song about a messy love triangle, was a self-contained musical tale hastily pieced together by Townshend to fill up a side of their second LP. Tagged by critic Dave Marsh as 'halfway between Gilbert and Sullivan and a stag film,' the effect was an amateurish jumble of country and western, surf sounds, and full-tilt rock.

Further antecedents stemmed from actual stories Townshend was writing. 'Happy Jack' was actually born from an aborted fairy tale, while 'I'm a Boy' was but a fragment extracted from *Quads* (not to be confused with *Quadrophenia*), about a futuristic civilization wherein the sex of all offspring is scientifically predetermined. A couple 'orders' four girls and mistakenly receives a son, who they nonetheless raise as female, and all grow up to form a Motown-style 'girl group.' Not exactly high art, but it clearly displayed Townshend's growing narrative mind-set.

Pete's real promise, though, was displayed with the six-minute quasi-pop march 'Rael' off the *Who Sell Out* album. This was an excerpt from a complex opera set in 1999 within a political landscape where the Communist Chinese become world conquerors, quashing all religion as they go. With its challenging tempo changes and operetta-like harmonies, Pete was steadily forging new territory.

His evolution was also displayed in a piece played by the Who during their performance at the never officially released Rolling Stones' *Rock 'n' Roll Circus*. 'You Are Forgiven' (complete with sizzling falsettos) was tagged by Kit Lambert as the first official 'mini-opera.'

Initially, Townshend's 'new' art form was born of sheer practicality. 'I suppose what I wanted was to rescue the pop song which seemed to me to be in serious trouble in the late sixties partly because of the kind of post-psychedelic wetness that seemed to be everywhere. You could write a song that went "Weee love you, Weee love you,"* and it would get to number four in the charts. I was outraged and desolate because I knew I was too much of a cynic to ever be able to do that. I was a believer in what a certain group of writers like Ray Davies, Bob Dylan and certain moments in Lennon and McCartney were occasionally uncovering.'

It was around this time too that the Who faced both bankruptcy and a long string of fiery identity battles that threatened a breakup. The band was now clearly at a crossroads. Townshend, though, had nothing much left to lose and so decided to gamble everything on one 'last ditch attempt.'

The idea began as merely a patchwork collective of songs he sought to weave together in some sort of artistic 'order.' 'That's why *Tommy* is so big,' he would later point out. 'It's actually [several] vignettes. It was supposed to be a series of singles and any departure from that was introduced by Kit Lambert's coaching: "keep that, write another tune, then repeat that." So I just wrote bits and stuck them into songs. It may appear to flow, but when I presented it to the band it was simply a series of songs.'

In fact, as Townshend pointed out years later, 'I think it's obvious that *Tommy* and "My Generation" were very similarly motivated entities. "Generation," in fact, says what *Tommy* does, only in a much shorter timespan.'

But there was still clearly a missing element. For the spiritually hungry Townshend, who had a year earlier begun to zealously follow Parsi spiritual master Meher Baba, he had himself become the archetypal Seeker, searching for something more. 'I was captivated by that [spiritual aspect], but felt the Who had absolutely no hope. Keith Moon and spiritual revolution? Roger Daltrey, a sheet metal worker from Acton, and spiritual revolution?

'But *I* could do it. Of course I could.'

In the summer of 1968 Townshend wrote a number called 'Glow Girl.' Written on a plane, it sang about the crash of young lovers in the campy mode of the Shangri-Las and Jan and Dean, complete with a trippy reincarnation ending. For his new project Townshend borrowed the line 'It's a girl, Mrs. Walker, it's a girl,' and duly changed the girl to a boy. He now had his protagonist, Tommy, after

---

* A reference to the Rolling Stones' 'We Love You,' off the much maligned *Satanic Majesties Request* LP issued in December of 1967.

the well-known moniker for British soldiers. His greatest project had now found direction.

On the popular *Michael Parkinson Show* in 1981, Townshend recounted the original synopsis of the story: 'Something pompous, crazy, ridiculous; a deaf, dumb, and blind boy who's given drugs by an acid queen, is raped by his own uncle, and then becomes the Messiah. I thought, "That'll make money!"'

As he got into it, though, it became something much more. 'I got about halfway through and became very serious about it. It was one of my most focused pieces because I was once again using the singles medium; each segment of the piece was like a short single.

'The pivotal song was "Amazing Journey": "Deaf, dumb and blind boy/He's in a quiet vibration land/Strange as it seems/His musical dreams ain't quite so bad." That song became the center; it tries to tell the whole story. As soon as I'd written it I had the shape for the piece.'

Lambert's input as executive producer and mentor cannot be overstated. It was his fascination with European classical music that swept Pete along the track of opera. The talented manager was likewise responsible for the overall organization and structure of the work, also coming up with the idea for the overture.

Since *Tommy* fuses conflicting themes of social alienation, senseless violence, molestation, and substance abuse, true Townshend aficionados realized long before even the artist himself its subtle autobiographical nature. His images are easily defined: the Pinball Wizard, a metaphor for Townshend the great guitar wizard; the Acid Queen, an embellishment of the trendy drug pushers prevalent around Shepherd's Bush; Cousin Kevin, an amalgam of every childhood thug who had ever bullied him; Mrs Walker, drawing shadowy parallels of Betty Townshend and her numerous infidelities. 'If Tommy is struck a blow,' notes Townshend, 'he does not feel pain, he experiences something like the chord of G. That's really what we want to do, create this feeling that when you listen to the music you can actually become aware of the boy and aware of what he is all about because we are *creating* him as we play. . . . We try to tell Tommy's story from both the inside – his musical interpretation of his dreams and secret thoughts – and from the outside, the terrible way he is treated by society. In a small way the album is also a solution to the way we might achieve divinity because I have no faith in evolution and science only reveals another two things to be discovered.'

Within this abstract framework, *Tommy* operates efficiently on several planes. '*Tommy* is a cross section of the way people are now and the way young people clutch at anything which seems as if it might help them along a bit quicker. They all want short cuts, the easy way out. Nobody is prepared to admit life has a purpose . . . that the individual is to blame for anything.

'In the story Tommy's fantastic miracle is something people appreciate, but also deeply resent. Why weren't we deaf, dumb and blind so that we could have become cured, purified and wonderful as Tommy? they asked.

'They say "We want to be like you, how did you do it?"'

In the end, however, Tommy's young followers could only simulate their master's perfection, and then only on the most superficial level. Tommy's disciples wanted purity without sacrifice, love without devotion and knowledge without introspection. Ernie's Holiday Camp, a kind of Billy Graham crusade run by money-hungry charlatans, represented the exploitation of religion or 'the decadence of the Temple,' as Townshend called it. Tommy, realizing the faithful are being scammed, lays down the law: 'No drinking, no drugs,' purposefully turning his followers against him. 'It's a sort of crucifixion thing; he sacrifices his own aura so they can go back to what they were doing before because he realizes that's the best thing they could be doing.'

On another level the piece stands as a rather obvious autobiographical account of the Who. 'Of their audience, of adolescence, of flower power, psychedelic drugs and finally of the spiritual revolution sweeping the young,' relates Townshend. 'The whole thing started with rock 'n' roll [which] is almost a religion to me. As an art form it has gripped me in a way I can't explain.

'You feel that celestial buzz. That's a spiritual thing and rock 'n' roll is spiritual in a different way. It makes people equal, it makes people selfless, it makes them forget themselves.'

Finally, *Tommy* operates too on a very personal plane. 'I am deaf dumb and blind in another sense. Closed up and alone in the belief that what I see and hear is all that exists unless it can be proven it didn't happen.'

The young protagonist (remembering only his name from his pre-trauma experience) allows Townshend to explore yet another familiar theme, that of the eternal search for identity. 'Practically every talented person spends most of his time hiding his talent or freakiness,' contends Pete. 'This fascinates me. Some hide it behind the aura of being a glittering superstar in show business. The reason is the remoteness it creates; the more remote they become, the more powerful they become.'

At the heart of the opera, though, lies the work's paramount concept: illusion versus reality as manifested in the image of the mirror. Townshend explains: 'In general terms, man is regarded as living in an unreal world of illusory values he's imposed on himself. He's feeling his way by evolution back to God, and thus the illusion is broken away bit by bit. You need the illusions, though, until you reach very pure saintly states. When you lose all contact with your illusory nature, you become totally dead, but also totally aware. You've died for the last time. You don't incarnate again, you just blend. It's the realization of what we all intellectually know, universal consciousness, but it's no good until you actually *realize* it.

'Tommy's real self represents the aim, God, and the illusory self is the teacher; life, the way, and the path. The coming together of these is what makes him aware. They make him see, hear, and speak [spiritually] so he becomes a great saint everybody flocks to.'

Adding a personal aside, 'I think somewhere deep down inside I can see myself too, my real self.'

The device of the mirror also demonstrates the interplay of illusion and reality that is a part of everyone's makeup and experience. A mirror, on one hand, represents distortion, a reverse image, as well as the fragility and fragmentary qualities of glass.

Yet for Pete Townshend it was the only place he could allow his true nature, the one he kept hidden even from himself, to be revealed. Remember those adolescent days when he stood before the mirror perfecting dance steps, honing guitar moves, trying desperately to alter his waggish appearance? Locked away before the mirror he could envision his enhanced perfected self. Here he was in control. It is a frustrating paradox, however, that the Pete of the looking glass becomes a reality only in the concentrated image of the mirror.

That's why the breaking of the glass is the opera's climactic turning point – Tommy's mother discovers a way to crack the shell he has built around himself. 'When he discovers that the vision he has been staring at is actually himself, he triumphs over his disabilities and is whole,' proclaims Townshend.

In the end, Tommy – his followers having long since deserted him – is once more all alone, having come full circle. 'Deep down in every human being is this feeling that nothing is ever going to be complete,' Townshend ventures. 'That the circle will never connect, and that in itself is the secret to eternity. The fact that the circle will never be complete is the real knowledge of infinity.

The more plain-speaking Daltrey sees it this way: '*Tommy* came along at a time in our lives when everyone was searching for answers in their life. The ambiguity of *Tommy* allowed it to answer many things for many different people. But in fact it didn't really answer anything. That was the beauty of it.'

Years later, in 1994, Townshend offered this somewhat more down-to-earth assessment of the finale: 'There is no ending. What I was doing at the time was attending to the fact that in rock 'n' roll what you don't do is make people's decisions for them. You share their ideas, difficulties, and frustrations. But you don't say, "The thing that you have to do now is . . ." You go for a beer and talk it over.'

In examining the nuts and bolts of the musical structure, one can see Townshend engaging in his familiar practice of nicking a few bits here and there. 'Eyesight to the Blind' was taken from 'The Hawker,' a Sonny Boy Williamson composition off a blues album called *Mose Alison Sings*. In particular, Williamson's phrase 'She can make the dumb speak, can make the blind see, the deaf hear' made an effective intro to the 'Acid Queen.'

The 'Underture' and 'Sparks' were built up from guitar lines Townshend used previously for 'A Quick One.' Even 'Rael' is reincarnated to lend melodic fragments to the moving overture.

One fascinating story formed the genesis of 'Sally Simpson,' Tommy's ultimate superfan, sycophant, groupie goddess. It evolved from an incident the night the Who shared the bill with the Doors at Madison Square Garden. 'The Doors had become meteoric,' relates Townshend, 'and Jim Morrison's Christ picture was all over fucking New York.' Townshend went on to express horror at Morrison's shoddy onstage behavior, punching a fan in the face while his bodyguards enthusiastically worked over another. One particular girl caught up in the frenzy tried to make her way to the stage and tumbled headfirst, slashing her face.

Ultimately, Townshend charged that people missed the innate satire and irony of the piece. 'We joked as a group about *Tommy* being true opera (which it isn't), but the Who's audience and many of the rock press took it very seriously. It was this seriousness that ultimately turned *Tommy* into light entertainment,' he said in 1977.

Townshend would be the first to agree that his cherished masterwork is deeply flawed. Most notably, the opera doesn't really stand on its own. Without explanation, the plot is incomprehensible and the libretto provides only the most roundabout clues to the foundation of the story line, including the significance of Tommy viewing the murder in the mirror, an essential key to the work. As journalist Al Aronowitz put it, '*Tommy* is the story of a boy who becomes deaf, dumb, and blind after witnessing the murder of his mother's lover by his natural father, who has just returned from among the missing at the close of World War II. Before he is cured to become a religious leader, Tommy gets molested by a perverted uncle and is slipped some LSD by an unscrupulous gypsy. We learn all this from the program. Otherwise the whole thing may as well be sung in Italian.'

Townshend also addressed the problem of using mere words to deliver the powerful feelings he first envisioned. This was true especially of the lines 'Listening to you I get the music/Gazing at you I get the heat.' 'It's meant to be extremely serious and plaintive, but words fail so miserably to represent emotions unless you skirt around the outside, and I didn't do it enough there. This one fails because it actually comes out and says it.'

In 1987, Townshend went so far as to say he regretted composing the album altogether, claiming that it was too caught up in 'Jungian spiritual analysis of our spiritual autism in a sense. It was sort of obtuse and measured.' Had not John Entwistle invented Cousin Kevin and Uncle Ernie, and Moon contributed the Holiday Camp idea, Pete concedes, 'it would have been the most unbelievably tedious and pretentious piece I've ever come up with.' Daltrey agrees. 'The most important songs in *Tommy*, which give it the kind of edge, are "Cousin Kevin" and "Uncle Ernie." Which were written by John Entwistle, not by Pete.'

From a technical standpoint, another flaw is the album's

somewhat hollow, primitive sound, which robbed the band of its usual fiery combustion. For some reason Lambert used the IBC Studios and rushed the boys through recording, allowing them no real time for overdubs. In addition, Lambert's poor mix had Townshend's piano sounding like a tinny saloon honky-tonk, and his decision to mix the voices up front at the sacrifice of the music was loudly criticized by Entwistle. 'The drums always seemed to sound like biscuit tins,' he cracked.

Standing up for his producer, Townshend claimed that Lambert had not actually meant to leave it so raw, intending to later overdub an orchestra. For the record, however, Pete knew better than to trust the technically deficient Lambert with the task (which created the first real rift between the two), and in the end the idea was scrapped.

The one major element Townshend remains most proud of, though, is his thematic use of Tommy's apparent disabilities. 'It is a metaphor of our own spiritual deaf, dumb, and blindness,' he says.

Hailed as 'the Who's *Sgt. Pepper*,' *Tommy* was released on May 23, 1969, to highly charged but mixed reviews. On one hand, elements of the conservative press labeled the work 'sick and pretentious.' Leonard Bernstein, though, gave it high praise. 'Now Pete Townshend of rock's toughest and most innovative group, has made the dream a reality with *Tommy*, a full-length rock opera that for sheer power, invention, and brilliance of performance outstrips anything that has ever come out of a recording studio.'

There was no doubt how the fans felt. The album rescued the Who financially, going on to sell some 10 million copies. It also soldered the band and redeemed Daltrey. 'There's one part of *Tommy* that's fifty percent Roger and fifty percent the Who,' confirmed Townshend. Not only did the piece allow Daltrey to shine as a vocalist, but it also provided a shot in the arm for his drooping ego. 'For me, *Tommy* was an absolute dream,' Daltrey explained. 'As a singer I was paranoid from having once been thrown out of the band. It was an amazing catalyst for me. I'd go on playing it forever. I think it's a masterpiece.'

Pete thought of the work as his first conscious departure from adolescence, but the composer himself couldn't have conceived that meant entry to the world's finest opera houses: the Royal

Theatre of Copenhagen, the Cologne Opera House and the New York Metropolitan, where they performed on June 7, 1970. Keith Moon quipped, 'It was rather like playing to an oil painting.' Pete too regarded the upper-crust venues with a jaundiced eye. 'The Met had that feeling of being full of dead ideas, dead people, and too much fucking reverence.'

Townshend promptly put an exclamation point on his statement during the second show when an audience member, disgruntled at the lack of an encore, shouted, 'Boo!' Pete shot back, 'After two fucking hours boo to you too, mate!'

The performances were seen as a triumph akin to the French storming the Bastille. 'It was an affirmation not only that rock had to be taken seriously but of our very existence as human beings,' he has said. 'It seemed to me to be a very mature and sensible gesture that we and our fans should be invited to a place like the Met. It's a wonderful notion, the idea of a snotty pop group playing opera houses. But we actually did it. . . . We shit in their toilet!'

Just four months after the release of *Tommy*, still basking in the headiness of the accomplishment, the Who flew to Bethel, New York, to play Woodstock. To say Pete disdained the experience is putting it mildly. 'I didn't at all like Haight-Ashbury. I didn't like fucking Abbie Hoffman. I didn't like Timothy Leary, and I didn't like Woodstock!'

Townshend certainly had his reasons: a fourteen-hour delay in their set spent sitting on a wooden plank in the rain and mud; having his coffee spiked with acid right before he went onstage; his more than reasonable demand for an appearance fee, which circulated around the camp and generated 'bad vibes.'

'All these hippies wandering about thinking the world was going to be different from that day on,' he groused. 'As a cynical English arsehole I walked through it all and felt like spitting on the lot of them and shaking them, trying to make them realize that nothing had changed and nothing was going to change. Not only that, what they thought was an alternative society was basically a field full of six-foot-deep mud laced with LSD. If that was the world they wanted to live in, then fuck the lot of them.'

With that attitude it's no wonder Townshend was in no mood for Yippie leader Abbie Hoffman storming the stage and grabbing the mike to protest the imprisonment of Detroit White Panther John

Sinclair. An enraged Townshend instinctively swung around to ramrod the activist, 'kicking his little ass in a proud rage,' though Hoffman later termed it merely 'a thump.' 'I feel the stage is a sacred platform,' declared Pete. 'If you're taking responsibility for it, you have to be sure it's used for the right purpose.' Years later he still maintained his position: 'I'd still kick the little fucker off!'

In 1987, though, a more reflective Townshend finally recanted, saying, 'I deeply regret that. Given the opportunity again, I would stop the show. Because I don't think rock is that important. Then I did. The show had to go on.'

The Who followed up their self-proclaimed 'worst ever performance' with a powerful show at the Isle of Wight Festival, Britain's answer to Woodstock. This last hurrah of the peace and love era proved a stunning success for the band, who outshone even headliner Bob Dylan, making a comeback after an absence of several years.

To his credit Townshend was perceptive enough to understand that the sixties promise had turned sour. Rolling Stones founder Brian Jones died mysteriously that July, for which Townshend penned the never released memorial, 'A Normal Day for Brian.'* 'Brian should have been put in a straitjacket and treated,' Pete said. 'I used to know Brian quite well. The Stones have always been a group I really dug. Dug all the dodgy aspects of them as well, and Brian Jones has always been what I've regarded as one of the dodgy aspects. The way he fitted in and the way he didn't was one of the strong dynamics of the group. When he stopped playing with them, I though that dynamic was going to be missing, but it still seems to be there. Perhaps the fact that he's dead has made that dynamic kind of permanent.

'A little bit of love might have sorted him out. I don't think his death was necessarily a bad thing for Brian. I think he'll do better next time. I believe in reincarnation.'

Over the next few years many more would fall: Janis Joplin, Jim Morrison, Alan Wilson of Canned Heat, and Jimi Hendrix, who was rapidly withering in a cloud of pharmaceutically induced paranoia. 'Hendrix was a psychological mess of a man,' observed Townshend. 'Nobody cared. People thought, "He can play such great guitar, so

---

* It has been only recently revealed that the ultratalented Jones was, in fact, brutally murdered at the behest of Stones' minder, the late Frank Thorogood and others.

he's obviously okay. What made me work so hard was seeing the condition Jimi was in. He was in such tragically bad condition physically and I remember thanking God as I walked on stage that I was healthy.'

On a personal level, Townshend was faced with the enormous problem of trying to top *Tommy*. It was hailed almost universally, and the band had just released the roaring LP, *Live at Leeds* in February 1970, still regarded today as one of the best live performances on record. How much higher could he go?

In the autumn of 1970, Townshend attempted an impossibly ambitious, revolutionary audience-participation piece he later termed 'the one that got away.' Called *Lifehouse*, it began simply as a story around which he wrote several songs. Townshend soon fleshed out a full-length film script about life in a programmed totalitarian society on the verge of collapse, where people wear 'experiment suits' and are fed through test tubes. Townshend termed it 'an allegory, a bit like *Close Encounters* or *ET*, about what's happening to us in the modern world, using music as a representation of good versus evil. The baddies were people who gave us entertainment intravenously, and the goodies were savages who'd kept rock 'n' roll as a primitive force and had gone to live with it in the woods. The story was about these two sides coming together and having a brief battle.'

Townshend's recurrent theme of rock as the divine healer of all ills once again comes into play, like *Tommy* though with a wider, more intricate metaphysical scope.

The climax of the piece, explained Townshend in 1974, involved the emergence of an ancient guru figure who recalls rock music and how through its power people could reach a state of spiritual release. 'The old man decides he's going to try to set it up so that the effect can be experienced eternally,' explains Pete. 'Everybody would be snapped out of their programmed environment through this rock 'n' roll-induced liberated selflessness.'

Townshend's project sparked a grandiose plan. Instead of merely acting out the script on a sound stage, why not actually play out the concept using a live audience in a concert setting and film the experience as part of the movie? He and Lambert sold Universal Pictures on the project and obtained an at-the-time staggering $1 million to finance it.

'The idea,' said Townshend, 'was to perform the songs over a period of two weeks. We were going to have an open-door policy. The band was gonna do this long, long concert with the doors open all the time.'

He went wild, working out a complex scenario whereby a personal profile of each concert-goer would be worked up, from the individual's astrological chart to his hobbies, even physical appearance. All the characteristics would then be fed into a computer at the same moment, leading to one musical note culminating in mass nirvana that Pete dubbed 'a kind of celestial cacophony.'

This philosophy was based on the writings of Inayat Khan, a Sufi master musician who espoused the theory that matter produces heat, light, and sound in the form of unique vibrations. Taking the idea one step further, making music, which was composed of vibrations, was the pervading force of all life. Elevating its purpose to the highest level, music represented the path to restoration, the search for the one perfect universal note, which once sounded would bring harmony to the entire world.*

Early rehearsals at the Young Vic Theatre, a venue in the round attached to the renowned and venerable Old Vic, proved an unequivocal disaster. Expecting an audience of enlightened, cooperative participants, instead, Townshend lamented, 'all we got were freaks and thirteen-year-old skinheads. If we had advertised the thing as a Who concert, we could have packed the place for a year. But we were just opening the door and playing, waiting to see who came in.'

The bizarre scene culminated in a drug-crazed hippie charging the stage yelling, 'Capitalist pigs! Bastards! Get off the fuckin' stage!' True to form, Townshend beat the unwelcome anarchist senseless, only afterward facing the disheartening truth. 'I thought, "Fuck it, I'm only fooling myself." It was a dream that was only fiction. It's never going to come true.

'It was a disaster. The self-control required to prevent my total nervous disintegration was absolutely unbelievable.' Admitting he

---

* Meher Baba, himself an admirer of Inayat Khan's teachings, mirrored many of these same tenets in his own philosophy. The universally held idea that sound is both the source of creation and sustainer of everything is mirrored in the Hindu concept of Nada Brama or 'the sound is God' and in the biblical injunction 'In the beginning was the word' from the book of Genesis.

had actually lost touch with reality, the experience led to a nervous breakdown, one he has never discussed.

Lifehouse did, however, form the basis of what Townshend and most fans termed the band's best album, *Who's Next*. 'The material had a thread to it, and a lot of blood and guts which was the *Lifehouse* story.' Originally conceived as a double album, it was pared down to nine first-rate songs. 'It has a silky quality to it, the only Who LP with near perfect sound.' This was thanks to engineer Glyn Johns's steady guidance. Also Townshend played a vintage orange Chet Atkins 1957 Gretsh guitar, with its single cutaway and double pickups, given to him by Joe Walsh (then of the James Gang). 'I used that guitar on every track on *Who's Next*. It's the finest guitar I've ever owned, and the loudest I've ever known.'

Who's Next contains three key songs; 'Baba O'Riley,' the album's slated opening; the autobiographical 'Behind Blue Eyes'; and 'Won't Get Fooled Again.' 'Baba O'Riley,' named for Townshend's spiritual master, and electronic musical wizard Terry Riley,* featured the memorable cry of post-teenage anguish, 'We're all wasted!' This lament over the bleak badlands of adolescence was rooted in the storyline's overt reference to pollution, both environmentally as a result of overpopulation, and mentally/spiritually at the hands of the neofascist Big Brother government.

The powerful song, with its stirring violin break by Dave Arbus, was originally intended as a twenty-piece instrumental synthesizer piece written in the studio. This, along with 'Won't Get Fooled Again,' was jettisoned by a prerecorded synthesizer track. Here Townshend once again displayed his knack for parlaying the latest musical gadgetry (in this case the spanking new ARP 2600, whose technology he first encountered at Cambridge University) into a phenomenon. 'This definitive classic seventies rock song actually came from an indulgent experiment in electronic music.' It was more than a mere experiment, however. Townshend spun popular music into the techno era when many artists laid down their guitars for the more versatile keyboard.

'Pete came up with synthesizer basics for the tracks which were just unbelievable', recalled Glyn Johns. 'Nobody had done it that

---

* Riley, an American musician-composer who'd studied in India, gained a following playing avant-garde music in European cabarets. His innovative use of keyboards and tapes was incorporated by Townshend on *Who's Next*.

way before, and it was amazing to work with. . . . Everything on that record was an incredible inspiration.'

'I like synthesizers,' said Townshend, 'because they bring into my hands things that aren't in my hands: the sound of the orchestra, French horns, strings. There are gadgets on synthesizers which enable one to become a virtuoso of the keyboard. You can play something slowly and you press a switch and it plays it back at double speed. Whereas on the guitar you're stuck with as fast as you can play and I don't play fast, I just play hard. So when it comes to playing something fast I go to the synth.'

In the haunting and exquisitely crafted 'Behind Blue Eyes,' Townshend once again returns to the mirror as a symbol. Many have taken this to be an autobiographical song, but actually it owes more to the villain Jumbo in the *Lifehouse* story. The lyric depicts Jumbo's lament about being misunderstood by those around him as he gazes into the mirror trying to justify his deeds. Here Townshend utilizes the mirror as a strictly reflective device, exploring how others view us and how we view ourselves.

That's not to say Townshend didn't find a personal link. 'I think there's a lot of vengeance involved in the insecurities writers have. I used the word *vengeance* in 'Behind Blue Eyes,' and the vengeance in a sense is saying, "Listen, why don't you understand me without me saying all this stuff? Why don't you love me as I really am without me demonstrating who I really am?"'

'Won't Get Fooled Again,' was never the political anthem the masses took it for, but was, in fact, just the opposite, a refutation of revolution, which Townshend dubbed 'the ultimate betrayal.' 'It was the dumbest song I've ever written,' he later revealed. 'It was dumb to deny the political role of the individual. Burning your draft card is a purely political act. Throwing your vote away is an apolitical act, and "Won't Get Fooled Again" was an apolitical song. Luckily, the people didn't listen to the verses: "There's nothing in the street/Looks any different to me/And the slogans are all replaced, by the by . . ." They just listened to the catch.

'It was an irresponsible song. It was quite clear during that period that rock had the ear of the people, and people were saying to me, "Pete, you've got to use the Who. You've got to get the message across."'

The track tells of the rebels being offered amnesty to abandon their anarchic ways and join up with conventional forces, accepting the status quo and thereby receiving power in return. 'The hero of the piece,' states Townshend, 'warns, "Don't be fooled, don't get taken in." It's interesting it's been taken up in an anthemic sense when in fact it's such a cautionary piece.'

Although Pete was happy to see *Who's Next* sell over 4 million albums he was devastated by the *Lifehouse* debacle. In a certain sense he would never really recover. This marked the first tiny cracks in Pete's eventual dissolution of the Who.

Pete did keep pursuing the project over the years, and the script was rewritten several times over. Nicolas Roeg was even set to direct the project at one point in the eighties. But inevitably it was too complex an undertaking.

'The most important development was that a treatment was sent to Ray Bradbury, because I fancied getting someone like him to finish it off. I'd done a couple of scripts for it, but I can't see the wood for the fucking trees anymore. Anyway, he's interested, and if he did the script, then maybe someone like Nic Roeg would probably be a great director for it, but I don't think he'd agree to do it without having control over the script. . . .

'What excites me about it is that it does contain a concert and a story, and it does contain a lot of my feelings about what rock and music is, and why music has a spiritual value and why the effect of rock music has a spiritual value.' These days Townshend is considering turning it into a novel.

In the meantime, he was faced with the problem of topping *Who's Next*. Townshend, on the suggestion of Daltrey, began exploring the possibility of incorporating his old mod heritage. 'Mods were one thing that held me together, gave me a feeling of belonging. I always felt alienated by the Woodstock generation, felt out of psychedelia because like most pop musicians I was into it before the masses, and when it became big I was extremely ill.'

He remembered how much more involved he'd been in the old days. 'Being a mod was a way of getting back my working-class roots. I was fascinated by working-class expressions like that. The Who were working too hard for me to get really involved, but sometimes I'd jump offstage between sets and just disappear. In retrospect, these were the moments I treasure most.'

The idea spawned the four-headed monster *Quadrophenia*, which its composer designated 'a Townshend solo album performed by the Who.' This time the story was simple enough, about a mod named Jimmy who becomes lost when the movement folds, to the point that his parents all but disown him and his psychiatrist finds he has four personalities.

Thematically, the device provided Townshend with a perfect opportunity to instill the four distinct energies of the Who into the piece: Roger the fighter, John the romantic, Keith the lunatic and Pete the self-dubbed 'beggar and hypocrite.' *Quadrophenia* was closer than *Tommy* to an actual opera. This time the songs were carefully integrated into characterizations and plotline.

The characterization of Jimmy on the album's liner notes offer glimpses of Townshend's own complex personality: 'There's a part of me that hates people. Not the actual people but how useless they are, how stupid. They sit and stew while the world gets worse and worse. Wars and battles. People dying of starvation. Old people are dying because their kids have got their own kids and they ain't got time. That's what makes me smash things up. My shrink says I ain't mad. He should see me when I'm pissed.'

Yet this view can't be taken too far. Pete claimed following *Quadrophenia*, '[Jimmy's] a workshop figure. An invention. And while he may seem more real than Tommy, he isn't. *Tommy* was set in fantasy, but there was something very real about its structure. Jimmy, on the surface, looks like a simple kid with straightforward hang-ups, but he's far more surrealistic.'

A number of literal-minded critics missed this point. To them the ending of *Quadrophenia*, in which Jimmy drifts out to sea, having contemplated suicide, signified his death. Townshend was quick to point out that, in fact, his protagonist, at least for that moment, chooses life and that the closing was left purposefully vague. 'It is about the Who and what happens to us. It starts out in 1965 and ends now, and I left it open-ended on a note of spiritual desperation because we're in the middle of nowhere, not sure where we're going.' As Townshend told audiences, 'It's about growing up. At the end of the album the hero is in grave danger of maturing.'

As ambitious as the work was, Townshend encountered monumental problems in recording. Kit Lambert was out. Of late, the flamboyant manager was recklessly indulging in cocaine and heroin, running up gambling debts, and pursuing young men in Venice, where he kept a grand palazzo. Lambert began to show up late at the studio, if at all, and came to blows with Roger Daltrey, with whom there'd been friction from the beginning. As a result, Townshend was left alone to produce.

Although elated with his initial demos, he faced a gargantuan problem with transferring his tapes to acetate, including the tricky sound effects, a feat that never quite came off. Moreover, Pete was targeting the work for quadraphonic sound; he was one of the pioneers to experiment with this format. In the end, however, quadraphonic sound was not ready for *Quadrophenia*.

The band was unhappy as well. Entwistle contended that every track sounded the same, and his bass lines were all but lost in the mix, while Daltrey's vocal abilities were not at all suited to several of the songs.

From a performance standpoint, *Quadrophenia* immediately proved a technical nightmare. To start, some twenty tons of equipment had to be hauled in three forty-five-foot trucks, and a sound and light crew numbering thirty was also needed. Glitches appeared during the debut performance in the Midlands on October 28, 1973, where five numbers had to be cut. Then at the very next stop, in Newcastle, there was a fifteen-second delay in the tape sync from the accompanying prerecorded material coming through Moon's headphones, throwing his drumming into a chaotic jumble. An exasperated Townshend exploded, jumping sound engineer Bobby Pridden and hauling him across the soundboard before kicking over an amp and stomping offstage. *Quadrophenia* had to be abandoned that night in favor of playing old Who standbys.

Their American tour (November 19 through December 6) proved to be trying in other ways. The band was jailed in Montreal for a particularly inspired hotel smash-up, Townshend freely joining the mayhem by helping Moon chuck a marble table out a window. Roger got a scare that the constant wear on his vocal cords might induce cancer. Then on opening night in San Francisco someone spiked Moon's drink with PCP and the drummer collapsed twice, causing the band to enlist a member of the audience to fill in, bestowing upon one Scott Halpin permanent cult status.

There were also problems with the work itself, which Townshend conceded was 'a little weak dynamically.' Finding audiences couldn't always follow the storyline, Daltrey took it upon himself to narrate long-winded transitions between songs, which exasperated Townshend. Also once again the elaborate tapes of prerecorded sound effects and synth orchestrations broke down and finally had to be discarded.

The work elicited both hot and cold reviews from critics. After its release on October 19, 1973, the *Toronto Star* deemed it 'Townshend's most self-indulgent work . . . wrapped in a techno gloss (synthesizers, tape and rhythm loops, symphonic texturing) that achieves a hyperbole of Wagnerian proportions and yet deprives the rest of the band of significant input.'

The ambitious piece elicited an uneven response from audiences as well. Americans didn't understand mods at all, noted Pete, and the fans in general were changing. 'Audiences seem more demanding, more skeptical, more levelheaded, less likely to accept myths. There was a time when an audience would come to a concert and be satisfied with the myth of the Who while we could be doing fuck-all in the way of music.'

After a few follow-up European performances, the passionate opera was laid permanently to rest. 'It was too difficult, too intangible,' Pete grimly acknowledged. What was especially sad for him was that he had purposely written the music as a vehicle for live performance. All of the songs were guitar based to lend a 'Who aggression with bite.' Ultimately, though, it just didn't stand up on stage.

Quadrophenia sold a million copies in three weeks, largely on the strength of the tour, but two singles fared abysmally, reaching no higher than number fifty in the charts. In fact, out of seventeen tracks, only three became Who staples: 'Bell Boy,' primarily inserted to give Moon a vocal; '5.15,' a superb rocker, and Jimmy's theme song, the regal 'Love Reign o'er Me,' one of his finest moments ever.

The past two years had exacted an exorbitant toll on Townshend. He was now on the verge of physical and mental collapse. 'In 1973 and '74 I was the aging daddy of punk. I was bearing a standard I could barely hold up anymore. My cheeks were stuffed, not with cotton wool in the Brando-Mafioso image, but with scores of uppers I had taken with a sneer and failed to swallow.'

Tony Bramwell, former press liaison for the Beatles, remembers, 'You'd bump into them in town, and they'd be totally under the influence of everything. They'd look like they were sixty: Keith Richards, and Pete Townshend of the Who. They were old men in their twenties.'

A stark casualty in this period was Eric Clapton. Even though Pete was suffering from problems of his own, his unflagging devotion to help extricate his old mate from his savage addiction to heroin is a heartening story. 'I spent a tremendous time with him during his heroin cure and earned his love as a result.' He admitted to being shocked after first seeing how debilitated Clapton and his girlfriend, Alice Ormsby Gore had become. 'It was a typical junkie scene,' Pete remembers. 'It was the first encounter I'd had with addicts. I wasn't prepared for the lies, the duplicity, but even through all that I decided they definitely seemed worth the effort.'

From the autumn of 1972, when he lured the guitarist back into recording, to well into 1974, when Clapton sought a controversial electro-acupuncture treatment cure, Townshend remained unwavering in both his friendship and his goal to see Eric through the crisis. 'Pete has been very close, and I owe him a lot,' acknowledged Clapton. 'The reason for that is he really took a lot of time to help out because he thought I was worth it when I didn't think I was. He gave me faith in myself again.'

Townshend insider Kathy points out it's an example of the artist's keen sense of loyalty. 'People he's known throughout the years, he always makes a point of doing things for them. When he's in town, he'll take them to dinner, give them tickets and backstage passes. He's truly a loving person; it's his best quality.' It should be noted that it was Doctor Meg Patterson, who was to play a pivotal part in Pete's own rehabilitation years later, who weaned Clapton off his addiction.

While Townshend was cementing a friendship with his onetime rival, he concedes his reclamation of Clapton not only took a heavy toll on his marriage but on the time he spent with his two young daughters, Emma, then five, and Aminta, two years younger. 'My wife measured it against time spent with her. . . . There's no point pretending that it is possible to help bring a man off heroin while you're doing a nine-to-five job. Tea and the wife don't mix with three a.m. phone calls and Rainbow reunion rehearsals that actually start at six in the morning.'

His troubles at home were amply reflected in the dissension in the band. At this time Townshend's treasured friendship with Kit Lambert was about to be shattered. The managerial situation had been in precarious flux since March 1971, when Lambert had been called upon to remix the *Lifehouse* demos and failed, forcing Townshend to bring in Glyn Johns. Lambert, for all his creative ideas, simply lacked a knowledge of studio production, and Johns deemed him an amateur. 'Kit Lambert didn't have any idea whatever about how to make a record.'

Technical prowess aside, Townshend had outgrown his Svengali, whose concoctions, such as concerts on the moon, now seemed ludicrous and outlandish for the serious-minded Pete. Lambert had become increasingly involved in the Who's Track label, which also stabled Jimi Hendrix and Arthur Brown, and the success had gone to his head. There were also rumors of financial mismanagement. By 1974 he and Stamp were operating in name only while Bill Curbishley, an organization insider, had taken over management of the group. Kit, for his part, felt miffed for not being allowing to orchestrate *Tommy*, for being shunted aside for Glyn Johns, and for not being 'properly' credited for the band's skyrocketing career. Clearly, Lambert felt underappreciated for all he had done for the band. According to Townshend, 'Kit did great work for the Who, not realizing that we were satisfied that he should be thanked, credited, and presumably made to feel quite happy by his royalty check each month.'

Although Townshend realized that the time had come to end the association, the decision was acutely painful owing to his closeness to Lambert. 'He wasn't just my manager, he was my friend.'

Demoralized, Townshend also harbored resentment that his cohorts weren't keeping pace with his advancing musical evolution. They were simply three working-class London blokes who couldn't share his intellectual grasp. 'Paranoia does not adequately describe my feelings, though I suppose all of the Who were to a degree paranoid toward one another', he says. 'But my trouble was also manifestly spiritual. I felt I had let myself down morally and artistically. I felt quite genuinely a hypocrite. I complained a lot about things I felt I was doing from the goodness of my heart but wasn't receiving enough credit for.'

His alienation had been growing for some time. It had begun, noted Townshend, in the post-LSD period with 'Roger's development as a separate ego wearing fucking shawls' and each member beginning to 'define their images,' which Pete felt diluted the music. More and more they had begun to go their separate ways, personally and professionally. Roger had turned his talents to successful solo projects as well as acting, landing starring roles in the upcoming film version of *Tommy* as well as *Lisztomania*, based on the life of composer Franz Liszt. Keith too found a comfortable niche in film, appearing in *That'll Be the Day* and *Stardust*, and had even moved to Los Angeles. John, in a situation very similar to that of George Harrison, a talented composer never allowed to grow with the Beatles, issued a series of solo albums. Unlike Harrison, however, all of John's works sank without a trace.

Inevitably, matters came to a head between Townshend and longtime sparring partner Daltrey. Roger had been recently, and quite justifiably, upset over Kit's rejection of his solo album, which Bill Curbishley had subsequently taken over. Pete felt that Roger had been unduly critical of *Quadrophenia* and hadn't really appreciated the work he'd put into it. They warred too over the direction of the band. Daltrey made no secret of wanting to return to the well-traveled Who tradition of touring, while his partner slaved over several grandiose projects that didn't quite come off.

An eruption finally took place in October 1973. In the midst of a heated argument over the recording of a track, tensions exploded and Townshend cracked Daltrey over the head with his guitar. It only took one power punch from an infuriated Daltrey to render Townshend unconscious and on his way to the hospital. As Townshend remembers, 'Roger caught me with a proper bang on the jaw. I went out for about four hours.'

What Townshend hadn't seen coming was a marked change in Daltrey. A combination of his own successful solo projects and his renewed, formidable position as the Who's front man, set against Pete's monumental failures, had launched a new confidence, one ready to challenge Pete's authority. 'Maybe it was better when I used to bully him and he'd hit me if he disagreed,' Pete suggested sarcastically at the time. 'Maybe it was better when I was the "intellectual genius behind the group" and he was just "a cardboard cutout puppet singer" I used to manipulate from behind the scenes.'

Music had always been Townshend's saving grace, but even that was failing him. Since *Tommy* his compositions, including 'The Seeker,' 'Let's See Action,' and 'Relay,' had barely cracked the top twenty. *Tommy* had become the lovable but overbearing aunt who comes for a visit and never leaves. There was the Canadian ballet version, a sappy orchestration by Lou Reizner; then came *Electric Tommy* played on synthesizers and even *Marching Tommy*.

'I've no control over the beast,' Townshend anguished. With the debacles of *Lifehouse* and *Quadrophenia* still festering and the singles avenue having shut down for the band, Townshend feared he would soon be considered nothing but a one-trick pony.

In the meantime he signed on as musical director for Ken Russell's eccentric film version of *Tommy*. Soon, however, Townshend questioned the wisdom of his decision. Although Pete was happy to be working with the white-haired 'enfant terrible' of the British film industry, whom Entwistle aptly dubbed 'a psychopathic Father Christmas,' he admitted Russell's blowsy extravaganza was far from his own more internal interpretation. 'The result was a much more literal film than I expected,' he said at the time. 'It's an exaggeration in some ways, almost burlesque at times.'

Creative differences aside, it was while working on the movie that an emotionally wrought Townshend found himself in a deep crisis. 'I was mixed up by my two professions: as writer and musical director on the film and as a performer with the Who. I think I blamed the Who's live work for bringing me to such an emotional abyss.' Rolling over him too were swells of immense guilt for having very publicly set himself up as a messenger of a divine, greater good. Peering into his looking glass, though, he found himself no paragon of virtue.

'When you come on like I do, which is like some saint and intellectual genius sitting on some extremely high chair, you've bloody well got to deliver. I'd done that with *Tommy*, where I'd taken a heavily spiritual stance to suggest there might be a better way to live. . . . What I felt made me a hypocrite was not living the kind of life I felt capable of living and the way I had in fact told people it should be lived. That's why I felt so awful.'

With nowhere to run, he soon found escape in the bottom of a brandy glass, adhering to the old show business edict 'When in or out of trouble: drink.' 'Drinking round the Who,' he has said, 'is the greatest thing gutter-level life can offer. The bawdiness of the humor, the sheer decadence of the amount put away, the incredible emotional release of violent outbursts against innocent hotel room sofas; all these count to get a body through a lot of trouble. But at the end of the orgy the real cancer still lies untackled deep within the heart.'

What Townshend was just beginning to discover was that alcohol was no longer simply part of the MO of the consummate rock 'n' roller, but a symptom of deeper problems. Although he had been able to hold his liquor over the years – in hefty amounts at that – he was now sinking beneath the weight of incredible stress. His over-the-top consumption had snowballed to a crisis point.

He nearly drank himself into oblivion, often hallucinating and suffering terrifying memory lapses. He once woke up in the back of a limo, not knowing how he got there. He signed several critical managerial and recording contracts 'in a complete fog.' When he vowed to stop and in fact did, his hair began falling out and he continued drinking without even realizing it.

'At the end of one [recording] session which I had gotten through by pulling incessantly at a total of about twenty cans of Coke, I wished everyone good night, walked up to a makeshift bar, and drank a bottle of vodka. I just don't remember doing that. . . . The only event I remember is quietly screaming for help deep inside.'

In his alcoholic haze, Townshend even stepped out of character to launch into an indiscriminate womanizing spree. '[I was] getting drunk, having a good time and screwing birds. . . . I was waking up in bed with somebody and not knowing what had led up to that particular point. Then I was going home and trying to face me old lady.'

But even Townshend hadn't fully realized how close he was to the breaking point until a harrowing experience in mid-June 1974 during a performance at New York's Madison Square Garden. The arena was packed with Who fans crowding around the stage, not there to see the show, Pete contended, but to let everyone know they were card-carrying fanatics. 'It was dreadful. They were telling us what to play. Every time I tried to make an announcement they all yelled out, 'Shhhrrruppp Townshend and let Entwistle play "Boris the Spider." If that wasn't bad enough, during the other songs they'd all start chanting, "Jump, jump, jump." I had no instinct left. I had to do it from memory. I was so brought down by it all. I mean, is this what it had all degenerated to?'

Townshend confessed the episode so paralyzed him he could not have gone on stage for the next three shows without getting roaring drunk. 'I felt old, finished. I thought, "This is it. The End. I don't want to go on."'

Over the next year the band retreated to their separate corners. Keith was off to L. A. and John and Roger went to work on solo projects. Daltrey seemed to be sending a message to Townshend via his album *Ride a Rock Horse*, with its raw, heavy sound that harkened back to the Who's glory days.

Pete, meanwhile, hunkered down in the isolation of his home studio, trying to work up songs for the group's next album. Recounting his precarious state of mind, he said, 'Paranoia does not adequately describe my feelings, though I suppose all of the Who were to a degree paranoid toward one another. I felt down . . . empty, tired, and defeated.'

By May 1975 his relationship with Daltrey had grown extremely tense, and he leveled some high-octane remarks to the press out of 'my weakness and indulgence': how the Who had become stale, how he felt taken aback by Daltrey's comments about the Who 'rocking in our wheelchairs.' He snobbishly commented that he had sacrificed his own best material for the band, an obvious stab at both Roger and John.

Daltrey, justifiably incensed, retaliated via the *New Music Express*. 'Don't talk to me about booze because I've never been onstage drunk in seven years, Mr. Townshend! I'm just getting a bit fed up with these left-handed attacks.' He went on to attack Pete's recent subpar performances and even accused him of outright deceit: 'You can't live on lies forever.'

Pete would later admit that the backstabbing fiasco, however manipulated by the press, was the best thing that could have happened. 'It hurt me at the time, but when you're so far down, the gutter looks up. I had, after all, been derisive of Roger in print many times.'

Townshend channeled his despair and eroding confidence into the 'shoot from the hip' *Who by Numbers*, penning material that was darkly forlorn, cuttingly acerbic, and highly revealing. 'They were written with me stoned out of my brain in my living room crying my eyes out. All the songs were different, some more aggressive than others, but they were all somehow negative in direction. I felt detached from my own work and from the whole project . . . I felt empty.' So distanced from the project were Keith, John, and Roger that they couldn't even identify the tunes from their titles. Townshend later called the bloodletting an exorcism with titles such as 'However Much I Booze' and 'How Many Friends Have I Really Got.' 'I forced the band into a corner with that material. When I first played the demos, Keith burst into tears. He came and put his arms around me. I suppose he was thinking, "Poor

Pete," but that was the kind of material I was dishing up. The group recoiled from the stuff.'

Released in October 1975, the album was generally dismissed as substandard. Critic Roy Carr called it 'Pete Townshend's suicide note,' while Simon Firth perceptively noted, 'Like any other rock fan he won't get fooled again; rock ain't going to save his life and sometimes . . . he can't remember why his band seemed so necessary, what part they played for him.'

Ironically, the album, with its anguished, cynical themes, spawned a top ten single with the bouncy 'Squeezebox,' a puerile play on words Townshend later dismissed as juvenile piffle.

More representative of Pete's deep decline, however, was the embittered and sarcastic 'They Are All in Love.' The song encapsulated the bitter, intractable situation with Stamp and Lambert, as well as Townshend's on-going litigation battles to retrieve unpaid royalties. But its pungent lyric, 'Goodbye, all you punks/Stay young and stay high/Hand me my checkbook/And I'll crawl off to die,' suggested something far more insidious. For the first time since he had encountered Bill Haley twenty years back, Townshend was no longer sure his beloved rock 'n' roll could remain vital.

'For kids rock means nothing,' he told the press. 'They're not really listening. It's become a spectator sport; something could easily replace it. Rock music is not really contemporary to these times. It's really the music of yesteryear.'

Townshend must have thought back to that regiment of original Who fans, how they resembled a thousand Jimmys, still frozen in that moment of glorious purpose, never having moved on. Pete Townshend was now just thirty years old, but he felt fifty. He was lost, confused, and bone-weary. Was he so different from his old fans? After all, he hadn't kept his promise. He hadn't died before he'd grown old.

Or had he? The way he was talking in mid-1975, there was precious little life left in him. He spoke of his disenchantment with the stage, not being able to perform, being tired of the band. 'The Who is a difficult band to write for. It is very tied to tradition and to its audiences and very slow to change. It's like swimming in your own wake.'

As he surveyed the landscape, he saw no new mavericks, no one to pass the torch to. Rock, and the kinetic culture around it, had now become a wasteland of excess and degradation. 'I saw people like Electric Light Orchestra and ELP. I thought about what we were up to and the Stones and Mick Jagger's silk pajamas and Elton John and Rod Stewart. I thought, "Hell, it really is dead!"

'I felt the band was finished, I was finished, and the music was dying. I really felt like crawling off and dying.'

In the midst of his despair, Townshend found himself precariously clinging to something bigger than himself, bigger than his battered, failing ego, bigger even than rock 'n' roll. It was the one lifeboat that might just help keep him afloat.

5

Ragged Heart:
Loving Meher Baba

I am the Divine Beloved who loves you more than you could ever love yourself.

– Avatar Meher Baba

Never will I be able to stand back from myself and pretend anymore that God is a myth. That Christ was just another man. That Baba was simply a hypnotic personality. The facts are coming home to me like sledgehammers, not through the words I read in books about Baba, not through even his own words. But through my ordinary daily existence. Meher Baba is the avatar, God incarnate on our planet. The Awakener.

– Pete Townshend

Merwan Sheriar Irani was born at Sassoon Hospital in Poona, India, on February 25, 1894. By the time Merwan was born, his family was already well established with its own modest home and business, but eventually fell on hard times after his father's business partner defrauded him. Still, the family held together and Merwan's childhood was reportedly a happy one.

On a bright May morning in 1913, Merwan was riding his bicycle on his way to college when a local female saint by the name of Hazrat Babajan beckoned to him. The elderly master, who lived outside under a large tree, rose and embraced him. 'It was like steel to a magnet,' Merwan later commented.

Some months later, after spending a lot of time with this mysterious woman, Babajan kissed him on the forehead one night in January 1914. It was the tender key that unlocked his divine destiny. At that moment, the story goes, young Merwan instantly became God-realized. More than that even, for it was then he realized he was God himself.

'At the time Babajan gave me the *nirvikalp* [inconceptual] experience of my own reality, the illusory physical, subtle and mental bodies – mind, worlds, and one and all created things – ceased to exist for me even as illusion,' Baba later recalled. 'Then I began to see that only I and nothing else existed.'

According to his family, Merwan ate nothing for some nine months and lost all attraction for ordinary life. Thereafter his avatarhood was further confirmed by 'perfect' masters Narayan Maharaj, Tajuddin Baba, Sai Baba, and Upasni Maharaja. Meher Baba later remembered the momentous transformation. 'Despite my resistance the five Perfect Masters kept "pulling me down" to ordinary consciousness for my destined manifestation as avatar; and in this excruciating agony I went through this "tussle." I used to knock my forehead on a stone in my room at home, during the nine months before Upasni Maharaja brought me down to normal consciousness.'

As the years passed, Merwan (now called Meher Baba, or 'Compassionate Father,' by his disciples) gathered around him a core of disciples who served him with unflinching loyalty and devotion. On July 10, 1925, Meher Baba formally began what would become an astounding forty-three years of complete silence of which he has said, 'You have had enough of words. I have had enough of words. It is not through words that I give what I have to give. My love, which is always silent, can flow to you to be yours to keep and to share with those who seek me.'

Over the years Meher Baba's Western devotees largely fell into one of two categories: artists and intellectuals, and the upper-crust unfulfilled of Park Avenue, Forest Hills, and Bel Air. As the sixties unfolded, however, the emphasis changed. Suddenly Haight-Ashbury was flooded with little cards with the guru's smiling face proclaiming, 'Don't worry, be happy,' and flower children everywhere were reading his discourses alongside the works of Huxley, Hesse, Tolkein and Kerouac.

Of course, they were also tripping their asses off on various psychedelics and thus posting some very strange letters to Baba and his mandali (inner core of disciples). A few of the more determined made their way to the master's front door. One of those, Dr. Richard Alpert, alias Baba Ram Das, the errant ex-Harvard associate of bad-boy philosopher Timothy Leary, wrote and asked Baba to elucidate on the emerging promise of LSD as a key to the legendary doors of perception. Baba wrote back to the aspiring yogi, making clear his stand on the spiritual repercussions of acid use. 'No drug, whatever its great promise, can help one attain the spiritual goal,' he said. 'There is no shortcut to the goal except through the grace of the perfect master; and drugs, LSD more than others, give only a semblance of "spiritual experience," a glimpse of false reality.'

For Pete Townshend, the hard-drinking, hard-rocking, hard-living mod king, the mere suggestion of ever humbling himself at the feet of *anyone* would seem laughable. Townshend, with his well-honed irreverence, and arrogant disdain for authority was an unlikely disciple for the kindly, grandfatherly Meher Baba.

Or was he? Perhaps those are exactly the qualities required for such a life-shaking change of direction. Although the avatar is for everyone, perhaps he is a little *more* for the directionless, the angry, the lost, and perpetually insecure. All these are prime adjectives to describe the young Pete Townshend. He was a man who would later make millions from mirroring his own oceanic insecurities and mile-high pain in his consciousness-rousing music. In short, he was ripe for plucking by the old master.

In 1968, while leafing through an imported copy of the *Observer* one evening, Baba reportedly happened on a photo of Townshend and the Who breaking it up with their usual keen precision. He signed something in the air never recorded and then placed his thumb squarely on Townshend's brilliant nose.

Meanwhile, in London Pete was gradually coming to the conclusion that all he really knew was nothing. His hollow confidence and faithless bravado was dissipating with every pointless toke, lusty pint, or power chord. Spiritually, he was very much alone. At twenty-three Townshend was just about at the end of his tether.

'I'd been in the pop business two years, and I was rich and famous,' Townshend later commented. 'But I had got there through frustration. I felt as if a bomb had gone off in my head, and there was just a demolition site inside. I had to find *something* to fill the empty space.'

A highly intelligent, philosophically inclined young man, Townshend had thought long and hard about such widely ranging subjects as UFOs, reincarnation, God, and Utopian politics. Perhaps a bit too hard.

'Every time I came up with a worldwise theory that had taken me years to get clear, [a friend of mine] would say, "That's such a coincidence, man, this guy Meher Baba said something similar in this book *The God Man*," ' Townshend recalls of his evolution toward his inscrutable master. 'I just had to look at this book. What I saw, apart from a photo in the front cover of a strange and elderly man, was shattering.

'Sure enough, each theory I expounded, many to do with reincarnation and its inevitability when considered in the light of the law of averages, were summed up in one sentence. . . .

'What was so sneaky about the whole affair was the way Baba crept into my life. At first his words were encouraging, his state of consciousness and his claims to be the Christ exciting and daring; later they became scary. I began to read of his astoundingly simple relationship with his disciples and of his silence for forty years. It became clear that the party was over. If I read any more lines like "What I want from my lovers is real unadulterated love, and from my genuine workers I expect real work done," I would have to decide once and for all whether the whole thing was really for me or not.'

Encouraged by his first brush with Baba, Townshend still had a long way to go to conform to Baba's fairly rigid dictates. First to go was dope, which was a big step for the rowdy guitarist. It was during a visit with longtime follower Rick Chapman in California, about six months after he first learned of Baba, that the hammer came down.

'As we sat in a shared hotel room in San Diego, I rolled a joint, spouting some high-flown guff about being a happy Baba lover,' remembers Pete. 'Rick took it very calmly, considering he spends a good part of his time lecturing on the spiritual side effects of 'soft' drugs and what Baba had said about them. Anyway, that was my last stoned day in the normal sense. It was easy to give it up. Like a lot of others, I was getting a little bored with pot highs, which seemed limited to the strength of my imagination at any given moment. In other words, I was looking for an excuse to say no to the joint as it came round to me.'

Tripping also rapidly went by the wayside. There was a downside to LSD that Townshend was finding increasingly tiresome, and scary. 'One thing I do know,' he says, 'the last acid trip I took (on a plane coming back from the Monterey Pop Festival) would have been my last whether I'd heard about Baba or not. Acid had taken me apart but not put me back together again.'

With his newfound devotion to Meher Baba, Pete was on top of the world, in 'the honeymoon,' as Baba people call it. Still, like many who have heard the word, there would be a long, rough road ahead. His first big hurdle in his zeal to spread the good news of Baba's avatarhood was the Who itself. Roger Daltrey, for one, found the whole thing pathetic, running down Townshend's master to his face and referring to him sarcastically as 'Ali Baba.'

Keith Moon apparently quite regularly took the piss while John Entwistle characteristically kept quiet, from time to time rolling his eyes skyward in disbelief of his old friend's newest mania.

But all such negativism only served to strengthen Townshend's resolve that he had truly found *the answer*. Fortunately, Pete was not completely alone on the amazing journey, as Karen too was sufficiently attracted to Baba to consider herself a follower – though perhaps not with quite the same neophyte zeal as her highly impressionable new husband.

Townshend even curtailed his often reckless drinking too out of deference to Baba's teachings. Frankly, Meher Baba never did anything but good for the emotionally frail young man. The measure of tranquillity alone his faith afforded him was worth the hefty price of admission. Besides, within months, having a guru would become a very attractive feature of Pete's overall persona to the fans. A fact which almost certainly ultimately brought thousands of people to some knowledge of Baba, or at least of their own latent spiritual nature.

'My view on Meher Baba is one of total blindness at the moment,' Townshend stated. 'I have been attempting to love Baba and serve him in my daily life for nearly two and a half years, and I think other Baba devotees will understand me when I say that the path grows brighter and darker at the same time. Baba has brought me to my senses in many ways, most of all in my normal life. My work as a pop musician had taken me through all phases of excess and indulgence, and it is one of my proudest boasts to be able to say that I can look back at those days and know that not one minute was wasted in catching up with my past, finding the magnificent present in Meher Baba.'

Strange to many, however, is the fact that Townshend never made the trip to India to seek an audience with the master. True, Baba kept strict rules relating to visits of this kind. Even letters were discouraged except in cases of real emergency, but still, if he had pushed the issue, he stood a pretty good chance of a private audience with the messiah.

'I never met Baba,' acknowledges Pete. 'Never wrote him a letter or received one. How am I hanging on? I'm *stuck* on. People could easily get the idea that I'm an unwilling Baba lover, or "Baba tryer" as I prefer to call myself. No, it's just that I was unwilling to let go of that incredible piece of happiness, that unqualified stab of love that I didn't even ask for, didn't expect, and it's made my life, which I know to be as colorful as any, gray in comparison.'

He began to attend weekly meetings of the faithful. In this case they often took place in Townshend's own flat. Led, more often than not, by senior disciple Don Stevens, author of the enlightening *Listen Humanity*, the sessions started out with a congregational recitation of Baba's Universal Prayer and then generally moved on to a lecture by Stevens on one of Baba's many discourses. Often the faithful were then treated to some of Townshend's latest Baba-inspired compositions via acoustic guitar.

'The first [Baba center] I was involved in was actually one of my old pads,' Townshend confirms. 'Right in the heart of Soho, it was on the top floor of an office block. It was an incredible experience to walk into the sun streaming up there through big half-circle windows, and hear Don Stevens, our London father figure [he's actually from San Francisco], give a talk. . . . In the back of my mind were memories of the times I had spent there. Listening to records on a giant system at two hundred watts. Making love in the bed built up near the ceiling, watching *Alice in Wonderland* on the telly, eating baked beans straight out of the tin. . . .

'The second center is still in use. This one was, believe it or not, my wife's flat. We are a many-flatted couple. Though we do manage to live in only one building today. This one is in Victoria in a basement. . . . A hundred people have been known to squeeze in there. Only about twenty of them got served tea. The center is run and financed by a committee which includes myself. The committee sees to it that it is open a couple of days a week and keeps the bills paid and the library full. It also drinks a lot of tea.

'Baba sees you knocking at the door of his basement center in the once-sooty air of Victoria where the steam trains used to play, and pulls you in by your ears. When you first hear about Baba, and your heart warms to him, he shows you an aspect of himself that floors you, astounds you.'

Meher Baba himself, however, was suffering from failing health.

In March 1968 a circular was distributed to Baba's followers worldwide informing them that Baba's prolonged period of 'seclusion' would continue until May 21 of that year. 'None can have the least idea of the intensity of the work I am doing in this seclusion,' explained Baba. 'The only hint I can give is that compared with the work I do in seclusion, all the important work of the world put together is completely insignificant. Although for me the burden of my work is crushing, the result will be intensely felt by all people in the world.'

On July 30, 1968, Meher Baba declared that his work was 'one hundred percent done' and that his lovers would be permitted to visit him from April 10 to June 10, 1969. At this time Baba also planned to end his four decades of silence and draw the multitudes toward him by finally uttering his 'word of words.' 'This is the time for my lovers,' he explained. 'The time for the world's crowds to come to me will be when I break my silence and manifest my divinity.'

In mid-January 1969 Baba again communicated with his followers via yet another declaration stating that this darshan would be his last in silence and that despite his increasingly ill health the event would proceed. Back in England, busily engaged in his exploding career with the Who, Townshend looked forward to finally meeting his famous master face-to-face.

Baba's physical condition, however, deteriorated fast and the seventy-four-year-old teacher suffered a traumatic seizure of unknown origin. The next afternoon Baba said, 'Do not forget that I am God,' and then after yet another slight tremor Meher Baba, the self-proclaimed avatar of the age, 'dropped his body.'

'I am not limited by this form,' Baba had pronounced sometime earlier. 'I use it like a garment to make myself visible to you, and I communicate with you through words best fitted to your understanding. If I used the language of my own consciousness, you would not know what I was talking about. Don't try to understand me. My depth is unfathomable. Just love me.'

Back in England Pete was busy working with the Who when Baba suddenly departed. But what about the great teacher's legendary silence? Was it somehow finally broken before he passed away or was it at all conceivable that Meher Baba was somehow simply an extravagant, charismatic fraud? Both views were widely considered.

'I held that Baba's word has been spoken, probably about the time of his death,' Townshend later projected. 'I was suffering from a bout of flu when Baba was about to drop his earthly body. We were playing Newcastle the day he died, and when I got home the news was broken to me, I felt as if I had betrayed myself. I felt as if I hadn't had enough time to really make myself ready, to learn to love Baba and hang tightly to his apron strings as the whirlwind of spiritual events around the closing of his manifestation speeded up.

'Today I understand a little better. I am not the spiritually advanced seeker I imagined myself to be. Reading too much Herman Hesse and Idries Shah can be a bad thing in that respect. One builds a sort of hero worship for the "Seeker" in the same way one would a film star. It's only recently I've begun to see that Baba's word is an eternal word. Its impact reaches well into the past and the future. The wave of spiritual fervor and obsession that sweeps youth today is a reflection of the force of that word, that expression of his almighty loneliness. . . .

'Baba washed the religious preconceptions from my heart with my own tears. I love Jesus far more now than I ever did at infant school as I sang, "Yes, Jesus loves me." Now I know he really was the Christ.'

At the time Tommy Walker, the profoundly deaf, dumb, and blind boy turned pinball messiah, was born, changing forever the face of rock and instantly making his creator, Pete Townshend, a millionaire. 'My kind of religion!' Keith Moon quipped to the media at the time.

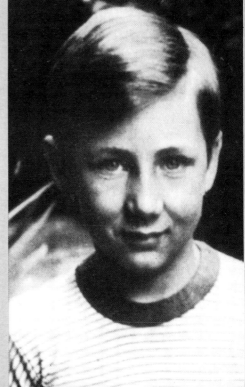

The No. 1 Hip Record
in Town . . .

"ZOOT SUIT"

By the

HIGH-NUMBERS

ON FONTANA TF480

Release date

JULY 3rd 1964

Order your copy of this Record
NOW from your Record Shop

A 1964 music magazine ad for the High Numbers. (© *The Who Fan Club of America*)

An early sixties publicity photo for the High Numbers. (© *The Who Fan Club of America*)

An early sixties ad for the Detours. (© *The Who Fan Club of America*)

Three moody shots of the boys in the mid-sixties. (© Sage Photos)

Keith playing hard at
a mid-sixties gig.
(© Sage Photos)

Mischievous Moonie
listening intently for
any tell-tale rumblings.
(© *The JoAnn
Newburg Agency*)

Pete participates in a
typical mid-sixties pop
star photo op. (© *The
JoAnn Newburg
Agency*)

Pete poses in his private studio in 1967. (© The JoAnn Newburg Agency)

As with many who followed him, Meher Baba's death strengthened Townshend's resolve to live a truly spiritual life despite the trappings and distractions of his superstar status. 'When the Who play the States, I am constantly reminded of Baba by the many, many people I meet there who are also followers,' Townshend has said. 'Obviously it is fairly common knowledge that I am a Baba follower, and despite the fact that I owe my fame ostensibly to physical and not spiritual efforts, I am treated as much of a Baba celebrity, like, say, an Indian visitor who has been with Baba for many years.

'The questions I get asked by these people, the majority of them young, and into rock, are like: When did you first hear of Baba; how is your life affected as a rock star? etc., but often they take pleasure in commandeering me into long storytelling sessions. Many of the people I meet in the States have followed Baba far longer than I. Many have met him and his intimate mandali, and have hundreds of semi-hearsay stories to tell about Baba's dealings with the local people in his area and with themselves when they visited, or tried to visit, Baba in India. Some younger ones look to me as some kind of spiritually together superstar adviser, to be hugged carefully and regarded with awe. In fact, worldly success and spiritual advancement are totally unconnected.'

Western lovers should stick to their responsibilities, work hard, and realize that before society could ever be improved it needed the grace of a Messiah like Baba.

'[Sixties singer] Melanie, who used to be very interested in what Baba had done and said, became thoroughly repulsed by overly gushy Baba lovers. Perhaps she saw hypocrisy in their eyes. Saw people that talk about love but squabble among themselves and gather in centers like so many ministers of the Church, forming a religion that would discolor and taint the words of The Master as sure as it had happened a hundred times before. . . . But I like Baba lovers. Perhaps even a little more than I like any other kinds of people. It is only with them that I can talk about my love for Baba with complete abandon.'

On March 1, 1970, Pete penned a rambling editorial in the *Sunday Telegraph* touting Baba's conservative philosophy on drugs. It was a brave step for a professional hippie like Townshend to take:

Sterility of Drug Taking

From Pete Townshend, Leader of The Who Pop Group

Dr. Allan Cohen's work with students in particular, is unique as far as I know. He is well acquainted with not only the effects of drugs but also the terminology and slang used by drug abusers. This is very, very important. It is not a good idea to insist that the problems of a young drug user are obvious and that the course of action is clear.

The very fact that a young person is willing to take the chance of using drugs indicates a fairly desperate state of mind. Perhaps more desperate than even the young person himself realizes or cares to admit. However, the desperation is of a spiritual nature. The spirit is the unknown quantity and the drug user tends to regard all other aspects of life with less respect.

Thus, a man like Cohen who has used drugs and can *really* talk to users on their own 'level' (whether that be high or low) can inform people of *why* they use or wish to use drugs, not tell them what the drugs are going to do. They *know* what the drugs are going to do: the extreme nature of experience and the risks involved are all part of the fun, dreadful though that may seem to the general public and myself in recall. Dr. Cohen and his aides in the States are directly responsible for my own drug-free condition at present. The use of drugs had led me, some would say inevitably, to an interest in religion once again, and rather than fight the preconceptions I had learned during childhood to Christianity I turned to Indian mysticism. On coming into contact with Meher Baba's followers, I came to realize that drug use could no longer fit into my life as a sincere, soul-seeking person.

I feel that the general public and the authorities believe that to go from a life of drug taking to a life of devotion to an Indian avatar is going from the sublime to the ridiculous. But, of course, it is not true. Dr. Allan Cohen and his aides, and possibly myself on occasion, have encouraged many young people to refrain from drug use by giving them an idea of what it is they are really after. What, of course, they are after is nothing really new, they are searching for their own true identity in the divine scheme, they are, in essence, searching for God . . .

I really believe that the answer to the drug problem lies in the hands of men like Dr Cohen. Men who realize the motivations of drug users and can offer them an alternative way of life; that of devoting one's whole life and existence to the only *real* search, the search for God. I hope that young people everywhere, playing games with their own destiny, will realize sooner than I did that the real game is already in process, has been always, and will be always. Your move. – PETE TOWNSHEND, Twickenham, Middlesex

In late November of that same year Pete once again went to print with a cover story in *Rolling Stone* entitled 'In Love with Meher Baba.' Still, the most personally moving Baba adventure for Pete had to be his February 1972 trip to Arangaon, India, to meet with Baba's mandali and bow down at the tomb of his avatar. It was here, standing alone on the windy hill at Meherazad, that Townshend finally made peace with himself for the first time in his short, eventful life. Surrounded by the miracle of love only those closest to Meher Baba freely share, all he could say when asked to describe the experience was, 'It felt like home.'

Pete made a heart-felt contribution to Baba followers with two thousand privately distributed albums he produced in cooperation with the London Baba group. *Happy Birthday* featured an eclectic, illustrated twenty-eight-page booklet and an album that mirrored the emerging youthful element inherent in the organization.

In 1972 the LP was reviewed by *Rolling Stone*: 'The music is mostly Pete Townshend productions: "The Seeker," which has been released as a single; "Content" and "Day of Silence," peaceful ballads with acoustic guitar and buzzing mandolin; "Maryjane" and "The Love Man," bouncy songs with a Whoish touch of psychodrama and comedy ("Maryjane, get your tingly fingers off me"). And then, of all things, Pete Townshend does a charmingly artless rendition of Cole Porter's "Begin the Beguine." It was Meher Baba's favorite song.'

Townshend followed up this venture. In October 1972 the still pristine and challenging *Who Came First*, part of the trilogy of 'Baba' albums he produced prior to his turbulent Oceanic period. The clever cover depicted Pete resplendent in his trademark white boiler suit, Doc Martens and Meher Baba button standing thoughtfully and definitely on a floor of eggs

121

(a play on the old 'which came first' theme) by artist Graham Hughes.

The first tune, 'Pure & Easy,' was originally intended for inclusion on the *Lifehouse* project, but ended up here. It was the swirling, upbeat, defining anthem for Pete's new musical declaration of independence. With its 'in the beginning was the word' message and convincing vocals, the song ranks as one of Townshend's most soulful and eloquent works.

'From the peace of the original note, the single unmultiplied breath of life, the eternal silent singing that pervaded all, came this,' Townshend has said of the lofty theme of the song. 'What are we supposed to be doing? Here am I, in suburban Twickenham, skinny, vain, and obsessed by the word "forward"; how am I equipped to begin to understand Infinite Love?'

Another song, 'Nothing Is Everything (Let's See Action),' is one of the purest and most complete pop statements made by any artist. Here Townshend summons up potent images held together by a sometimes honky tonk, sometimes hard rock, sometimes folky mix of passionate musical mediums. Sleeping quietly all these years on this little known album it is Townshend's barrier busting 'Day in the Life,' 'Stairway to Heaven,' or 'All Along the Watchtower.'

Although Roger Daltrey took a stab at the tune with the Who, it landed like the *Hindenburg* on that infamous misty New Jersey morning. Only Townshend's version hits the mark with an intricate web of complex lyrical assaults heralding the cause of spiritual freedom as well as the profound hypocrisy of everyday society, the collective power of the individual, the apathy of ignorance, man's quest to see God face-to-face, the hope of expanded consciousness, the eternality and majesty of the soul, the expansive nature of nothingness, surrender of the finite ego to the Great Oversoul, and finally the simple, plaintive, pitiful plea for some kind of direction home. Quite a lot to be accomplished by one three minute so-called pop song!

Once again intended as part of *Lifehouse*, this song bores into the mind, a stinging jewel of street-smart spirituality and hip prophecy. This piece illustrates, perhaps more clearly than any other, exactly what following Meher Baba did for Pete Townshend's art.

'Time Is Passing,' on the other hand, ping pongs directly to the heart of the matter, outlining more directly Townshend's Meher Baba model of spiritual gnosis and ultimate surrender to the Divine

Ocean within. Here everything is alive and tingling with trippy life force: the singer's imaginary sister, empty jam jars, simple laughter, the sea, starfish, the rocks, seagulls, trees, an 'empire' of 'dead men,', faith and even time itself. The message? 'Time will teach us all,' scoundrels that we are.

'I played this to Baba's mandali when I went to India this year,' Townshend comments in the album's helpful, handwritten liner notes.

The second song on side two, 'Heartache' (better known as 'There's a Heartache Following Me'), was one of Baba's favorite songs by his favorite contemporary singer country gentleman, the late Jim Reeves. Pete's rendition, however, is somehow strangely out of place in comparison to the rest of the album. It's not the obvious fact that it's a circa 1950s-something C. and W. ballad sung by a willowy English boy to his Persian-Indian messiah. That only makes it more intriguing. Perhaps it's the hollow chords, extraordinarily up-front vocals, and piercing keyboards that somehow grate.

Although Townshend depicts 'Sheraton Gibson' as a simple 'on the road again' ditty, one wonders, What road? The road home to Twickenham or the long and winding, infinitely tricky road to self?

In 'Content' Townshend sings a song (with lyrics by Maud Kennedy) that examines the primal yearning of man for God. 'I put it to music and sing it like Vera Lynn,' says Pete.

Finally, 'Parvardigar' (adapted from Meher Baba's *Universal Prayer*) caps off the innovative album with a spiritual bullet right between the eyes, a masterpiece of poetics, devotion, and the musical art. Listening carefully it can bring one to tears.

Over the next three years, however, Townshend would lose his way, a body and mind spent from the excesses of 'living in the material world,' as George Harrison, also a follower of Eastern mysticism himself, once wrote. By mid-1975 Townshend found himself floundering in spiritual darkness, light years away from his beloved master.

The only road home was to go back to the beginning, to unearth his Baba roots, Townshend decided. In the summer of 1975 he packed up his family and a few friends to visit the Meher Center in Myrtle Beach, South Carolina, Baba's Western home. 'My family, particularly, of course, my wife (who, as a matter of personal policy, tries to avoid aspects of the music world that I still find exciting), had suffered a lot from my pathetic behavior of the previous year, but they would naturally be by my side on any trip other than Who tours. So they came with me, or rather I went with them to Myrtle Beach.'

Awed by Baba's Western home and by resident matriarchs Kitty Davey and Elizabeth Patterson, Pete and his family slowly wound down at the five-hundred-acre retreat. Wandering the shoreline and woodlands, with its teeming wildlife, spending time in meditation and prayer, Townshend felt the soothing presence of the avatar flood him with peace. 'We were all staggered by the impact of the love that literally filled the air,' he later declared.

But it was only a beginning. Ten days later Townshend continued his spiritual journey, moving along to Walnut Creek, California, for a six-week study with Murshida Ivy O. Duce, the Baba-appointed head of an organization called Sufism Reoriented. Despite a tongue-wagging from the seventy-something Duce about what she perceived as the 'frivolousness' of Pete's two Baba albums, he stood at rapt attention as she held forth on the intricacies of Meher Baba's philosophy.

There the final transformation began. Townshend found himself pouring out his heart to this wise woman. 'I told her every grisly detail: the paranoia, the drunken orgies, the financial chaos, the indulgent self-analysis, and, of course, the dreamy hope for the future.'

Totally mystified, he found his spiritual cup immediately begin to fill. By the end of his stay Townshend was fully energized, strengthened, and 'feeling fairly certain that I could now rock 'n' roll right into my grave,' he stated.

Back home in England as he strode into the band's rehearsal hall, an incredulous Keith Moon remarked, 'Hey, mate, you're smiling again.'

'Something positive happened to me,' grinned Pete in reply.

By the time Pete made his second trip to India to visit Baba's mandali, he knew this was the path he would follow the rest of his life. While there he walked the many places favored by his master, played guitar for the devotees, and even took part in a documentary produced by Baba's Australian followers.

While he was careful to avoid any public pronouncements on the subject, Townshend also made it known to the Baba elite that he was planning to open a formal center dedicated to their master in upper-crust suburban Twickenham. 'For a few years I had toyed with the idea of opening a London house dedicated to Meher Baba,' recalls Pete. 'In the eight years I had followed him, I'd donated only coppers to foundations set up around the world to carry out the Master's wishes and decided it was about time I put myself on the line. The Who set up a strong charitable trust of its own which appeased, to an extent, the feeling I had that Baba would rather have seen me give to the poor than to the establishment of yet another so-called "spiritual center."'

As 1976 wore on Townshend was busily engaged establishing Meher Baba Oceanic. The ambitious, multifaceted venture would further publicly link the star with Meher Baba. First in a list of projects he undertook was discussed in a 1976 press release.

Right now the most important thing in hand is the film we have underway about Delia de Leon. This will be called simply *Delia*, and is about Delia and her recollections of Baba and His effect on her life. It also illustrates how Pete Townshend's coming to Meher Baba was very much accelerated by her example and openness.

The film is in the rough-cut stage at present, and is about an hour long. We are going to include film of the *Tommy* London premiere, which Delia attended, Kew Gardens, a garden party held for Baba lovers at Pete's home, and plenty of beautiful film of Baba Himself, courtesy of many of you reading this memo.

The music in the film is composed by Billy Nicholls, but there is also music recorded live in India by Pete, including his own Parvardigar prayer (recorded by Baba's tomb), and Indian music recorded at the Armatithi gathering 1972. This music will probably be released on a limited-edition stereo record in the future.

Pete has been directing and editing the film, with heavy research and media co-ordination work by John Annuziato. Friends of Delia have spontaneously flooded to offer their services in the film, and to help in any way they can. . . .

This film has taught us many hard lessons. Most of all, that film making is both fun and terrifyingly hard work in the bargain. Most of all, it has installed in us a new respect for attention to detail in and around the story of the life of the Avatar; a powerful sense of Baba's Presence pushing us toward His own nameless goal.

Delia, as always, has been enchanting us with her stories about Baba, and her impatience to see things moving at the kind of pace we feel only the Master Himself is capable of keeping up.

Nevertheless, staggered as we are by the showering of Love and Energy, we find it all interesting and stimulating even at a basic day-to-day level. Film is an evocative and powerful medium as Baba so rightly pointed out – and there is no better medium for spreading His message of Truth. . . .

Much Love in Him
AVATAR MEHER BABA – KI   JAI:
The Film Department at Meher Baba Oceanic

Seldom does a biographer share a page in the life of his subject, but it was at this point that Townshend's life intersected with mine.

I was at the State University of New York at Brockport, just outside Rochester. After following the Hare Krishna movement for some time I was now a wanna-be transcendentalist, forsaking meat and all manner of drugs.

I became attracted to the teachings of Meher Baba when the orthodoxy of Krishna consciousness became a little too taxing. To hear Baba boldly pronounce that I too was intrinsically a boundless spiritual entity only temporarily tied to this disappointing material realm was big news. To meditate on his beaming, heavily mustached face was uplifting, and to be part of my local Baba group was a joy.

So wrapped up in Meher Baba had I become that I soon longed for a more intimate 'connection' and thus piled into our late-model Plymouth station wagon with my long-suffering consort, Brenda, and headed off in search of the ultimate Baba buzz at Meher Center.

Banging an old eight track of *Who Came First* into the stereo we flew down the highway cushioned by the high volume presence of Pete's moving compositions in praise of Baba, 'Let's See Action', 'Sheraton Gibson', and the largely unsung devotional masterwork, 'Parvardigar.' A 6:48 spiritual orgasm adapted from Baba's *Universal Prayer*. A song that either made me shout out the lyrics in a passionate out-of-tune tirade, or simply sit in silence as Townshend's shimmering acoustic guitar drilled into my soul only to fill me up again with Baba's empire exploding words.

Ultimately one of the Baba lovers suggested I drop Townshend a line. I immediately wrote a long, rambling letter to Pete, and then cycled around the corner and slammed it in the mailbox. Thereafter, I suddenly got very busy at school and immediately forgot all about it. A couple of weeks later, however, my mother pulled a long khaki colored envelope from her purse and wordlessly deposited it on my grandmother's vintage fifties kitchen table. As I looked at the humble typewritten missive with no return address I wondered out loud whom it might be from. Nineteen years later I remember my excitement as I carefully opened it to find an equally long, wordy letter from Mr Townshend dated February 25.

'What I am very keen to do is to meet somebody who I feel is capable of running things for Oceanic in the USA. We have talked to several people with the right technical qualifications, but the problem is that individuals are *over* keen. They see this as their opportunity to both work for Baba, and make a good living doing something creative. It shades the internal vision. . . .

'I don't drink anymore. It nearly killed me. Occasionally, though, despite the fact that the dizziness nauseates me, and the memory of the way I was appalls me, I take a small drink. I remember Baba and do it so that I don't become just as habitual a non-drinker as I was a drinker. I don't do that with dope, Meher Baba gave us clear *orders* in that respect. The chance to obey an order is obviously something we should jump on. So, despite some George Harrison rumors to the contrary, I haven't smoked dope since 1967. . . .

'Much love to you brother, brother in generation and Master. (The only two things I have ever really cared about.)

As I read and then reread the letter it dawned on me that Pete was obviously a very nice, approachable, concerned human being.

From there several letters whizzed back and forth across the Atlantic in rapid succession until Townshend invited me to fly over for the opening of Meher Baba Oceanic in July 1976. Even more exciting was Townshend's hint in a letter dated 'Easter Saturday' that perhaps I might even end up with a job out of it all. 'I will remember your "toward camera" aptitude,' he wrote. 'In fact, when John Annuziato starts his American filming work, we will need an interviewer, someone skilled at making people feel at ease, with a bit of screen grace in their own right.'

After a long, tiring journey, I arrived at Townshend's doorstep at Number 3, The Embankment, several days later. I bravely rang the doorbell, and immediately the door swung open. A tall, attractive woman briskly informed me that Pete wasn't in, but only just down the road in his office at Number 24. Before I could thank her, the door snapped shut and I stood there alone, gathering up my bags for the quick walk to the long brick building that housed Eel Pie Productions and the gritty legacy of the Who.

Ducking my head through the front door, I was met by a friendly fellow who introduced himself as John Purdue, coordinator on the Oceanic project and all-around fixer. Scraping together my last few pennies, I bought a pint of milk and a Swiss roll and munched away while we talked. I recall the one big room was bare but for a few scattered pieces of office equipment and a series of framed eleven by fourteen prints from the inside booklet of *Quadrophenia* hanging high over the streetside picture window.

After only a few minutes Pete turned up. I stood up and held out my hand as he moved forward to say hello. Unbelievably, the first thing I did after shaking hands was to spill my milk all over the polished hardwood floors.

Pete was a very tall, powerful-looking geezer in white shoes and a striped jumper. His highly individual, angular face was at the same time very gentle, but somehow slightly disturbing. He certainly didn't look like a pop star. Somebody's gangly, grizzled road manager maybe. But a poncy, guitar-playing front man, no way.

Following a bit of small talk he motioned me to follow him outside, where we walked silently together back to Number 3 to do a 'little job,' as he put it.

Once inside I waited in the lived-in-looking front room with fancy ceilings while Pete wandered off only to amble back a few minutes later with the same young woman I'd spoken to earlier. 'This is my wife, Karen,' he offered. 'This is Geoffrey, from the States. His lady is just about to have a baby and he's come over for the opening.'

'You should be at home,' Mrs. Townshend snapped as we nodded hello.

Of course she was right, but it was still embarrassing to hear it put so bluntly. Even Pete felt it, and quickly changed the subject by beckoning me upstairs. Making our way to the second floor, past the bedrooms of Pete and Karen and their two young daughters, Aminta and Emma, Pete finally explained what was up.

'Baba's personal secretary, Adi K. Irani, is coming for the opening, and he's getting on a bit. I've got an old air conditioner in the attic which might make it a bit easier for him in this hot weather. Actually, it's probably the only bloody working air conditioner in all of Great Britain!'

Bounding up two more floors we finally stood beneath a tiny entryway in the ceiling. He gave me a boost and before I knew it I was crawling around in Pete Townshend's attic in search of an air conditioner for God's secretary!

'You see it?' he called out laughing.

'Yeah. It's here. If I can get hold of the damn thing,' I answered. Poking around on my hands and knees, I spied several badly broken guitars stacked haphazardly in a heap against the wall. I suddenly realized that here must be keepsakes from Pete's stormy days of rage with the Who.

Getting that air conditioner out of that tiny hole, down four narrow flights of stairs, and into Pete's old van outside was a gritty, sweaty business, but we laughed a lot and quickly developed an easy-going, friendly rapport.

My sense that Pete was a good guy was confirmed when we were joined by an American teen whose name I have forgotten. Townshend told me he had rung up from Heathrow one day with his girlfriend to say that he had arrived. Just like that. Immigration apparently required confirmation that the couple were indeed 'guests' of the great Pete Townshend, which, to his credit, he confirmed. When they turned up at his home he graciously invited them in and subsequently put the girl to work in the house and the kid as a gofer. All of this for total strangers.

At any rate, the three of us set off for the new Oceanic building on Ranleigh Drive, Richmond, to drop off the air conditioner and show me my new digs in a guest room on site. The impressive structure was not yet completed and I remember the builders (mostly longhaired young guys) all trying to impress Pete with their hard work as he strode by. Once inside I peeked out an upstairs window to see them sitting about in the hot sun swilling beers and eating sandwiches. Some things, anyway, never change.

After I dropped my bags in the small but comfortable room –

which in a few days would house the venerable Sri Adi K. Irani – Pete invited me to a rehearsal for the upcoming opening in a nearby church hall. By this time, of course, I was fading fast and desperately needed sleep, but here was a chance to witness the Who's senior powerhouse go through his paces.

During the twenty-minute ride there Pete talked about the difficulties of following Meher Baba, the spiritual power of music, and his desire to produce a series of film documentaries recording the intimate recollections of Baba's now elderly mandali. 'Pretty soon they'll all be gone, you know,' he confided. 'It's important that their knowledge and memories are preserved. If not for us, but for the future. After all, these are the people Baba chose to be around him.'

Upon our arrival I walked to the back of the van and carefully picked up Pete's double-neck electric twelve-string and began to carry it inside. 'Let me get that,' said Pete, overtaking me on the way in. 'It's a very expensive guitar.'

'Sure,' I nodded. And this from a man who made his fortune wrecking a small mountain of the things.

Soon after the band let loose (consisting of longtime Townshend pal Billy Nicholls on bass, Pete on lead, and an unnamed trio of backup vocalists, a neighbor lady with a thick accent and her hair in curlers barged in and gave Pete a piece of her mind.

'Some people have children sleeping round here, you know!' she exploded.

'Do you realize who you're talking to like that?' said one of the bystanders.

'Easy,' Townshend diplomatically interjected. 'We're very sorry, luv. We'll turn it down for you.'

Unfortunately, however, the old dear wasn't willing to let it go at that. 'Turn *off*, you mean! I don't know why we should have to hear *any* of it. We pay to live round here, and I'm sick of having to stay indoors with the windows shut for a bit of peace. Does that seem fair?'

'No, I suppose it doesn't,' Pete calmly replied. 'I'll tell you what. This is our last day and we'll only be playing for another couple of hours or so, then that's it. Do you think you can live with that?'

'Well, in that case,' she replied, her anger suddenly diffused. 'Ta ra, then,' and with that she turned and walked out.

As the rehearsal progressed Pete had to stop several times to admonish the American for playing 'too much' on the drums. 'Just keep it simple,' he patiently intoned. The kid didn't really seem to get it, and Pete carried on, pretending not to notice.

After about an hour, from out of nowhere, Townshend stopped between songs and asked if I wanted to join the chorus jamming away at the back of the hall. The music to be performed was woven around an abbreviated version of Hermann Hesse's *Siddhartha* called *The River of Life*. I remember, we spent quite a long time working on a harmony that went:

> Oil from Persia silk from Siam
> Options on the sale of watermelon jam.

What it was all about I don't really remember, but with Pete's driving guitar it sounded fucking great.

The next number was the more familiar 'The Seeker,' the heavy-weight spiritual rocker first recorded by the Who several years earlier. Gearing up for the challenge, we sailed through about half the song when Pete suddenly shouted for me to take over the vocal from him!

Stunned, I nevertheless dove straight in without missing a beat:

> They call me the seeker
> I been searching low and high
> I won't get what I'm after
> Till the day I die.

I looked over at Pete, who was smiling broadly as he strummed away, his foot propped on a small amp. Much to my amazement I even hit all the high notes.

Following my few minutes of reflected glory Pete signaled for everyone to break while a quick rehearsal was organized to firm up the dramatic portion of the piece. Once again, he called on me to help out, this time by reading the part of the Buddha for some guy who hadn't turned up and then later tutoring the entire cast on how to convincingly chant the Hare Krishna mantra in a scene that featured a wandering tribe of mendicant Vaishnavas.

As we were packing up getting ready to leave, Pete mentioned that the Who were popular in just about every country in the civilized world with the exception of Israel. 'I can't understand it,' mused Townshend. 'I guess the kids are too busy working on kibbutzim and dodging bullets in the military.'

After dropping Pete and me at Oceanic, the American drove off in the van back to Twickenham, leaving us alone in the rambling, only partially completed building. I remember Pete making sure all the bathrooms were equipped with toilet paper and nervously fussing over the list of Baba VIPs expected at the grand opening.

Wandering into his spacious office overlooking the muddy, narrow Thames, I propped myself on a box and tried to somehow look occupied while Pete pored over the mountains of paper on his desk. Eventually he looked up, and we talked for a few minutes before he bolted out the door and down the short staircase to the recording studio/rehearsal hall/theater on the ground floor.

I quickly noticed that unless you were listening to him or responding directly to something he'd just said, he had a way of not really connecting. We could be chatting away when he'd suddenly jump up and leave the room without a word.

Another of Pete's Baba pen pals (and there were many in those days), Dawn Rippa, once said that after corresponding with him for several years quite intimately, when she finally met him at Oceanic en route to Baba's tomb in India, instead of the warm welcome his letters led her to expect, he hardly even acknowledged her presence before summarily walking out on her.

'We met Pete in London,' she later wrote me from India. 'He was really busy that week so we didn't have time to develop any kind of rapport. We did manage one brief conversation. Your name wasn't brought up. I'll tell you more when we get home. We arrived on Tuesday and their weekly meeting took place. Pete didn't come but his mother did. She's who he takes after.'

Ironically, Pete's towering sense of self, the very thing that makes him so magnetic a composer and performer, also clearly exposes the often petulant child he carries within.

Personally, it was easy to forgive Pete his sometimes graceless preoccupation with Oceanic. No less a creative achievement than a record album, film, or book, and Townshend worked passionately to ensure that here would rise an orderly, working, tangible expression of his devotion to Meher Baba, and a selfless center of love and learning for those who shared his particular vision of truth.

Among rock stars only George Harrison had committed himself

as deeply, funding several projects for his adopted guru, His Divine Grace A. C. Bhaktivedanta Swami Prabhupada, including the publication of several books as well as a stylish London temple and sprawling country retreat.

In fact in his first letter to me Pete mentioned Harrison in a surprisingly brotherly, matey way. 'I know George Harrison very well,' he wrote, 'and claim to be one of the few people in show business who respects his devotion. But I find that despite the fact that Meher Baba so carefully illustrated how closely all the world's religions are related, we mortals take joy in the differences rather than the similarities.'

My first night alone at the soon-to-be Oceanic was precipitated by Pete offhandedly announcing that while there was a small kitchen upstairs there wasn't any food and nowhere really close to buy any. 'What about restaurants?' I asked, once again in the money after my mom wired over a couple of hundred bucks via American Express.

'Not really,' he declared, weakly shaking his head. 'This is pretty residential round here. I don't know where the hell you can eat.'

'Never mind,' I broke in, not wanting to put him out, 'all I really want anyway is some sleep. My head is pounding from the trip.'

'Right,' he said thoughtfully, 'are you sure you're okay then?'

'Absolutely. I'll see you tomorrow.'

'All right, mate,' he tossed off softly.

'Hey!' I called out as he skipped down the stairs to the wide front door, his keys jangling.

'Yeah?' he said turning back.

'Jai Baba, man!' I loudly proclaimed.

'Jai Baba,' he answered, smiling quietly.

I bolted the door behind him and walked back up to my room just in time to see him jet off down the quiet, tree-lined street in his long silver four-door Mercedes.

Meher Baba Oceanic after dark was a little like staying in a shiny new airport lounge after the last flight had gone. Despite the expensively framed paintings of Baba hanging everywhere by blind artist and Meher Center resident Lynn Ott, this was essentially an office building and thus conveyed all the warmth and comfort one might expect from bedding down in the lobby of a fancy solicitor's.

My first order of business was to unlock the office (Pete had left

133

me with the keys in case I wanted to go out) and try and call home. Unfortunately, I couldn't figure out how to use the phone, so I whiled away a couple of hours reading first a book on Baba, and then, regrettably, some of Pete's personal correspondence left lying atop his desk.

In hindsight, I realize that this was the beginning of the end for Pete and me. I should have simply gone to bed, but I was keyed up from all the excitement and at the same time bored stiff with the prospect of the long dull evening before me. It wasn't any major plot to systematically invade Pete's life or anything. I was just 'snooping,' as my mother used to call it. I am, however, cogniscent of how shoddy it looks now in cold hard type. Still, the worst was yet to come.

My first full day in Townshendland started with the din of swinging hammers as the builders got under way early, followed shortly thereafter by the arrival of Pete's PA, Judy Waring, and then around 11:00 a.m. the big man himself. As always, John Purdue was around, efficiently carrying out Pete's instructions, as was an aging hipster by the name of John Annuziato, whom I couldn't help but dislike the minute I laid eyes on him for his smarmy, insincere charm. He too was American, and immediately buddied up to me, telling me stories about working the sponge boats in Tarpon Springs, Florida, and traveling the rock circuit with this and that superstar band. I was not impressed.

I remember watching Purdue, Annuziato, and Townshend huddled together on a metal bench at the end of the street deep in conversation about the millions of last-minute things that needed doing for the opening, now only days away. After finally summoning up the courage to interrupt, I strolled over, clearly in the middle of something important, but Pete was still very gracious.

'There he is!' Townshend intoned brightly. 'Sleep okay?'

'You bet. Listen, man,' I ventured, charging ahead as if to justify my boldness, 'I know an incredible sitarist who lives here in London and I was thinking maybe you might like to hire him to play for Adi. He's an English guy, Clem Alford. I used to take lessons from him a couple of years back. What do you think?'

'How much would he want?' Annuziato asked.

'I dunno. Shall I call him?'

'Yeah, sure,' said Pete. 'But you know . . . be cool. See what he wants. If we can swing it, then great, if not, then it's not really a big deal. It's getting pretty late to add anything new anyway.'

Turning to John, he told him to give me a tentative schedule of the festivities so I could try and find a good spot for Alford to perform. 'Night time would be nice,' Townshend suggested. 'Maybe around sunset.'

As I walked away clutching the long mimeographed sheet, I suddenly hoped I could really deliver on my big idea. It wouldn't be the first time I'd talked myself into a corner. At this point all I wanted was to be part of Team Baba and make a good impression. Neither of which would come to pass.

Reading through the five-day calendar of events, I was greatly impressed by the genuinely terrific program Townshend and Company had put together. It read in part:

Wednesday July 7

3.00 p.m.   Picnic in Kew Gardens. Meeting at Oceanic, thence to Kew by car and transport provided. It is not yet known whether Adi will be able to enjoy this picnic, if not we will bring him some leftover cakes! Please bring food for yourself or a culinary contribution. Some basics will be provided. R.S.V.P.

7.30 p.m.   ADI K. IRANI. Second major talk.

8.45 p.m.   Tea.

9.15 p.m.   John Horder will read HAFIZ.

9.40 p.m.   Adi will talk about Baba's love of Hafiz and Jigger and quote some of his favorite Ghazals.

Thursday July 8

7.30 p.m.   Premiere showing of Martin Cook and Dudley Edwards' film *Fred*. Fred Marks himself will be present.

8.15 p.m.   Live music. Tea.

9.00 p.m.   John Annuziato present two films about Allan Cohen. These are 'educational' films designed to help introduce young people to Meher Baba; we are showing them for your interest and to hear your reactions on this type of work.

Friday July 9

8.00 p.m.   *River of Life* – a Rock Musical and spiritual odyssey performed by the Meher Baba Strolling Players. There will be an intermission. Please take your seats early. The play is written by Ken Graham, directed by Sue Hunt.

10.00 p.m.   A Prayer and short talk from Adi K. Irani, before Silence Day.

Saturday July 10

4.00 p.m.   SILENCE DAY. We will gather and keep Silence (or fast), and remember Meher Baba. The *Disc Magazine* is 'premiered' today, and with luck (lots of it), copies will be on sale. The music will anyway be played, and the artwork available for inspection and enjoyment. Various videotapes and music tapes will be played throughout the afternoon to entertain.

6.00 p.m.   Supper will be provided for all who are not fasting.

7.30 p.m.   Films of Meher Baba from India will be happening. We break our silence at 10.00 p.m.

Sunday July 11

4.00 p.m.   Premiere of Carrie Hamblett's film about Mike DaCosta, *Mike's Poem.*

4.30 p.m.   Live music.

4.55 p.m.   Pete will introduce his film about Delia de Leon. Another premiere, the film is called simply *Delia.*

6.00 p.m.   Supper will be provided for all.

7.30 p.m.   ADI K. IRANI's closing talk.

9.00 p.m.   Pete Townshend will thank all concerned in the emerging of the 'OCEANIC' project.

9.15 p.m.   Tea.

9.30 p.m.   Pete Townshend's LIVE MUSIC CONCERT.

10.00 p.m.   Parvardigar Prayer, and Goodnight.

It was now Friday, July 2, and by the time I returned to Ranleigh Drive the only souls around were Pete and a couple of middle-aged masons fussing with the ornamental brickwork along the front of the building. When Pete saw me he asked if I would help him move some boxes of books into the library. We worked for a good couple of hours at the end of which he offered to give me an old chair that was sitting in an upstairs storeroom.

'It's Jacobean,' he explained, spinning it around on one leg for me to examine. I told him no thanks as it was a little big to fit in a suitcase and I was a very long way from home. The truth is, at the time I had absolutely no idea what the hell Jacobean meant and have often regretted not accepting the prize. God knows what it was worth.

For those unfamiliar with the trappings of Indo-based philosophies, it might be worthwhile to describe the interior of the library. It was a long, though not overly wide room on the upper floor facing the street, and the walls were lined with volumes of books by, about, and dedicated to Meher Baba and his expansive, nonsectarian teachings. Here and there were photos of Baba at various stages of his life. Leaning against a wall was Baba in Hollywood in 1932. On a shelf was an older Baba from the fifties leaning out the window of his ashram planting a full frontal kiss on the lips of a horse, believe it or not.

Most interesting, however, and perhaps telling about the level of Pete's devotion to Baba, was a floor-to-ceiling glass case in the corner reverentially displaying life-size plaster casts of the master's feet and hands, even a cherished lock of his beautiful reddish brown hair.

As Meher Baba himself instructs in his 1955 collection of spiritual discourses, God to Man and Man to God: 'Dwelling on the form of the Master often facilitates concentration of the form of the Master. . . . This is responsible for removing such barriers as may exist between the aspirant and the Master and gives rise to unrestrained love for the Master, leading to the meditation of the heart which consists in constant thinking about the Master with an uninterrupted flow of love.'

Once again, to a spiritual hayseed like myself this was pretty heady stuff. Although I'd spent time in the Hare Krishna Movement and had seen such things from a distance I was touched by Townshend's efforts to give Baba and his followers a permanent home in London.

Later that evening Pete and I took a long ride around Richmond.

I can't remember where we went or why, but I do know what we talked about. Many times over the years I've referred back to that night, going over and over Pete's words as we made our way through the rain-swept streets of Richmond.

'It's very hard to put into words,' he began, 'but I feel I'm definitely in contact with Baba and that right now, he's more important to me than the band, the money, my home, my family, even my own life. As far as I'm concerned, this whole rock star thing is a burden. It's almost killed me several times: I feel like my nine lives are just about used up.'

'Don't forget,' I tossed back, 'how Baba uses people for his work. Remember back in the early days in Europe with his first Western disciples how he'd order everyone to the cinema or the theater just to work through the concentrated consciousness of the audience. Maybe it's the same with the Who. Perhaps somehow Baba's working through that sea of humanity all focused on you up there prancing around. As for me, I feel almost totally disconnected most of the time. I don't feel Baba at all, but still I can't let go.'

'What does the Bible say?' Townshend carried on. 'More blessed is he who has not seen and yet believes.'

Meanwhile, back at the ranch, we did the old hippie handshake in the front seat and Pete dropped me off, warning me that as it was Friday no one was apt to be around again until Monday.

'In that case,' I said thoughtfully, 'perhaps I'll take the train to Coventry tomorrow and visit my old pal, Tom Gerrard.'

'That might be good,' Pete agreed, 'just make sure you're back for Monday morning so we can get started on those oceanic T-shirts you're going to silk-screen.'

I promised him I would and sprinted inside. It was great a evening, I thought to myself. So great, in fact, I was about to fuck it all up by making one of the stupidest mistakes of my entire goddam miserable life.

Once inside the building I rang Gerrard (Judy had very kindly showed me how to use the phones earlier in the day) to tell him I would be coming up in the morning. Following that I shuffled around for a bit and then reached into my pocket for the keys. I noticed a locked door just to the right of Pete's office and suddenly got very curious about what might be inside. I fiddled for the right key, and the lock finally clicked. Inside were yet more boxes, which didn't really inflame my curiosity too much, so I switched off the light and went back to my room. After a half hour or so, though, I got to wondering about the content of the containers and decided to take a more concentrated look.

The first box I laid my hands on held literally dozens of small reels of tape. Many were unmarked, but two stood out as potentially interesting. They were labeled *Tommy* Edits One and Two. I instinctively scooped them up and went right for the phone. Once again, I rang Gerrard.

'Hey Tom,' I began excitedly, 'you'll never guess what I've got. Townshend's *personal* copy of *Tommy*. Better yet, I think they're fuckin' outtakes, man! The only problem is they're reel-to-reel. If I bring them up can you find somewhere for me to hear them?'

'Probably, yeah,' Tom replied coolly. 'But if I were you I'd put them back. You're onto a good thing here, man. It's obvious Townshend really likes you. I wouldn't jeopardize that for a fucking tape.'

'I'm not gonna keep the fuckers, man, I just want to listen to them, that's all. Don't be such a fuckin' Boy Scout!'

'It's your call, mate, it's got fuck all to do with me. I'll see you when you get here. Call me from the station and I'll pick you up.'

The next morning I grabbed my knapsack and hiked to Richmond Tube, making my way to Euston Station. Some two hours later I was sitting in Gerrard's grandmotherly front room sipping a glass of what the British foolishly call lemonade.

'So what's the deal on these tapes then?' I inquired. 'Where we gonna listen to them?'

'Where are *you* going to listen to them, you mean. I don't want to know.'

'Yeah, beautiful. That's a beautiful sentiment, buddy. So where can we go?'

'Rog Loamis has all kinds of recording gear at his place. If anyone can figure it out he can, I guess. But I still think you're fucking stupid.'

Loamis was an old mate from our hippie days down at the Dive Bar and the Golden Cross back in '71. I used to fly over summers to stay with my sister Sheila and her British husband, Pip, and met these guys through my regular excursions into the city center in pursuit of chicks and dope.

'Right then!' I answered. 'Let's do it!'

Unfortunately, all Loamis could tell us was that they were

professionally recorded tapes playable at 30ips, a speed available only at a proper recording studio.

'So what's the big mystery then?' Roger inquired. 'Who's on the tapes, then?'

'Exactly!' I shot back, paraphrasing the old Abbot and Costello routine. 'Forget it, man. It's probably better you don't know.'

And that was that. As they were impossible to play I tucked them into my backpack and summarily forgot the whole thing, intending to put them back upon my return to London. Unfortunately, I left them at Tom's.

Arriving at Oceanic around ten o'clock Monday morning I was surprised to see that Pete wasn't in. Entering my room I noticed my bags were gone, the bed stripped and my few books packed neatly in a corner. It was like I'd died or something and some hospital orderly had erased every last trace of my existence.

'So where's my stuff, Judy?' I inquired from the handsome redhead seated at her desk next to Townshend's in the big office.

'Pete thought you might be more comfortable at a proper hotel so he's moving you to the Star & Garter in Deer Park.'

'Great,' I replied smiling. Deep inside, though, my heart sunk.

Something was going on. The British are fucking hopeless liars and Ms Waring's obvious reticence to make eye contact was a dead giveaway.

After about an hour I saw Pete's Mercedes winding along Ranleigh Drive.

Gliding to a stop outside Oceanic, Pete silently got out of the car, walked around to the boot, and removed my bags. With that he angrily tossed them at my feet, screaming, 'Now take yer fucking bags and get!'

Springing to my feet I lunged forward, pleading with Pete to tell me what was wrong.

'You know fuckin' very well what's wrong,' Townshend growled. 'What about my tapes then, huh? Do you have them or don't you?' His mood softened for a quick moment. 'Well?'

It was my one and only chance to come clean. If I had, I'm sure now we would somehow have been able to work through it and perhaps even salvaged the relationship.

'Well?' he demanded, staring me straight in the eye.

'What tapes, Pete?'

It was all he had to hear.

'You're not only a cunt, you're a lying cunt as well!' he screamed. And then raising his fist in a fury, 'Get the fuck out of here or you'll taste it!'

'But, Pete! Listen man, *please*. I don't know what people have told you, but you've got it wrong. I only wanted to listen to them . . .'

Townshend, however, didn't reply. The conversation was over. Our relationship was over. And I was out on my ass.

As I struggled with my bags across the nearby common toward Richmond Tube I cried softly. I did not turn back to look at Pete, but I was later told he stood there for several minutes trying to compose himself before going upstairs to work.

Once out on the main drag I flagged a cab and took off for Heathrow and hopefully a quick flight home via Toronto. Upon reaching the airport the cab sputtered up to the departures level and the driver snapped down the meter. Just then I somehow decided that given time to think Pete might calm down and welcome me back into the fold.

'Hey listen, man,' I cautiously began. 'I've changed my mind. I think I'd like to go back to Twickenham.' He gave me a long suspicious look and then slowly turned around and wordlessly took off.

On the way to Oceanic I decided I probably had a better chance of catching Pete if I went directly to his home. I wasn't at all sure if this was the right thing to do. But I was genuinely very sorry and thought he might at least sense my sincerity. By the time the taxi dropped me down the road from his house though I was perceptibly shaking. Once again poised at his front door I thought I was going to be sick.

In the end I lost my nerve and quietly slipped down the few steep steps and into the rainy cobblestone street. There I rummaged through my bags and pulled out a carefully rolled silkscreen print I had done of Baba for Oceanic called *The Everything and the Nothing*. With that I bounded to his door once again, quickly rang the bell, and then ran off, taking shelter just around the corner.

Almost immediately the front door opened and an emotionless Karen Townshend scooped up the rolled print and ducked back inside. The whole thing was over in about three seconds and I was still profoundly fucked. Thank God I didn't hang around for yet another confrontation with the dour Mrs Townshend. There was nothing left to do now but grab yet another cab out to airport, wait for a flight, and fly home.

Once back in my home town of Albion New York, I exchanged several letters with Townshend over the incident, outlining the whole sorry mess again and again in excruciating detail. Pete too apparently suffered from the ordeal, writing on July 15: 'I don't condemn you, I am far, far worse than you will ever be. If we are both punks, well alright, for to me a punk is close to God. Perhaps *I'm* too old to be a punk now. . . . But the future is the same for all of us, to become like dust at His Feet. . . . He hurt both of us, or let us hurt one another because he cares about us, loves us . . . I am behaving like a caged man now. I lock my office every second, nothing is left around. . . . Privacy is vital, more to my wife than me, I love having people around.'

Four days later, on July 19, he apparently felt the need to further define his feelings, offering this prophetic bit of sage advice. 'You must lower your sights and work. Not acting, not writing, not stealing, just working. I can't moralize as I am not a "good" person in the eyes of society anyway, but I feel you are a good person inside, and I think you only know what you are truly capable of . . . Don't write to me with explanations, I know what happened. Write to Baba, or pray to God, tell Him we're both very sorry for making so much noise in the street outside *His New House*.'

With that final word from above I was left to stew in the quagmire of my own outrageously stupid actions. I continued to feel badly about it for many years, hardly able to face up to my own often out-of-control curiosity and innate ruthlessness. Eighteen years later, however, I'm pretty much unmoved by the whole tawdry episode, yet strangely, it still seems to prey on Townshend a bit.

'Let me say that once and for all I forgive you for what went on when you were my guest at Oceanic,' he wrote me in December 1994. 'It is not forgotten, because it was obviously important for us both to go through it (it made me aware at the time that keeping open house was not entirely wise for someone in my position and, without being cynical I hope, I stopped trusting everyone). You learned your own stuff I know.'

In reply, on December 29 I wrote that although it was certainly good to be forgiven it was even nicer to at last have grown up. 'I was cast in the role of Judas once eighteen years ago and have no desire to ever be there again. . . . I'm now forty-one and with every passing day realize my opportunity to try and live the insights I have been *allowed* diminish with every tick of the clock. . . .

'When people caution me about saying "this or that" about much of your controversial behavior I always say, "Hey, this isn't like writing about Paul McCartney or Cliff Richard, who presumably spend a good deal of money trying to keep their image 'G' rated to the general public. It's not necessary to dig up dirt on Pete Townshend because he's always announced it to the world himself! To be blunt, you've made my job much easier as you've addressed almost every question ever put to you in a no-nonsense, straight-ahead fashion. Something I find very admirable (I do it too, by the way). . . .

'Remember, I'm the one who's going to be publicly portrayed [in this book] as a thief and a hypocrite, someone who accepted your hospitality and then stabbed you in the back! I'm guaranteed to look like a total cunt to tens of thousands. But the way I see it, that's the only way to really get clean. Put *everything* out on the table and then hopefully have the balls to transcend it.

'I emanate from roughly the same kind of dysfunctional family as you. The odds were ardently against both of us on every level. Materially, I should have been a fucking plumber and spiritually as a Westerner and born-again beef eater, should have lived my entire life never hearing a peep about any of the many Avatars, the process of self-realization, nor the chance to associate with the many spiritually advanced people I have known. I suspect it's much the same for you. To be honest, from outward appearances, you've done about as much with your good fortune as I! I've made a fucking career out of taking the path of least resistance. Steadily forsaking my singular chance at real devotion for chicks, drugs, cars, cash, CD players, good reviews, pats on the back, etc. Personally, I'm sick of it all!

'You once called us both 'a couple of ripe bastards' and I agreed. I once called us 'punks' and you agreed. I just hope that down the road, no one will be able to refer to us as a couple of sad old men who sold out their one real chance to really get off the Wheel.

'I appreciate you *formally* forgiving me in your letter and that you will judge my book on you on its own merits (or lack thereof). There's no real reason the two of us should ever have even met, let alone enacted that clever little scenario in the tawny side streets of Richmond. To be honest, the whole thing stinks of Meher Baba! [By

the way,] eighteen years is a very long time. I am happy to report
that I am now a perfectly socially acceptable houseguest. No more
sticky fingers!'

Free of my participation in the grand Oceanic experiment, Pete
carried on like a man possessed. Unfortunately, according to a
Townshend intimate, Richard Barnes, Meher Baba Oceanic fell
into a hopeless tailspin shortly after the grand and auspicious
opening.

'Pete's intentions were highly laudable,' he has stated. 'He had
hopes for the project and was very ambitious. He even had the
cash to back all his grand schemes and was doing so. However,
he never really saw things through to the end. He was constantly
initiating new ideas and projects, but in a few days or weeks his
mind would have raced ahead to something new and he'd be
changing everything again. He'd have builders in to alter the
place, pull down a wall and then erect another somewhere else.
A few weeks after the paint was dry, he'd have the new wall taken
down and the place altered again. At first there were facilities for
filming and editing, then it was video, then it was recording. Pete
was like a rich kid with too many toys.

'The place was supposed to be an English Baba center, but
apart from Pete's secretary, it was, for the first year or so, full
of Americans. Many were very sycophantic, and I fully expected
one day to see the photographs of Baba on the walls replaced by
those of Pete. Pete was only trying to give people the opportunity
and the facilities to carry out their own creative Baba projects.

'He also set up a number of companies under the banner of "Eel
Pie Ltd." I was staggered at the stupidity of some of the people
Pete had given key jobs. By mistake, the tape would be wiped off
after a day's recording session, or a video would be ruined because
somebody forgot some vital function. The whole place was deadly
amateurish but with the budgets of professionals.

'Many people took advantage of his idealistic good nature;
not that they were calculating, but, in the main, just inept and
hopelessly disorganized – someone would quite gladly spend all
day in a company car looking for a box of staples. The Baba Center
evolved just like one of Baba's parables. It became far removed
from having any real feeling of love surrounding it, as mountains
of expensive technology seemed to amass itself. The incongruous
combination of recording studio and Baba workshop under one

roof was a typical, badly thought-out move by Pete. The whole place seemed to be a reflection of his own confused state of mind at that time.'

In the research stage of this book, Seriar Press, the publishing arm of the Meher Baba movement, was contacted in reference to obtaining copies of Oceanic's various cinematic works. Amazingly, only two videos seem to have made it to the mainstream of Baba devotees. One, a collage of Baba's often inscrutable avataric activities over the years called *Parvardigar*, treats the viewer to a live rendition of Townshend's masterful adaptation of Meher Baba's unabridged homage to himself. The other, a more ambitious feature entitled *The East-West Gathering*, chronicles a four-day open house held by Baba for his lovers in the fifties.

Like the Beatles' ill-fated Apple Corp, the Stones' ambitious *Rock 'n' Roll Circus*, or the Moody Blues' rudderless Threshold Records, Townshend's Meher Baba Oceanic remains an entity of unfulfilled promise on the fickle landscape of pop culture.

Still, on the surface, the grand plan of Oceanic producing (as their letterhead boldly declared) 'a series of films about Meher Baba and His Disciples' never quite came about. A reality most unfortunate in view of the enormous potential the concept originally portrayed.

Ironically, the most lasting thing to come out of Oceanic wasn't a film at all, but rather a record (now highly collectible). At the opening in July 1976 an all-new Baba LP was distributed to guests; it featured three powerful, carefully crafted Townshend compositions, 'His Hands,' 'Sleeping Dog,' and the instrumental 'Lantern Cabin.'

With a beautiful color cover of Baba taken off a film by Pete and a well-designed booklet, the collection features three tunes by longtime Townshend chum Billy Nichols as well as selections from Ronnie Lane and Peter Hope Evans of Medicine Head, among others.

'This album is produced as a gift of love dedicated to Meher Baba,' the album's brief liner notes announce. 'It is a limited edition of 4,000. Any profit will help future similar projects. However, all material contained herein is strictly copyright and is solely reserved by Eel Pie Recording Productions Ltd.'

Although I wrote Pete and asked him to send me a copy, he refused in a letter dated July 15, 1976 saying, 'You'll just have to find it in Baba stores as best you can. I feel we "owe" you in a sense for the T-shirts you made, etc., but your actions wiped out any sense of propriety I might have had.

'For your own sake you have to get your life together. . . . You have responsibilities to Brenda, you should marry her if her child is yours and look after them. You must keep out of dope totally, it will affect your child if you don't. . . . Even though you lied to me once or twice, I don't think you are a hypocrite. . . . Baba didn't let you get away with it . . . because you have already given Him your heart. Don't waste another lifetime.'

Despite his investment in Meher Baba and his worldwide movement, Townshend himself ultimately 'let go' of the master's *dahman* [dress] and slowly drifted back into drugs, drink, and occasional womanizing. By early 1977, although he still paid lip service to Baba's philosophy, Pete was finding it very difficult to adhere to the strict lifestyle.

'Yesterday was Meher Baba's "Amartithi,"' he wrote in yet another extended Baba/Townshend article published in *Rolling Stone*. 'Followers of this great Master (to whom I remain committed) celebrate the anniversary of his passing in 1969. In the afternoon, I saw a film of his entombment and felt a most powerful feeling of his presence throughout the day.'

As time passed, Townshend's enthusiasm for all things Baba faded along with his own once jubilant sense of self. One witness to Townshend's waning devotion was former John Lennon minder Fred Seaman, who at the time was dating Jodi Linscot, the high-profile percussionist to everyone from Eric Clapton to Paul McCartney and Pete. 'In 1982 I went over to England on some business for Yoko and was hanging out with Jodi, who at the time was working with Pete on his *Empty Glass* album,' says Fred. 'I stayed with her first at Owen Rogin's house, one of the Who roadies, and later we moved into the Boathouse for a few days. It was a quiet place with several devotees of Meher Baba. They were very pleasant, friendly people. Pete would show up occasionally. I don't think he was too involved with Baba at that point, but obviously still owned the building.

'When Pete was dealing with the Baba people it seemed like a fairly businesslike relationship. They were deferential to him, and he was respectful of them.

'The first time I met him was when we all went out to a pub on the outskirts of London. It was Jodi and I, Pete, and some of his old buddies from the sixties. It was a very casual scene, he played video games with his friends. Pete and I had a few Rémy Martins and he seemed like a very down-to-earth, friendly bloke.

'I remember Lennon used to speak about Pete sometimes. He considered him one of the really great lyricists of the sixties, one of the top British musicians. John also liked the Who, because they were the greatest-ever live band.

'Pete is obviously a very smart man, but not particularly open in general. He was hanging out with some of the so-called New Romantics. He wouldn't actually talk much. He had a cynical sense of humor and didn't take himself too seriously. He didn't take the fans or his body of work too seriously either. In fact, I think he harbored a bit of contempt for the fans who treated him like some kind of demigod. He felt like he was a talented guy who had a lot of luck and made the most of it, but there was nothing really extraordinary about his accomplishments. He seemed like a very humble guy. He didn't put on airs or anything.'

Townshend was obviously incredibly enriched by his Baba period, and this new strength would be powerfully displayed over the next few years. He was entering a period in which he would throw his full energies once again into the Who. He would compose some of his most moving work. He would explode on a whole range of fronts with a new surge of creativity. To the world at large, Pete Townshend was back.

6

Thunder and Silence: *Disillusionment*

I've read that stars and punks take themselves too seriously. I am both star and punk, therefore I take myself so seriously sometimes I actually believe I matter to the world.

– Pete Townshend

He would remember the eighteen-month period from the autumn of 1975 through to the spring of 1977 as among the happiest times of his turbulent life. His devotion to Meher Baba and growing dissatisfaction with the often unhealthy perks of fame gave him a deeper understanding of his mercurial introspective nature.

Real change could only come about, he finally realized, by distancing himself from what had become a fifteen-year obsession. 'I went barmy with rock 'n' roll and the Who,' he admitted. 'So I went away and got my head together. I needed to go through that kind of catharsis . . . I had to tighten up and discipline myself. I had to decide to get my priorities right. I had to own up that the Who was the thing I was all about and that I should make my first commitment my family because I wouldn't be able to work properly for the Who without a stable home life.'

Toward that goal Pete made several significant changes. The first was to go ahead finally with legal proceedings to dissolve all managerial ties with Lambert and Stamp, which came about in March 1977. 'I felt myself being pulled in two directions,' says Pete, 'and in the end I had to let go of my friendship with Kit and Chris and run with the band. If two of your kids are drowning, which one do you save? You don't necessarily save the nearest. Somewhere along the line you make a choice which may be deemed selfish. In retrospect, I made the right choice.'

Pete's decision coincided with a significant recommitment to his wife Karen and their family. While he was out 'playing a young man's game,' his family was on the sidelines catching his comings and goings in the papers, which inevitably focused on his latest public outrage. 'After a month away I'd walk through the door like some sea captain . . . I walked back to kids who didn't know who I was. They were very cagey and intimidated by me.'

Townshend's marriage staggered on for a time before leading to a showdown. 'My old lady just broke down one day and said she'd run out of energy and that was it.' He heard what she was saying: 'I don't really love you as you are. I don't care whether you go or stay. I don't give a damn about you or your life or the way you think about us.'

Stung by Karen's painful pronouncements, Pete retired for some hard reflection. 'I saw that if I lost Karen and the family, I wouldn't be able to face life. What's more, I wouldn't be able to do anything for the Who either. I suddenly realized I could very easily lose what I value most in life.'

As a result, he once again quit drinking and became a more involved husband and father, taking the kids to school, staying home weekends, and spending his free time in various literary pursuits. 'It's tough,' Townshend conceded, 'because I really do love my life. I like my life on the road with the band, I like the guys in the band, I love rock 'n' roll.' This precarious tightrope between family, career, and self would continue to remain a near lifelong dilemma.

During his sabbatical, Townshend also came to the discovery that he no longer had any use for heroes, with the exception of Meher Baba. Early icons like Jimmy Reed, Chuck Berry, and Mick Jagger systematically tumbled off their pedestals, becoming mere talents in their field. This was best demonstrated by Townshend's attitude toward Bob Dylan. 'I couldn't wait for the day when somebody would do that in-depth interview when everybody would find out what was really going on in the back of his head. When I discovered that there was nothing there at all, I was incredibly disappointed. From that day on he ceased to be my hero.'

Several years later, when Dylan announced his conversion to Christianity, Townshend was not only suspicious but felt that the move was a reaction to the singer's upside-down personal life. 'I scorn him,' Pete proclaimed in 1980. 'When I saw him let go of a nice wife and kids, I lost a lot of respect for him. If anyone's going to be a hero, it's Jesus Christ downward and I'm not going too far down.'

Pete's recommitment to the band was linked with his constant and fervent self-examination. He soon concluded he'd been too much the boss, a role in part born of being the primary songwriter; his compositions were enmeshed in his feelings and life experiences. He decided, therefore, the ultimate direction of the group. Townshend remembers: 'I took the band over when they asked me to write for them in 1964 in order to pass the Decca audition and used them as a mouthpiece, hitting out at anyone who tried to have a say (mainly Roger) and then grumbling when they didn't appreciate my dictatorship. Daltrey often sang songs I'd written that he didn't care for with complete commitment, and I took him for granted. I said what I wanted to say, often ignoring or being terribly patronizing about the rest of the group's suggestions, then sulked when they didn't worship me for making life financially viable.'

Patching up his differences with Daltrey proved perhaps the greatest concession of all. 'Let Roger win,' advised a friend in New York. It was that simple. 'He dropped his armor,' proclaimed Pete, 'and we immediately became close.'

Interestingly, Townshend's old band mate came up with quite a lot of very good creative ideas. 'That was the magic,' says Daltrey, 'being there as Pete actually began to make his ideas work. We used to talk things over. But eventually Pete and I didn't have to say anything. We'd just communicate and it'd be very intense and we'd get ideas across.'

'We still often disagree,' adds Townshend, 'but there isn't as much tension over it. Some people seem to think tension is one of the things that made the Who tick. I can tell you the exact opposite is true. It wasted a lot of time, caused an incredible amount of agony, and made road work together miserable. The closer we get now, the better things are.'

Pete continued, 'I was jealous of Roger's charisma, and he was probably jealous of talents I had that he didn't. We have both risen above that. The fact is, I feel deeply for Roger now.'

With this new understanding also came an appreciation of Daltrey's talents, highlighted by his pulverizing vocal delivery. 'That's what's always great about Roger doing the stuff,' he admitted, 'he can smash through things. My delivery always comes across as cynical rather than real guts.'

For Daltrey, the simple joy of interpreting Townshend's material was highly satisfying. 'I'm just pleased I can give Pete's songs the airing he wants them to have,' he has said. '[He] is really a genius. His writing has such meaning and generates such energy. It's hard for me to explain. I can't do Pete's material for more than two hours without a break because of the amount of energy I have to put into it. . . . Nobody ever does Townshend's songs. The Who are the only people who can play them. That's one reason we've survived. No one of us is very good on his own. It's only as part of the Who that we're great.'

Entwistle too submitted, 'The balance of power was always shifting with me in the middle . . . I'd have to sit there while Pete and Roger changed their minds a few hundred times. Eventually they always came around to what I wanted anyway. The power structure was distorted by the media from day one. No way could I be as powerful as Pete. He was the one with the gift of the gab. It was a bit depressing when people would come up to me and say, "You're the best bass player in the world," and I was at the bottom of the pecking order.'

Nothing, however, could shake Townshend's belief that the Who was fated to hold a special role in the ever widening circle of rock culture. The Beatles had long since imploded, and the Stones were too far gone into sex, drugs, and God knows what. 'The Who,' he concluded, 'knew what rock was all about in a spiritual and societal sense; [they were] not the thinkers of rock, but the ones who cared about it most.'

All this good feeling manifested itself throughout the 1975 Back to Basics tour of Europe and America beginning on October 3 and running until Christmas. Shunning both the conceptual trappings of *Quadrophenia* and the dour *Who by Numbers*, Townshend and

Company took to the stage in the hard-driving mode reminiscent of *Live at Leeds*. One tradition, however, was noticeably absent: the obligatory climactic guitar smashing, of which Townshend had grown understandably weary.

Looking back, Pete conceded, 'I think it was the healthiest period for the Who, even though a lot of people look back and say, "What a pointless waste of energy, what a foolish thing to have done!" But in a way it got rid of some of the anger, the vengeance, and allowed us to concentrate on what really mattered, which at the time was probably strictly entertainment.'

By this time heavy metal had become a distinct branch of rock, and the Who concerts brought up the question of whether the band were the true forerunners of this sound. On this question Townshend has waffled over the years. In 1980 he stated, 'We probably pioneered that early heavy-metal lineup which relies a lot on very, very high volume to actually convey any kind of tone, color, and excitement.' Ten years later, however, he was hedging. 'The guitar-smashing, loud rock 'n' roll, eyes-down, full-house guitar playing, that's only a very small part of what the Who is about,' he said. 'You only have to listen to our early albums and singles . . . they're not heavy metal, they're pop. Later, we were a bit heavier; the guitar was fairly raunchy for the time, but not really that distinct. . . . The thing the Who always had was a passion for lyrics with a certain amount of bittersweetness, irony, and humor. You have to have a sense of humor to take on such serious issues.'

Pete was also pleased with the way his guitar playing was evolving. He admitted it came from simply being unable to play like he used to. 'I've knocked down that wall of screaming and shouting so often it's no fun anymore. . . . Nowadays when I write, I push myself in another direction. I try to work out chord changes that turn your head inside out; I might spend a month messing around with a particular synth sound to try to get something that's gonna last for ten years and not sound jaded in a week. I'm trying to discover something else that's as good as a wound-up electric guitar.'

Guitar acrobat Eddie Van Halen liked to tease his elder colleague about his often less than sterling soloing. He'd phone Townshend and quip, 'Pete, I've just been listening to *Live at Leeds*. Christ, man, that's one great album. You play some fantastic mistakes!'

Other musicians, though, pointed to his well-developed strengths.

Terence Trent D'Arby once acknowledged Townshend's desperate sense of passion. 'He plays rhythm guitar as if his very life depended on it. He has come out of his experiences wiser and now has the air of a teacher. On each occasion we've spoken I feel I've learned something. You must respect a man who's been through so much and came back.'

As popular as the band was, it took the Who's conquest of the world's major arenas to turn them into a genuine phenomenon. 'There can be no equal to an enormous stadium with people seething around when you know it's you who brought them there,' said Townshend. 'It [also] makes a difference acoustically. Outdoor sound can often be a lot better.

'Large audiences, though, can be distracting, the bedlam that goes on very close to the front of the stage, seeing people being pulled out. It's not very pleasant. From the stage you get a perfect view of the suffering people go through. People gasping for breath and turning strange colors.'

The Who were among the first to implement a laser light show on a grand scale, honed to perfection by their affable lighting wiz, John 'Wiggy' Wolf. While Townshend defended as a necessary evil the 'camp and glossy show business side of rock today,' he also feared it marked the beginning of the Who losing control of their integrity and becoming a mere parody. 'It led to theatrical pomposity,' he stated. 'It had to be larger than life because the audience was larger than life.'

The vast fan base of the Who, at one time arguably the most loyal in all of rock, was a rowdy, inarticulate contingent growing with each performance. As part of his long love-hate relationship with his fans, Pete found both positive and negative sides to this. On the one hand, he noted:

'All I can tell you is that I meet kids on the road, from about sixteen to twenty, and they treat me just like the guy next door, they've got no deep respect for me, no fanaticism. It's an absolute one-to-one relationship. There's a familiarity and a sense of naturalness. I think that could only come about if they felt close to me. It doesn't happen with everybody, but it happens with quite a few people.'

Responding to the reams of fan mail sent to Pete's sanctuary at the Boathouse, Townshend generously spent hours not only reading, but providing admirers with coveted, sometimes multiple personal responses. Fans would pour out their many problems, explaining how Pete's music had helped heal them. It became part of his campaign to 'change people's lives by applying a complete total dedication to [them].'

That correspondence, according to Kathy, was Townshend's way of being a fan himself, being part of the entire Who experience, and most important, overcoming those old childhood hangups about fitting in. 'By writing back to people,' she theorized, 'he could connect with them. But by writing back to so many people he also created a country full of obsessed fans as well.'

His efforts were in part a battle against the insulation that comes with being so pervasively rich and powerful. 'If you're in that position you've got to face up to the fact that it carries a lot of responsibilities you might not want,' Pete contends. 'You can't just say, "I'll have those responsibilities, but not those."

'When it comes down to it the feedback I need most is letters. That's why I try to reply, so people know they can get through if they want. I hate being externalized.'

Yet for all the inviting closeness, there was a downside for Townshend, who referred to a certain contingent of New York fans as 'punks who used to try to get you by the ears and pin you down, then take you home in a cardboard box.'

Further irritating him were fans who would often gather at his house, standing beneath the window for hours hoping for a glimpse. 'As though I were Salvador Dali,' he scoffs. Inevitably, after a successful sighting they would run off, unable to handle the shock of actually seeing their idol.

'I've been rude to people almost as often as I've been nice to them,' Townshend admits. 'I'm often rude to women because I find that if you're in a rock band and you smile or are courteous, she seems to think that's a come-on.'

On a deeper level, suggests Kathy, Townshend is an extremely reticent individual who can't really abide fan worship and would rather keep a safe distance from potentially embarrassing face-to-face encounters. Correspondence is infinitely 'safer'. Notes Kathy, 'I've been with a lot of people when they meet the Who and they just can't handle it. People meet Pete and they're never heard from again. You develop a fantasy, and he's only a human being. When that happens, I feel so sorry for Pete. He's a normal guy, but people think he's this god. They get face to face with him and think, I've got to you, so you carry the conversation. And Pete's really shy; he can't. So they freak out. I think that's why Pete finds it so difficult to be around Who fans because they all just stare at him. He doesn't know what to say.'

One particular time Kathy remembers joining friends at the Boathouse to present Townshend with a birthday present. 'When he came out, he was literally jumping around the room he was so nervous. When we came in, he went behind a counter, backed against the wall like he was in front of a firing squad. After about twenty minutes, when he realized we were just there to talk, he calmed down.'

Townshend's letter writing, then, provided a safe way of keeping in touch, but not too close, filling his need to be accessible but never really exposed. 'There is a difference,' insists Pete. 'If I were a fan of the band, I would like the fact there was a feeling of closeness without feeling like you were infringing on somebody's privacy.'

Even as Townshend's relationship with his fans was maturing, the year 1976 would see a new underground revolt – from a new generation of youth. With their spiked hair and dog collars, snarling, spitting, and brawling against conventionality, came rock's latest incarnation, the punks.

'I used to wake up in the night praying to be destroyed,' said Pete. 'In the end I actually thought of inventing a new form of music which would take over from where the Who left off. In my imagination I invented punk rock a thousand times. I thought the hypocrisy of the position we were in was just unbelievable. Where are the young people of today? Where are the heroes of today?'

On one level, Townshend did not see much promise in the New Wave. With names like X Ray Spex, the Buzzcocks, and the Vibrators, they were automatically limited, according to him, to a three-year career. As Ronnie Lane once quipped, 'What's Rat Scabies gonna look like when he's thirty-one years old and still called Rat Scabies?'

On the larger scale, though, Townshend welcomed punk rock with both a sense of joy and, more important, relief. 'When the New Wave came along, it was a great affirmation. Aye, we're not dead yet! It freed me and allowed me to be myself. It dignified and allowed me to be cast to one side. I felt very uneasy with the way the Who were inevitably on the road to megastardom. I believed that the punk movement would free me from that. It did.

'It was the closing of a circle,' he went on to say. 'It was part of what had been nagging at me; it didn't seem the music business was ever gonna get back to rock again. . . . We were getting older, more mature and settling down.'

Townshend recounts an afternoon at a football match with some punks at which one threatened to kill a supporter from the opposing team. Pete reconciled the overtly violent attitude this way: 'Punk had to be destructive because what it was coming up against was a bunch of people who were turning out lightweight entertainment but pretending it was globally important when it wasn't.'

Townshend was referring to the inane drivel being trotted out by the likes of Donny and Marie Osmond, the Bee Gees, and Paul McCartney and Wings. 'All they're really doing,' Pete charged, 'is getting together and working out the most complex ideas they can handle, packaging it with pretentious marketing appeal, and unloading it on their fans.' Even the more respected acts, Yes, Genesis, and Pink Floyd, came under attack for their stagnant brand of stadium rock, rotely churning out their greatest hits for a million-dollar paycheck. The Western world had become comfortable, complacent, and nihilistic, about to spawn the 'Me Generation' in an era of overt conservatism led by Margaret Thatcher and Ronald Reagan. The world was ripe for punks like the Sex Pistols, Boomtown Rats, and the Clash, restless, sneering anarchists pointing their rapid-fire, guitar-slashing, brazen, raunchy rock guns against all that was safe and conventional. They were getting attention too, as evidenced by the Sex Pistols' 1977 number-one anthem 'Anarchy in the UK,' sounding perhaps not coincidentally quite like 'I Can See for Miles.'

While other bands were intimidated by the arrival of the punks, Townshend was rejuvenated by that sincerest form of flattery, their often blatant imitation of the Who. He took it as a validation of what he and the band stood for. 'The roots of practically every New Wave act I saw seemed to be the Who. Then I realized that just made more of us.'

In a familiar theme, he saw in their nihilism the rage that made rock 'n' roll a genuine social force. He noted, 'Divine desperation is at the root of every punk's scream for blood and vengeance.

'Damage, damage, damage! It's a great way to shake society's values. It makes mothers disown their children. It makes school teachers puke. . . . The crucifixion is what these people stand for. They humiliate themselves, their peers and care nothing for any accolades. These are true stars; they are part of an audience of stars.

'I am with them. I want nothing more than to go with them to their desperate hell, because that loneliness they suffer is soon to be over. Deep inside they know.'

Townshend's favorite groups were pop's reigning anarchists, the Clash and the Jam, both of whom were viewed in critical circles as 'surrogate Who.' 'My argument with Paul Weller,'* Pete noted, 'is that he never rated American audiences. He said they were spoiled; "Fuck America and their Cadillacs." For a long time he wouldn't tour America because he kind of sneered at it.' Weller, a philosophical throwback to the sixties, once confided he was more thrilled by finding his old Who badge than procuring a record contract. He deemed 'My Generation' 'the most socially significant thing ever written.'

These new young lions cuffed the aging king back into fighting spirit. 'Rock,' proclaimed Pete, 'is music about adolescence. The old rock establishment has really had it too long. But I'm not giving up. Let them try to stop me.'

Townshend funneled his newfound enthusiasm into the Who's autumn North American tour of 1976. 'When I walk onstage I feel timeless,' he has said. 'I feel abundantly athletic, free and liberated, unfettered and completely unself-conscious.'

He went on to say, 'I know that only from the Who's live concerts I get energy freely for doing practically nothing. I play guitar, I jump and dance, and come off stronger than when I went on. Walking offstage after a concert, we feel like superhumans.'

The tour was capped by a memorable bash thrown by the road crew after the final show in Toronto. 'It was the first party I had been to for at least five years which meant anything to me,' Townshend recalled. 'I don't go to a lot of parties, but I'm glad I made this one. I suddenly realized that behind every Who show are people who care as much as, or even more than, we do. Talking to the individuals who help get the show together enabled me to remember that audiences care too.'

Superfan Irish Jack recalls that following one of the gigs, several people in Townshend's party were left waiting while he chatted away with a cleaning woman who had come into the dressing

* Weller was the lead singer of first the Jam and then the Style Council.

room to sweep up. 'The four of us had to hang around while Pete had this conversation with the cleaning lady, and it wasn't an act at all. It was simply the Townshend way.'

Pete's income, however, was anything but humble. He was a very wealthy man, and his enthusiasm for new projects expanded in a dizzying variety of directions. The band, at his urging, branched out to invest £350,000 in London's waning Shepperton Studios to use for their own filmmaking projects. Their efforts spun a trio of compelling releases, all in some phase of production during the late seventies. *The Kids Are Alright*, released on May 12, 1979, was a Who documentary, a serio-comic 'history of the band,' as Townshend put it, produced by an American, Jeff Stein. It became a cult film on every Who fan's must-see list. Dave Marsh lauded it as 'one of the great rock 'n' roll movies, capturing all of the Who's sass and humor while taking the wind out of the band's pomposities at each and every opportunity.' Townshend, by contrast, pronounced it as simply 'All right.'

Quadrophenia, debuting that same year, was a major British hit, capitalizing on the short-lived but energized neo-mod resurgence. Unfortunately, director Franc Roddam homed in on the more violent elements, which was directly opposed to Pete's original concept, which was a study in 'spiritual desperation,' as he put it. 'The problem with a film like *Quadrophenia* is that it's exploited something that's already there. . . . I suppose the responsibility lies in direct proportion to everybody who makes money off it.'

The Who's interest in Shepperton also produced 1981's *McVicar*, a rugged, revealing Roger Daltrey vehicle about Britain's notorious bank robber turned author whose criticism against the penal system earned him celebrity status and won him an early release. It was a fine effort, despite several less than glowing reviews, and proved once and for all that Daltrey could really act.

Townshend, meanwhile was steadily spreading out into still other areas. He unveiled a number of companies under the umbrella of Eel Pie, which incorporated two recording studios: a leased facility in Soho and Eel Pie Oceanic on the first floor of the Boathouse. Among the notables who have recorded there have been Pink Floyd, Eric Clapton, and Phil Collins. In addition, Townshend formed his own Eel Pie Records and Eel Pie Sound, a PA hire company.

Apart from music, Pete parlayed his great love of literature into Magic Bus, a quaint but exhaustive bookshop tucked away in suburban Richmond. One of the best-stocked shops in London, Magic Bus boasted modern novels and classics, as well as many metaphysical texts, holistic medical titles, and health-conscious cookbooks. The shop became most renowned, though, for its impressive children's section. This emanated from his daughters' voracious reading, led by his eldest, Emma, who showed an early penchant for the novels of spiritual scholar C.S. Lewis. 'The girls read anything at the moment,' Pete said at the time, 'and rush into Magic Bus yelling, "Goody, free books!" But we don't let them become gluttons. We used to have an account in a shop near here, and every week they would get one book.'

The bookshop went hand in hand with his new Eel Pie Publishing venture. The company's first work, a British best-seller, was the whimsical *Hepzibah*, about a zany girl who stables a cow in her bathroom. The company would go on to publish several children's books as well as titles on Elvis Presley, P. G. Wodehouse, Pablo Casals, former Beatle Pete Best, plus Townshend's personal projects, *The Story of Tommy* and *Thirty Years Maximum R&B*, the exhaustive Who chronicle by Richard Barnes.

Pete was now a man of significant wealth. Although his spending didn't approach Keith Moon's excesses (a cavalcade of sportscars, a pub, even a mansion in the shape of a pyramid), he nonetheless enjoyed luxuries well out of the reach of most. Over the years he was free to indulge his reputation as a natty dresser as well as his obsession for boating, buying a fifty-five-foot custom-built wooden yacht and an eighty-year-old Dutch barge formally used to transport eels on the Thames. Purchasing the latter craft for thirty-five thousand pounds, Townshend subsequently poured another eleven thousand pounds into it before proclaiming it 'a folly.'

Jo Jo Laine, flamboyant wife of Moody Blues founder Denny Laine, fondly remembers racing Pete down the Thames and partying together at Bates Boatyard in Chertsey. He was also a frequent guest at their infamous swimming parties beneath the Laines' air-filled aquatic dome. 'I found him to be an incredibly nice fellow, very down to earth with no silly come-ons,' she said.

Finally, vast sums were spent on real estate: a two-bedroom Georgian cottage purchased in 1974 to house his children's nanny, a six-acre forest-retreat log cabin in Goring, Oxfordshire, and a homey summer cottage in Cornwall. He also acquired a nineteenth-century four-story Georgian mansion that was once owned by poet laureate Alfred Lord Tennyson and contained a library of first-edition books and a 150-foot garden and coach house. The punk, it seemed, had now become the Godfather.

Townshend, however, was clearly uncomfortable with being identified as a member of the new aristocracy. 'It bothers me a little because it bothers my family and the people around me,' he says. 'It's intimidating. I feel pretty ordinary, and the people close to me think I'm pretty ordinary, if not *very* ordinary.'

Nor was wealth something he had particularly aspired to. 'I don't think any band worth its salt picked up a guitar because it wanted wealth and fame. . . . We wanted to play because we were into the music and into the fact that the only reality that existed was in losing yourself in people's reaction to you. . . . It's got nothing to do with money, or even success. It's some kind of need to be looked at, to be respected, and the need to find yourself through your audience's reaction. You've got to discover what makes an audience tick to discover what makes you tick.'

He could not resist adding an ironic note, though. 'Too much money can be harmful, but too much fame I don't think is necessarily bad. . . . People need heroes and you're doing a job in being a hero. You're performing a public service.'

According to Richard Barnes, Townshend's reconciliation of his wealth with the plight of the downtrodden continues to be a battle. 'He has always been very conscious of not living that middle-class mansion sort of lifestyle which so many pop stars do, sitting around worrying about their surtax. He has fallen into it himself from time to time, having friends round for Chocolate Oliver biscuits and chatting about property values, but at the same time he has always tried to maintain his progressive radical ideas about things. That contradiction is very marked in him: trying to stay true to what he believes has been a great factor in everything he does.'

Manager Curbishley went further, noting that the contradiction tore at him, causing him to be suspicious and uncommunicative, keeping his problems to himself. 'Pete has trouble coming to terms with being a star. He is a socialist, and although he shouldn't feel guilty about the rewards his own talents have brought him, he does. He can be quiet and moody offstage and explosive and violent on.'

To his credit, Townshend has never been one to flaunt his wealth, and in fact is the generous patron of many charities. A number of efforts have been directed at fostering new musical talents. He sponsored new groups like Rick Cassman and his band, Straight Eight, in 1978. Townshend invested thirty thousand pounds in launching them on his own Eel Pie label with their debut album, *No Noise from Here*. He also founded a studio called the Musicians' Co-op with the attached label of Propeller Records, a purely selfless endeavor. Townshend encouraged little-known bands to record, providing a PA system and van at their disposal for whatever they could afford or even at no charge.

Meanwhile, back in 1977, after their return from the American tour, Townshend sensed another collective slump coming on. 'We felt like a conquering army, it was so good, but then we rushed back to England and had no new album, nothing happening, no feeling of existing, and every time we picked up a paper there were snivelling little brats knocking us.'

Those brats were none other than the very punks who'd stirred Townshend's newfound sense of purpose not two years before.

'I came back like I achieved something amazing. I came back to an incredibly volatile, changing, exciting, but destructive scene. It seemed the lyrics of the Sex Pistols, the Vibrators, the Stranglers, were all designed and aimed at me.'

The New Wave upstarts were now calling Townshend 'a boring old fart,' blaming him and other rock musicians of the old guard for not remaining true rebels, but rather taking the money and running. Townshend fired back that their ideals had been strangled by music industry leeches, 'fleecing us, screwing us, exploiting us, insulting us.' Of these brash young guns, he hissed, 'They assume a lot don't they? They assume we've still got money. They assume they are going to get rich.'

Paul Weller charged that Townshend's writing had become largely self-indulgent, that he'd become a martyr and was living only off his past. Pete translated: 'He's really saying anybody over a certain age who's achieved anything should just go off and die!'

Nonetheless, privately the charges depressed him. 'So I started thinking, "Nobody really wants it, even if we are filling halls and winning the *Rolling Stone* award as the best live band." . . . We weren't creating anything new. All we'd done new was a few stage tricks with laser beams.

'I've been doubtful about the Who's road appearances for years,' he says, 'basically because we've gone on and played the same stuff. The Who, although they're sharp-edged, aren't particularly adventurous. We go on, and if it doesn't work straightaway, we go back to the old tricks. I'm not blaming anyone else in the band; I do it too. If I don't get an instant reaction, I start swinging my arms, smashing guitars, and they're on their feet. What am I going on stage for? To communicate something or simply to make people stand up?'

On a more personal note, a hearing problem that had begun to plague Townshend a few years earlier, was steadily growing worse, causing him terrifying earaches. Doctors warned that continuous exposure to the piercing decibels of the Who would leave him completely deaf in only a matter of years.

By this point Townshend's professional life was becoming bogged down in studio budgets and endless litigation. While the punks were out raving, Townshend was relegated to sitting behind a desk. 'All I've got to rebel against these days is board meetings and the old lady,' he groused. 'Sometimes I feel like an old gent going through menopause. . . . I prayed for it, and yet it's too late for me to truly participate. I feel like an engineer.'

Then someone came along to snap Townshend out of his lethargy: Ronnie Lane. The bassist, late of Rod Stewart's mod band, the Faces, had fallen on lean times, and he reached out to his old pal for help on his latest album. 'I was having a brain trauma,' quipped the affable East Ender. Pete snapped back, 'He nagged me to do it.'

It wasn't the first time Pete had teamed up with other artists. He had had a successful collaboration with both Thunderclap Newman and Arthur Brown, the quirky singer Townshend first met at the UFO Club back in 1968. He launched Brown's memorable 'Fire' to a number-one hit.

At first glance Townshend and Lane seemed an odd pairing. Ron favored lovelorn ballads in a pithy Dylanesque vein; Pete belted out hard nuggets of revelation and angst. Yet they had common ground as well. Both were ex-mod rockers and Ronnie had turned to Baba around the same time as Pete. Not to mention their self-deprecating sense of humor and instinctive, if contrasting, flair for composition.

Actually, theirs wasn't to be a collaboration in the true sense. Both came to the study with a cache of individual tunes more or less complete. Townshend was admittedly dubious. 'I've never written with anybody because I work unconsciously and tend to just let it spill out. If anybody says, "Why don't you change so-and-so," I don't know how to approach it. Because I haven't put it together in an intellectual way.'

Lane found out the extent of Townshend's convictions on the subject when he suggested they team up to compose a few tunes. Recalls Lane, 'He turned around and said, "What? And split the publishing?" I was floored. I never brought it up with him again.'

In the winter of 1976 and spring of '77, Townshend cautiously entered a world of gentle Gaelic influences of acoustic mandolins, violins, and accordions whose sounds still echo in the pastoral folds of the British countryside. With Eric Clapton and Charlie Watts adding their talents, Townshend and Lane combined efforts on each other's compositions, even playing on each other's tracks. Surprisingly, Lane had more influence on Townshend than the other way around. 'Ronnie's contribution to my stuff was much, much deeper,' he explained. 'He has always encouraged me to do stuff away from the mainstream Who clichés. You can get in a rut, and it must affect the way you work. On a song like "Street in the City" [the only piece Townshend wrote especially for the project], it's something I wouldn't have done before. Ron was knocked out when we heard the playbacks. It gave me a kick to see that.'

'Street in the City' was indeed a departure for its composer, with its lavish string orchestrations and clever lyrics seemingly snatched from a Sondheim musical. Ostensibly the story of a people watcher on a bustling London street, the piece showcases Pete's cynical side: a man on a ledge draws a crowd anticipating a suicide leap until they discover he's simply cleaning windows and hurry off about their business.

Of course, the real purport of the song and, indeed, much of the album is the composer's deep, unrequited spiritual longing. 'Street,' for example, illustrates the ultimate futility and irrelevancy of ordinary material life with its colorful descriptions of bank patrons carrying their 'very important paper,' seamy adolescent lust, and other equally mundane affairs. To the uninitiated the song may seem merely a witty description of one whimsical day in the life, but the fact is it meshes perfectly with Meher Baba's dictates on the nature of existence minus the so-called God principle or divine consciousness. Harkening back to the Bard's 'All the world's a stage,' Townshend's cutting wit and New Age politics are neatly cloaked beneath his cotton candy, lyrical descriptions and airy musical distractions. As with much of Townshend's work it is necessary to dig deeper to appreciate the actual content. In many ways, 'Street,' while sharing certain values with, say, the Beatles' 'Penny Lane,' strikes a far deeper chord in those ready to hear.

That is not to say, however, that everything on the album is as multifaceted and meaningful. Among the relative clunkers are 'My Baby Gives It Away' (far too clichéd, one would think, to have ever made it onto vinyl); the musically uninspired 'No Where To Run'; the witless 'Rough Mix'; the down and dirty wanna-be, 'Catmelody'; and the just plain boring 'April Fool.'

The album, though, featured a half dozen gems. 'Annie,' for one, is a poignant, folksy tune in which Lane's sincerity shines through, summoning visions of a lost relationship still piercing the heart of the singer.

'Keep Me Turning,' conversely, credited solely to Pete, is a straightforward cry for the grace of his guru and ultimate deliverance from the I, me, mine consciousness that's held him back from experiencing his higher nature. When he sings, 'Don't you leave me till the very last,' he is pleading with Baba to liberate him from his mundane mindset and ultimately time, space, matter, and everything that goes with this. Pete's way, however, does not encompass the fairly rigid fundamentalism recommended by sages from time immemorial, but rather a new kind of 'poppy' spirituality that allows one to enjoy the things of this world without garnering attachment to them – a philosophy that's certainly a lot easier than the kind of single pointed effort required by the practitioners of most mystical paths. Hence, Townshend's sneaky line about 'walking in backwards' like he's walking out. The joke is, of course, that while that might get you backstage somewhere it won't serve to bust open the fabled Doors Of Perception Pete has spent the better part of his life searching for.

This is not to say, however, that making the album was always harmonious. In fact, creative tensions between the two uncovered a startling and tragic revelation. 'I got angry with Ronnie about halfway through the sessions because I thought he was a drunk, just a drunken pig,' Townshend recalls. 'I don't know why I was being such a hypocrite, as I used to drink far more than he. But he was falling all over the place, and I got angry with him in the hallway and pushed him. I punched his right shoulder to emphasize a point, and he went flying down the hall. It was then I realized he was sick.'

The truth was, his old mate was in the initial stages of multiple sclerosis, a disease which would seriously impact both their lives in years to come.

The finished album, entitled *Rough Mix*, was released in September 1977 to great critical acclaim and was named Album of the Year by *Rolling Stone*. MCA, who had just negotiated a deal for three Who albums, did not promote it strongly, however. Townshend heard that the company feared he was going to leave and form a band with Lane, Clapton, John 'Rabbit' Bundrick and Charlie Watts. 'I think they kind of flushed the album,' he surmised. 'They printed seventy-five thousand copies and held back about fifty thousand. People were going out to buy it and couldn't find it. I suspected conspiracy. I think MCA were worried the money they invested in the Who would be lost if I went out and pursued a supergroup career.'

The *Rough Mix* project did give the world-weary Townshend a much-needed kick start. 'I was hanging on a peg, afraid of being musical or even mentioning the word . . . but we've got some shit-hot material now. I've never been so confident about my writing.'

Pete's composing had steadily evolved since those first heady days of the Who when he would sit penning potential singles on airplanes, buses, and vans. 'I often sit at a typewriter and knock out stream-of-consciousness stuff,' he said. 'It not only helps clear the head but brings forth ideas for songs. [They] were written on scraps of paper in the dead of night, at the lunch table with the kids on my lap, in hotel rooms, while filming or performing.

'I write first and think later. Someone like Irving Berlin has to write a song with a certain artist, subject, or even a whole show in mind. When you write a rock song, though, you just open your mouth and it pours out. If it fits, it's great. If it doesn't, no one plays it. You have to be impulsive. Music is easy. Words are far more important.'

Townshend noted that when he was most tranquil, he tended to look outward and come up with more universal material. 'In other words, I go looking for trouble elsewhere,' says Pete. An early example was 'Won't Get Fooled Again,' created at a point when he was at his happiest. 'The song is [written] from a position of a secure family: "I'll move myself and my family aside." That's the whole thing. I was writing in a sense to say, Don't fuck around with revolution for my benefit. I've seen them come and go and everything ends up the same. And I'd prefer it if my kids didn't get involved.'

During the late seventies Pete's writing reached the point where his subjects were very much the people around him. 'Misunderstood,' he revealed, was geared toward 'a Johnny Rotten type character. 'I wanna be misunderstood, wanna be feared in my neighborhood . . . [I wanna be] inscrutable, vague and so hard to pin down . . . want people to cry when I put them down.'

'Am I going to turn into Somerset Maugham writing secret stories about the people I know? It's surprising how far you can go before people recognize themselves.'

The truth is, the song is rather obviously about Townshend himself, no matter what he chooses to believe.

In November 1977 Townshend broke a two-year silence in the press with a rambling self-penned article in *Rolling Stone*. At its heart was a riveting account of a dream he had conjured up once again: the elusive search for the universal chord. It began quietly like 'a breath being gently sighed away' and soon grew into a 'roaring singing cascading sound that threw me into ecstasy. Its superficial simplicity only disguised a secret ingredient I felt must in itself contain all things.'

Plunging deeper to define the source, Townshend concluded that this extraordinary sound might belong to human voices, perhaps a heavenly choir. 'My skin crawled as I recognized the unique elements of this superficially wonderful noise,' he wrote. 'I could not believe what I heard . . . a vitiated and distorted ploy of my ego to stunt my trust in nature's beauty, kill my appetite for the One within the many and the many within the One.

'For the sound I was hearing was the roar of a billion humans screaming.'

He awoke, his body soaking and feverish, praying for protection. 'I now know,' he wrote solemnly, 'that of all things on earth, nothing is so inherently evil, so contemptuous, so vile, so conniving or worthless . . . as my own imagination.'

This humbling episode served to punctuate both his polarizing view of good versus evil and unshakable belief that top forty rock was somehow inexorably fused with the spiritual. From the depths too rose an awareness of his own frailties; he exposed his 'crime,' as he put it, that of letting down rock 'n' roll. 'I was failing friends, family, history, the future and most importantly, God. No one less could have invented this sublime music.'

Emerging slowly from his own self-made fetters, Townshend still fretted over the fact that there was 'no one to pick up the gauntlet of rock.' The answer, he said, came from a voice out of the sky he unequivocally recognized as Baba's: 'Keep playing the guitar with the Who until further notice!'

This impulse was given a great boost when Keith Moon returned after an extended stint in America. 'There is something very mystical and intangible about the energy that exists around the Who,' Pete once proclaimed. 'I couldn't ever hope to put my finger on it, but it's very vital and real. It costs the band a lot. But you just hope for those magic moments. Spill a bit of blood and do it honestly.'

Townshend gathered his mates around the table at a pub one night to outline their latest strategy. 'We were starting to cut at our individual egos, saying, "Look, this is a band. Let's not be afraid of being a band, of being the Who. Let's not be afraid to be different . . . to take stances. Let's not be afraid to be affected."'

Who Are You, released in August 1978 (and peaking at number two), made them, according to Townshend, 'a part of the American rock establishment.' Though cited by many fans as a triumphant return to the group's traditional MO, especially in light of Pete's uneven *The Who by Numbers*, the album also displayed signs of the path Townshend would follow once he finally went solo.

'New Song,' the album's measured opener, is 'about rock needing to say the same things again and again,' Pete explains. 'It never lets go, it always admits to the same thing.'

Optimism reigns on 'The Music Must Change' and the sizy 'Guitar and Pen.' On the latter, Townshend opts for a jazzy feel totally out of kilter with his lyrics; 'When your fingers are bleeding/And your knuckles are white/And you can ̶b̶e̶ ̶ door.' Moreover, with its operatic falsettos mixed in wi̶̶ ̶y's powerful delivery, the overall sound is muddled, yet.

'Love Is Coming Down,' a surging melodic ballad very much in the vein of the inspirational 'Love Reign o'er Me,' is first-rate. 'I feel my heart is really in this,' Pete later confirmed.

According to Townshend, however, the album's most inspired moments were left on the studio floor. His demos for the project show a progressive creativity, according to producer Glyn Johns, with his clever use of jazz, complex time signatures, and brave guitar runs. 'The demos were not really reproducible by the band,' affirmed Johns. 'In other words, he'd written grooves and certain sound ideas which were not really the Who.'

Added the vaunted producer, 'I would have loved to see the Who go in the direction of those demos. . . . But it wasn't to be.'

Keith Richards heartily agreed, commenting in 1985, 'In actual fact Pete Townshend made better Who records than the Who. He used to go there with the album already finished and the rest would simply come up with some dubs, but his was ten times better than the finished product. It was a matter of them imitating what Peter had already laid out, kinda Hitchcockish. After doing the storyboards, makin' the actual movie was a drag for Hitchcock. His whole thing was puttin' it all together. But I think in a way Peter is kind of like that. He *is* the Who . . . Pete knew what he wanted and made damned sure they did it, but I think he could have done it better himself.'

Townshend deemed the title track, 'Who Are You,' 'the archetypal old-fashioned Who-sounding track very much in the tradition of "Won't Get Fooled Again."' The song was based on an incident in mid-March 1977, when, as Townshend put it, 'I emotionally cracked.' He had been holding forth at a fourteen-hour business meeting with former manager Chris Stamp and the ubiquitous Allen Klein for his delinquent American songwriting royalties. This represented the final segment of a protracted six-month litigation. In the end Klein gleefully tore off a check to Pete.

'I don't fuckin' believe this!' Townshend snapped to Stamp. 'After all these years in the business I've sat through all this bullshit just to get a bloody check!'

then loudly proclaimed he'd lost all faith in the
indu... a...d felt 'like shit.' Retrieving a nearby bottle of Rémy
Martin, he headed off to the Speakeasy to catch John Otway and
Willie Barrett, two eccentric artists in whom he had invested.

Likening his behavior to 'a raging bull,' Townshend burst into
the club, tearing through the tables and viciously insulting old
friends. Spotting two of the Sex Pistols, he mistook drummer
Paul Cook for vocalist Johnny Rotten and cornered him against
the bar. He then fell to his knees and grabbed Cook's pant
leg, launching into a tirade: 'Thank God you've come. You've
saved us!'

'Actually, it would be really good if the Who stayed around so
we can keep attacking you dinosaurs,' Cook wryly replied.

'You've been manipulated,' Townshend screamed. 'Kick us out
now! You have the power!'

'The Who aren't really going to break up, are they?' a confused
Cook asked.

'We're fuckin' finished! It's a disaster. Rock has gone down
the fuckin' tubes!' With that he tore up his hard-won check and
stormed out.

The next thing he knew, he was being awakened in a nearby
Soho shop doorway by a policeman, having collapsed in a boozy
heap. 'Hello, Pete. If you can get up and walk away, you can sleep
in your own bed tonight.'

Karen was there to meet him 'with a rolling pin in her hand,' as
Townshend put it.

The nightmarish experience became the stirring 'Who Are You.'
Not only was it a top single for the band, but was also the
album's thematic centerpiece. Pete dubbed it 'an encyclopedia
for up-and-coming groups about how not to get caught. I think
it's important to show that it's possible to go through the rock
business, make money, and be successful while still remaining
relatively human.'

He'd also learned a valuable lesson about the limitations of
rock. 'I've got to the point where you can't do it all and rock
is not capable of changing society. The only thing capable of
doing that is power. So I'm more concerned now with trying to write music that makes people feel better rather than
worse.'

He cited the example of 'My Generation,' a song about gross

intimidation pointed at society's privileged top feeders who cruised about casually in Rolls-Royces. 'The stupidity of writing it,' he remembered, 'was that nobody in a Rolls ever listened to "My Generation." Nobody in a Rolls was ever even slightly scared of people with safety pins in their ears.

'I recognized very early on the thing that made rock work was that it was threatening. And yet it never carried out any of the threats that the media, my parents, and the establishment claimed it was going to.'

Still, Pete provided through his music a keen awareness of the human condition, to lend a voice to those who had none. 'Whether it's minority groups like blacks and gays or disturbed kids living in high-rise blocks, they want somebody to speak for them. . . . I'm more concerned with doing rather than pointing fingers saying, "That's wrong and that's wrong."'

For all of Townshend's renewed hopes, the Speakeasy incident represented an unsettling omen. Not only had he begun to drink again after three years, but Keith's return to London wasn't the joyous homecoming his band mates had hoped. The drummer was flat broke, overweight, in and out of hospitals, and rapidly alienating friends with his trademark off-the-wall behavior.

Despite his appointment as PR director for the Who's interests in Shepperton Studios and his ongoing role in the band, Moonie was bravely fighting alcoholism and the exhausting chore of being an aging Keith Moon. 'In the two years off,' he related, 'I was drifting away with no direction, no nothing. I'd try to do things and get involved in projects, but nothing ever came close to the feeling I get when I'm working with the guys. Because it's fun but at the same time I know I've gotta discipline myself again.'

Pete recalls the drummer's deterioration during the recording of *Who Are You*. He consistently arrived late for sessions after all-night clubbing, and it showed in his sluggish playing. 'I got him behind the drums,' he says, 'and he couldn't keep the song together. He couldn't play. . . . But before I said anything, he went, "See? I'm the best Keith Moon-type drummer in the world!" There was nobody to top him. But unless you wanted that, you were fucked, and it so happened on that song we didn't. . . . A couple of days after, he started to call me up just to say good night and I love you. He did that about ten times, and you could tell he was crying a little. He'd say, "You do believe me, don't you?" I'd say, "Yes, but you're still an asshole."

'It was terrible when we realized that Keith, though not actually dying, was somehow gone. He'd changed. And he was so much the epicenter of our life. The British regarded him as an eccentric loony like Ollie Reed. . . . When we lost that side of him, we thought, "Oh, bloody hell." What do you say to the guy, "Listen, sorry, we need you the way you were."'

In May of 1978 Moon participated in a staged concert for the closing segment of *The Kids Are Alright* film. At the end he is seen stumbling from his kit into Townshend's arms for a hearty embrace. It was to be his final performance.

Dougal Butler, an early Who roadie and later Keith's long-suffering personal assistant, remembered Moonie's confused and touching last days: 'I feel genuinely sorry for Keith. He is not capable of coping on his own, but at the same time I just do not feel able, any longer, to handle him. . . . I am beginning to feel the strain. Smashing up hotel rooms, driving about pissed, screwing in every conceivable place, with every conceivable type and using every conceivable variation, generally causing riots and behaving unlike a responsible and tax-paying citizen is a lot of fun. But in the end it begins to pall. It is clear to me when I decide to split that I have a choice in these matters, I can call it a day. But, sadly, Moonie does not have such a choice. He is a prisoner of his own nature. He is locked into a certain pattern of behavior, just as surely as swallows migrate, salmon spawn, and squirrels hibernate.

'It is just about a year after I leave Moonie that he dies, but before he dies I do see him a few times. There is one occasion when I am working full-time for Jeff Stein on *The Kids Are Alright*, and we are filming a Who gig at Kilburn State Theatre in London. At this time I am the official assistant director on the movie – or at least one of the official assistant directors – and I have to do a great deal of hustling about. . . .

'Anyway, it is inevitable that I meet up with the band,

including Moonie, on the shoot. . . . As it happens, I have no need to be concerned beforehand, because everyone gives me a very large "Hello!" indeed, none more so than Keith, and fairly soon we're hitting the brandies and ginger, and later we do without the ginger, as it seems to be getting in the way of the brandy. Well, eventually, I have to perform one of my functions as official assistant director, this function being to get the performers in front of the camera. So when the time comes, I stand up on my feet – a little uncertain in the balancing act, it's true – and speak as follows:

' "On set, please, gentlemen!"

'When this command is greeted with universal shouts of: "Fuck off, Dougal!" I know that it's business as usual, and I must say I am very happy about it.

'After this episode, Moonie says to me: "You fucking idiot, Dougal. Why don't you come back?" But I know I can't go back to Moonie. He knows it too. On the other hand, we both know we're mates again. . . .

'After this, I see Moonie a few times, and most of those times he asks me to come back. We meet up at Shepperton Studios, at his new flat, and have numerous phone conversations. But I stick to my chosen path, and I assume the role of Moonie's mate and confidant. Then he ups and dies.'

On August 7, 1978, Pete learned of the death of his early mentor, Pete Meaden, from a drug-induced suicide. The tragedy left him saddened and shaken, unprepared for the greater tragedy that would shortly follow.

One month later, on September 6, Moon attended Paul McCartney's annual Buddy Holly Week party (McCartney having purchased the artist's lucrative composing copyrights). That year the highlight was a screening of *The Buddy Holly Story*. Those in attendance found Moonie surprisingly fit and in great spirits, having shed some of his paunch, once again on the wagon, and looking forward to marrying Scandinavian model Annette Walter-Lax, closely resembling his former beloved wife, Kim, who had left him in October 1973. Actually, those close to Moon say his decline started with Kim's departure. Having lost the one true love of his life, he never really recovered.

In the early morning hours, however, Moon popped several handfuls of heminevrin, a potent sedative used both to curb his appetite for alcohol and control the epileptic fits the drummer experienced during his various institutionalized dry-outs.

The second dose proved fatal. Townshend received the devastating news from Bill Curbishley and quickly rang Daltrey. 'He's done it,' he choked, barely able to get the words out.

'Who?' Roger demanded.

'Keith.'

It was the news they had dreaded, always expected and yet could not accept. Surely their madcap pal would defy mortality once again and pop up behind them yelling, 'Gotcha!' In a chilling piece of irony, on the cover of *Who Are You* Moon is shown seated on an old studio chair that reads, 'Not to be taken away.'

'The worst thing,' according to Entwistle, 'was that none of us were there when he died. We must have saved his life thirty times picking him up when he was unconscious and walking him around, getting him to a doctor.'

Groping about for some rationale, Daltrey pinned Moon's self-destruction on his deep-seated unhappiness. 'If he wasn't channeling [his energy] through the drums, he had no place to put it. He had this desperation to be loved, really loved by the people he cared about. . . . Keith had the comedian's disease of trying to make people laugh all the time. But inside he was incredibly unhappy.'

Entwistle, always the closest to Keith, also remembers him as a sad clown. 'He never seemed able to get offstage. He always had to be Keith Moon. He was playing the part of Keith Moon because he couldn't remember what it was like to be normal. The only time he was normal was before two in the afternoon. After two he became his alter ego.'

In the end, incredible as it seemed, normalcy had done him in. 'He matured himself to death,' as one broadcaster put it. 'I helped him get back on his feet by getting his flat in London,' says Pete. 'And a couple days later he died in it. Funnily enough, he was at his most poised and contented . . . and I think there was something about that. He couldn't live with the new character he was. . . . He just let go.'

Moon's passing began a long, dark eclipse for the band, all their regenerated hopes suddenly extinguished. As for Townshend, he was about to enter his darkest period yet as the Great Pretender of rock 'n' roll. It was one role at which he would not only fail miserably but would very nearly cost him his life.

7

Second Coming:
Sex, Drugs and Death

I've been living in a garbage can all my life and so I remain. If you live in a garbage can, you just keep your mouth closed.

– Pete Townshend

Townshend wouldn't realize the harrowing ramifications of Moon's death until it was almost too late. Overshadowing the tragedy, however, were other urgent matters, chiefly whether or not the band should continue. The initial feeling was that this must be the end. The group's indelible four-way magic was now irretrievably lost. How could they possibly go on without their loony cohort?

'I wish the band had stopped when Keith died,' Pete would later confess. 'We were about to stop, but I felt we had to go on and finish off somehow.'

Instead the Who took no time to grieve, to heal. As Daltrey pointed out ten years later, 'We were on a treadmill, and when Keith died we stayed on that treadmill. We should have taken time and thought about what we were. But we just buried our heads in the sand and pretended we were the same band. But we weren't.'

Fans and critics would later point to the uncanny parallel of

Keith's death to that of Led Zeppelin's drummer, Jon Bonham. In the wake of Bonham's overdose in 1980, Led Zeppelin promptly elected to call it quits. Townshend, however, claims there was no comparison. Bonzo, he asserts, was much more a mainstay of the band, and his death came during a very active period for the group. By contrast, the Who had been on a hiatus of sorts. 'We felt responsible to go on playing so Keith's death didn't take the blame,' Pete reveals. 'People couldn't say, "Ah, that crazy Moon had an OD and the Who finished." We felt we had to keep going for him and make something positive out of it.'

In fact, it was Daltrey, caught up in the emotional turmoil of the moment, who was the first to venture, 'I think we should carry on for him.'

In one sense, the band was liberated, released from the old, overwrought sagging format. Moon had been a powerful character who was stubbornly resistant to change. The way Pete saw it, they were no longer weighed down with that responsibility. Rather than *waste* Moon's death, why not use it as an opportunity to develop? One thing, though, was certain, they weren't really the Who anymore.

'We don't think of ourselves as the Who,' Townshend was now telling the press, 'just performers and musicians . . . a normal band.' But what made the Who tick was precisely the fact that they were never, in any way, a normal group. A point Pete would stubbornly refuse to accept.

The appointment of a new drummer started when Ginger Baker, late of Cream, offered his services to Pete in the wake of Moon's passing. Unfortunately, he was virtually as problematic a character as Keith and thereby would have been equally controversial. Townshend politely declined.

As usual, Pete, in his self-appointed position as band leader, bulldozed through his choice as Keith's replacement: Kenney Jones. Another Faces alumnus, Jones was the polar opposite of Moonie both in temperament and playing style. The reliable and amenable drummer was a tidy, straightforward timekeeper with little fuss. Besides Pete's long-standing ties with his fellow mod (Jones was also the drummer on the *Tommy* film soundtrack) there was something deeper in his reasoning.

'I felt we should not try to replace Keith, not go down the same dynamic road,' Townshend recalled. '[The Who] isn't the name of a familiar group of musicians because once Keith died that was dead. It's become a kind of ideology, a sense of personal emancipation opposed to political or economic emancipation. We who are in the Who should know it's impossible to invoke that other kind of music without Keith. So I felt that without Moonie we were a new band.'

Entwistle heartily supported Townshend's selection, looking forward to a less frenetic rhythm section. 'I tended to play bass like Keith played drums. I got a lot more freedom playing with Kenney. I had to follow Keith every time he went into a break.'

The selection, though, was laced with bittersweet irony. Jones points out that he was with Moon that fateful night at the Buddy Holly do. 'We were talking with Paul and he said, "I've got this idea I want to call Rockestra, where I'll get a lot of musicians together. I want you, Kenney, Keith, and Jon Bonham with all these other guitarists, Pete Townshend and Eric Clapton." Keith and I were enjoying each other's company, and as we left we decided the idea was fantastic. The next day I woke up and he didn't.'

When offered the plum gig Jones didn't hesitate. 'Jesus, I've *got* to join the band. It's how I grew up, it's part of me, I know them and it's what I stand for.'

Daltrey, for his part, believed they should opt for a series of different drummers, always keeping the chair fresh. So when Townshend announced that Jones would not only be the new Who drummer, but should furthermore be installed with a full quarter partnership in the band, Roger bristled, insisting he should merely be put on a salary.

Pete fired back, 'I'm not ready for that. It means we're still running the Who. It's like we're on a pilgrimage to find Keith. To be really unpleasant about it, I'm kind of *glad* Keith is gone. He was a real pain in the ass. The band wasn't functioning. Can't you see, this is a chance to do something new?'

'I never thought he was the right drummer for the Who,' Daltrey always contended, 'I thought it totally unbalanced the way John plays. His playing evolved out of the chaotic way Keith played the drums while Kenney was simplicity itself. I never said that Kenney was a bad drummer or that we didn't get on socially.

'Kenney wasn't capable of doing any more than he did. What he did was very good. But when you put him with a bass player of John's stature who can play so much, who can move rhythms so

fast, the drummer has to do much more than boom-chi-chi-boom.
. . . Kenney's style was stifling. It was the same every night.'

Jones, caught solidly in the middle, was overtly conscious not
to mimic Keith in any way. 'The numbers kind of dictated the way
you should play anyway,' he noted. 'There wasn't a lot I could do
to bury it or do anything different.'

Paradoxically, the Who's latest configuration coincided with the
1979 Mod revival. Townshend recounts a story that took place at
the Rainbow Club where the band performed its first concert with
Jones in January. On his way to the venue, he spotted a line of
concert-goers all wearing parkas and original Who paraphernalia,
badges, and insignias bearing the group's sixties logo. Pete couldn't
resist strolling over to one of the kids in line and asking, 'Have you
ever seen the Who?'

The youth flashed him an uppity 'fuck you' look and snorted,
'Who are you?'

A great deal was conveyed to Townshend in that brief encounter.
The logo, which had meant so much to him and to their cadre of
early fans, was now just another symbol. 'Just like the bloody
swastika was to the Hell's Angels,' he lamented. 'It meant nothing
to them.'

More significant, the youngster's lack of recognition signaled a
changing of the guard. Rock was now, like it or not, in the hands
of the punk rockers, a generation not part of Who history. The
Who were growing further away from their once awesome and
unchallenged power base.

Still, at that point, Townshend wasn't really paying attention
to his instincts anyway. 'I cared about doing it for all the wrong
reasons,' he would later say. 'I carried on doing it for Roger, for
John, for the fans. I carried on doing it because I had a contract.
I carried on doing it because I had thirty employees. I carried on
doing it and I shouldn't have.'

But after fifteen years, letting go was still unthinkable. Deep
down Townshend stubbornly clung to the hope that they could
somehow renew themselves.

This all culminated in yet another major Townshend identity
crisis. For too long he and the band had been minders to the
childlike Moon, getting him on his feet after his latest bender,
seeing he made the gigs, careful not to drink around him, knowing
he was trying so desperately to quit. 'As a result of his death,' says

Pete, 'I felt kind of released from the responsibility of being straight myself and I very rapidly went downhill.

'For a long time I felt I was the one who was giving. I always seemed to be helping people. In the end I thought, "For God's sake, when is someone going to help me?"'

Despite all the exhortations about freeing himself from Keith's larger-than-life persona, Pete did precisely the opposite. Since 1964 he'd been Moonie's straight man, and now he was free to try on the platform shoes of a certified five-star looney. 'I felt, "Well, he's gone, that means I've got a bit more license." I was freer somehow.'

Trying to emulate Moon's superhuman feats, Townshend's newfound image coincided with an immediate moral collapse. 'I suddenly realized that this gawky kid who had a hard time even looking in the mirror was discovering a middle-age charisma which was hypnotizing women. I looked back at this terrible, troubled, self-obsessed life I'd had and it wasn't the ugly duckling turning into a swan, but rather the ugly duckling turning into Rambo.'

Townshend dove into a six-week binge of debauchery, focusing on London's high-class circle of groupies. 'It's not just about their firm voluptuousness,' he stated in 1993, 'there's the whole idea that you can penetrate not only the body, but also the mind. It's a form of vampirism.'

Instead of the anticipated freedom he expected from his newfound sexual exploits, Townshend's lascivious activities left him feeling empty, alone, and riddled with guilt. 'It confused me,' he said, 'wondering whether it had happened because of a genuine personal emergence, because women love a drunk, because I'm a superstar, or there's a chance they might get their hands on my money. It took me a long time to come to grips with it.'

The only way he knew how to cope was by hitting the sauce, a daily bottle of his favorite cognac, Rémy Martin. His pathetic indulgence quickly became apparent at the Secret Policeman's Ball in 1979 to benefit Amnesty International. It marked Townshend's first real solo appearance, and he was very nervous.

Following capable performances of 'Pinball Wizard' and 'Drowned,' Pete returned to the dressing room to finish off an enormous bottle of brandy before an encore duet with classical guitarist John Williams. According to producer Martin Lewis, Pete drifted idly through the song and finally slumped over his Gibson into a liquor-induced slumber in the middle of the number. 'Only three people noticed,' said Lewis, citing himself, Pete, and Williams. 'I thought, "Christ, how will they get out of this?"' The filmed concert, however, doesn't show the sleeping Townshend because as Lewis put it, 'Pete would have bits of my anatomy cut out.'

Even more disturbing, this period also marked a significant retreat from the artist's devotion to Meher Baba, though he wasn't consciously abandoning his beliefs. 'I made a commitment and I surrendered something when I first became acquainted with Meher Baba's life,' Townshend said. 'I just don't pursue the company of other followers anymore.'

One thing he openly resisted and fought mightily, however, was a return to the road. 'The Who,' he said at the time, 'is like a chicken with its head cut off. . . . I mean, I'll run around with it for a bit if they insist. But it wouldn't be determination and need that was getting me up there. It certainly would not be part of my purpose in life.'

He listed the reasons: his precarious state of hearing, the weariness of constant travel and hotel rooms, and not wanting to leave his family. The overriding factor, though, was his genuine fear of the road, where he turned into that *other* Pete Townshend: the boozing, raving, womanizing, aging rock idol. But as his recent behavior indicated, the road wasn't really causing his problem.

Beyond that, Pete feared the Who were turning into mere caricatures when they took the stage. 'It started to happen in 1976, and I don't think we even realized it,' he stated. 'I was really fucked up after that. They're trying to persuade me to agree to three three-week tours of America . . . but I'm not gonna do it!'

'You're barmy,' Daltrey shot back. 'I'm not gonna let your feelings of depression affect me.' Roger would go anywhere simply to perform while Entwistle was the consummate road rat. Their goal, they told the press, was to get Townshend out on the road 'dead or alive.'

Coaxed or, as he put it, 'bullied into it,' mainly on the strength of promoting their recently released *Quadrophenia* movie, Pete reluctantly complied. As a trade-off, he enlisted old mate keyboard wiz Rabbit Bundrick, plus three top brass players for a shot of new blood in the act.

Townshend's tour apprehensions proved portentous, but in a far different way. In October 1979 he told a magazine reporter, 'The kind of pressures we generate on stage and the intensity of the kind of audience we attract could conceivably someday precipitate a riot.'

Following several summer appearances in Europe and a week of September dates in New York, the Who returned to the States in late November 1979 for a month-long tour. In Cincinnati, knowing the band could pack in virtually unlimited hordes, the general-admission practice of festival seating was introduced. A first-come, first-serve policy, allegedly implemented to 'equalize' ticket holders, it was in fact designed to accommodate the greed of promoters who could take out floor seats and thereby pack in a few thousand more paying bodies.

On December 3, 1979, a raw, bitter wind was whipping off the water at Cincinnati's Riverfront Coliseum as fans began to line up at the doors hours before the eight o'clock curtain. By six, there was already a mob scene, with angry, half-frozen people ramming the entrances, crushing forward, jockeying for position. Finally the doors opened, but only four of the sixteen, unleashing a raging human stampede. Screaming pleas went unheard, silenced by the frenzied melee, as bodies were crushed and dragged in an undertow of madness. When it was all over, the floor was strewn with shoes, scarfs, hats, even clothing ripped off unfortunate victims. At the heart of the grisly scene lay eleven teenage bodies, a few of which were barely recognizable.

The band wasn't informed of the tragedy until the concert's end. Roger was left reeling, vowing never to step on stage again, while Kenney was so disoriented he was left behind when the band checked out and had to be escorted from the hotel.

Townshend, as spokesman, predictably had plenty to say, venting his outrage at pushers who peddled the explosive hallucinogen angel dust, which many believed was responsible for the volatile reactions of many concert-goers. The wholesale blame of festival seating, though, he charged was an overreaction. The famous Townshend temper reared when journalists constantly coerced an emotional, guilt-ridden response from the group. He charged that sending flowers to the funerals was only a hollow token. 'All wasted. I think when people are dead, they're dead.'

Pete would later contend that the Cincinnati tragedy needed to happen in order to force the band to see its audience in terms of real people and to permit outsiders to view the band as human beings. 'I think it only could have happened to the Who, only they could have survived it, the investigation and self-examination that obviously went on afterward.'

At the time Townshend's only coping mechanism was what he called 'tour armor,' which blotted out all feeling and sensitivity, thus allowing a more abandoned, tougher exterior. As he explains, 'It was, fuck! We're not gonna let a little thing like this stop us. That was the way we had to think, we *had* to reduce it because if we admitted to ourselves the true significance of the event . . . we could not possibly have gone on.'

Beneath the armor, though, Pete felt a sordid accessory to the 'show must go on' mentality. He later admitted that the event was directly responsible for his coming emotional collapse. 'I hated the feeling I was in a band on the downward slide that was killing people in Cincinnati, killing off its own members, killing its manager. We were making big money, and anybody who got in the way or had a problem, we dropped. Nobody seemed to notice. Nobody seemed to think this was a particularly bad thing, or we pretended it wasn't, anyway. I felt it start to kill me.'

In the wake of the incident, Townshend's drinking once more was displayed at the year-end Concerts for the People of Kampuchea. Pete and the other members of the Who joined such pop luminaries as the Clash, Wings, Elvis Costello, and Robert Plant as part of Paul McCartney's highly publicized Rockestra. On the final night, December 29, 1979, Wings drummer Steve Holly spins this yarn: 'It was during Pete's over-the-top cognac days. Just before we all went on, the poor wardrobe girl had popped into Townshend's dressing room to make sure everything was okay, when, to her horror, she discovered he wasn't wearing the gold lamé top hat and tux jacket Paul had made up for everybody, and what's more, had no intention of doing so. "I'm not wearing that fucking shit," the surly guitarist roared. Townshend was certain Paul was having him on and never actually expected that anyone else intended to appear on stage in the admittedly tacky outfit. Of course, everyone else was wearing the getup, which left Pete paranoid about being out of step with his colleagues.'

New Year 1980 saw the beginning of Townshend's notorious two-year 'big blast,' proving his dictum: 'Nothing in nature behaves so consistently and rigidly as a human being in pursuit of hell.'

A contributing factor to his waywardness stemmed from a core disagreement at home. Pete desperately tried to rationalize his need to drink by linking it to the boozy tradition of Fitzgerald and Hemingway. 'I always felt that drinking and work were tied together in a totally appropriate way,' he reasoned.

'This isn't me,' he told Karen, 'this is just some mechanism that drives me on. This is some ambition quotient.' Townshend's justification implied that being the songwriter and spokesman for the band created undue pressures that he wasn't allowed to bring home to the 'sacrosanct' circle of family life. 'This was the conspiracy my wife and I carried together,' he admitted in 1985. 'We were accomplices. It got to the point where the charade could go on no longer.'

Finally Karen, herself weary from all the stress, issued an ultimatum. 'Listen, Pete, your drinking is starting to affect the family. And I just won't have it.'

'Karen, I can't stop drinking. Particularly when I'm working.'

'Well then, when you work, you stay away.'

So began Townshend's progressive estrangement from his family. Hotels became home during periods of recording; he'd venture off to America for several weeks or hole up at his cabin on stilts in rural Oxfordshire. There were times too when he'd come back home, abstain for a period, then once again fall off the wagon. It was a pattern that began to control his life.

In the early part of 1980, Pete completed his first official solo work, *Empty Glass*. Despite the disarray of his private life, the project was a source of great joy and pride to the artist.

Interestingly, it was the perceptive Ronnie Lane who got him started. 'Listen, Pete,' he confided, 'the Who are finished. They were nice while they lasted, but they don't make music. They're power pop, they're pyrotechnics, they're showmanship. But you are a musician, and you should write songs and play a wider kind of music. I hear all kinds of stuff you do which the public doesn't, and that's wrong!'

The album's opening track, 'Empty Glass,' borrowed inspiration from the book of Ecclesiastes and sums up neatly what Pete was going through at the time. 'Spirituality to me is about the asking, not the answers. I still find it a very romantic proposition, that you hold up an empty glass and say, "Right. If you're there, fill it." The glass is empty because you emptied it. You were in it originally. That's why it's only when you're at your lowest, when you believe yourself to be worthless, when you're in a state of futility that you produce an empty glass.

'By emptying the glass you give God a chance to enter it. You get yourself out of the way. In a sense, it's to do with semantics, but ultimately you vacate. I can't really back this up, but I think that when I've sincerely prayed I've gotten an answer of some sort.'

Despite Townshend's growing state of despair, the introspective and elegant *Empty Glass* has a golden thread of hope woven throughout. In the liner notes is this piece of wisdom from Meher Baba: 'Desire for nothing except desirelessness, hope for nothing except to rise above all hopes, want nothing and you will have everything.'

Pete played guitar and synthesizer while recruiting Tony Butler (bassist for his brother Simon's latest band, On the Air) and four drummers, among them Kenney Jones. Recorded at London's Air Studios, the resulting clean, crisp sound drew high praise from *Musician* writer Vic Garbacini, who termed it: 'A near perfect blend of power, passion, and grace.'

Dedicated to his wife, the work contains a personal tribute, 'A Little Is Enough,' one of the few songs Townshend claims was 'truly inspired.' It dealt with coming off the road and his delicate readjustment to family life. 'She would always want a deeper, more sustained relationship than I,' remarks Townshend, 'but in the end I suppose we're lucky we love one another at all. Because love, by its very nature, is an infinite quality, an infinite emotion, just to experience that once in a lifetime is enough. Because a lot of people don't ever experience it.'

The swirling ballad 'I Am an Animal,' a Townshend favorite, offers a metaphor of climbing from animal to angel. 'It's a song about the evolution of the individual in a spiritual way, about all the different roles we go through in one lifetime.'

Townshend's generally good relationship with the print media took a decidedly bad turn with the acerbic 'Jools and Jim.' Here Pete took dead aim at Julie Burchill and Tony Parsons, vituperative writers for the *New Musical Express*, who'd compared Keith Moon to gutter bum Sid Vicious and said the world was better off without him. 'The only way I could get out the anger I felt was through writing a song.' Indeed Townshend held nothing back: 'Typewriter tappers/You're all just crappers/Everybody's human 'cept Jooles and Jim.'

A pair of songs, however, sparked immediate controversy. In the first, 'Rough Boys,' an aggressive, noisy rocker, which at the time Townshend dubbed 'an innocuous song,' he roams his old neighborhood recounting his youth, observing the kids in their leathers and wondering what he'd be like today.

'And I Moved' was originally written for Bette Midler, a request from her manager, as she liked Townshend's material. 'Make it a bit dirty, though,' he said, 'because that's the kind of thing she likes.' Pete penned the song, which he termed 'one of the purest pieces of schoolboy poetry I've ever written.'

But he didn't hear from Midler's manager for several months. 'I couldn't give that to her,' he complained to Pete. 'It's smutty.'

An aghast Townshend replied, 'But you asked for something dirty.'

'It's not dirty; it's *smutty*,' was the terse reply. And that was the end of that.

The pair of tunes spawned an onslaught of reaction from the gay community which congratulated Townshend for finally 'coming out of the closet.' In 'Rough Boys,' the line that sparked the controversy was: 'Come over here, I want to bite and kiss you.' Townshend explained that away by saying, 'It's about, "I can scare you! I can frighten you! I can hurt all you macho individuals simply by coming up and pretending to be gay!"'

The 'Midler' tune caused a stir, as well because Townshend chose to retain the female gender he'd originally written for Bette. Singing 'He laid me back just like an empty dress' was merely 'conveying the idea of surrender, of trust, not feelings of homosexuality,' he claimed.

However, in both cases Pete ultimately hedged, admitting, 'That's what I really meant, I think. It *could* have been what I meant, I don't know.' In effect, he was leaving ajar a door that would blast wide open ten years down the road.

Released in May 1980, *Empty Glass* was a unanimous critical and commercial triumph, becoming a top-ten hit driven by the fiery single, 'Let My Love Open the Door,' a bouncy, feel-good, spiritual ditty. Townshend noted this one could easily fit into a slot on Christian radio. 'Most of my songs are about Jesus. Most of my songs are about the idea that there is salvation and that there is a savior. But I won't directly mention his name in a song just to get some cheap play.'

One pleasant surprise for him was his singing. Before he started, he was apprehensive about his ability to carry an entire album. A subtle approach by producer Chris Thomas, though, put him at ease. 'Just keep singing,' he told Pete. 'I'll keep taping and we'll put one together.'

'I suddenly realized,' says Pete, 'he was saying that if I just kept singing, I would forget I was trying to sing and find my voice. What was strange was that when I found my voice, it was a little bit like Andy Williams!'

Another benefit of the project was that it freed him to write different sorts of songs. 'It didn't cost a lot in terms of me and the band. In a way it helped because it cleared my head and allowed me to realize that writing is not something you should do with any kind of hat on.'

For all the album's success, though, Townshend saw the rest of his life quickly unraveling. Having broken off from Karen, their life and mutual friends, he moved into a King's Road flat above a shoe shop. Making the dizzying rounds of London's trendiest clubs, he invariably made a drunken nuisance of himself. He also jumped on a merry-go-round of disposable girlfriends.

'I felt I was hurting other women I came across because I was such a pathetic mess,' he would later explain. 'I'd wake up in the morning, and there would be a beautiful twenty-five-year-old woman running around. And I would think, "What am I doing to this person? She should be out finding a young man."'

A further step in his downward spiral occurred when he was persuaded by the husband of a friend in New York to try cocaine. It happened at a party when Townshend observed the guests disappearing to the bathroom to snort their lines. 'I just thought this is ridiculous. I'm actually missing out because I don't use drugs. Thereafter, I made an absolutely positive decision to use drugs again.

'Having plenty of money I was able to supply myself and also about fifty other people who followed me around London.'

His real friends of course tried to warn him about these hangers-on. 'Pete, don't you see it's that sick bunch of assholes you hang around with that are screwing you up?'

'Hey, I sought them out, they didn't find me,' he would shoot back.

The coke began to seriously affect his work. During the Who's final Southern California shows in July 1980, he'd wander off into private jams at the end of numbers, leaving Daltrey standing bewildered while Jones and Entwistle scrambled to follow these bizarre impromptu, often extended solos.

On top of his brandy-cocaine cocktail Townshend, finding it increasingly difficult to make it through the tour, began to add an amphetamine chaser. Popping speed in large quantities turned him into an obnoxious backstage Foster Brooks, stumbling, spilling drinks, and blathering nonstop to anyone within hearing distance until early in the morning. Spewing this nonsense to fans who'd managed to get backstage so turned many of them off they immediately fled.

One unhappy episode brought it all home. On a flight from New York to London on board Concorde, Townshend was a one-man show of lunacy, lunging at stewardesses who passed, standing up in the aisle to make impromptu speeches ('We are sitting here traveling faster than a bullet in this supersonic rocket I paid for with my fuckin' taxes') before dipping into someone's meal, chewing on a wad of food, and then spitting it out at surrounding passengers.

The outrageous climax occurred when Townshend drew out a bag of cocaine, ripped it open, and proceeded to toss the contents at his nose, which cascaded in a shower of white dust all over him.

Following several weeks of this, a concerned Richard Barnes cornered his old mate in the dressing room one night and raged, 'God, you're pathetic! Do you realize what you're doing to yourself?' Townshend's eyes were a wasted glaze. He gnawed at the side of his mouth and mumbled how he was in control and knew what he was doing. 'I don't wanna be a bloody wimp,' he cried. 'It's all right for Keith. Why should he have all the fuckin' glory?'

Pete's desperate condition was manifested during one performance of 'Drowned,' off *Quadrophenia* in which Townshend's rambling solo was groggily punctuated with an ad-lib of the tell-tale words, 'I don't wanna die/I don't wanna die. I ain't scared of it/I just don't wanna die.'

The episode underscored the same deep-rooted matter-versus-spirit conflict he'd been battling for years, still woefully unresolved and growing increasingly more problematic. In his more lucid moments he would fess up: 'I'm very heavily into Meher Baba, but I also drink like a fish. I'm not the most honest person in the world. It's difficult, but I do at least know what's happening to me. I accept there is a larger reason for me being alive than just being a rock star.

'It's not just because I need something to hang on to that I believe in God. If all there was as a pinnacle of human achievement was what I've achieved then there's not enough . . . it's not pure enough.'

As 1981 rolled in, his troubles spilled over to the recording studio. When offered an early copy of the album, the Who's first for their new label, Warner Brothers, Pete refused, saying, 'I didn't like the mix, so why should I like the pressing?'

Both Townshend and Daltrey conceded there was something they couldn't really put their finger on, a chemistry that just wasn't there. Part of the blame was placed on Kenney Jones. On stage he was able to handle the established tunes well enough, but when it came to the challenge of creating sounds he was unable to chart any new territory as had Keith.

The album's critical failure was apparent within the title, *Face Dances*. It was supposedly a new band, a new era, a time to throw off the Who of old, but the album sounded more like David Bowie, or perhaps Phil Collins, than a ballsy rock 'n' roll band. On the whole, *Face Dances* offered a mishmash of musical styles and ideas. Trying to be true to his pledge of exploration, Townshend flung the band into a misguided rock, funk, pop, and jazz potpourri that sent any trace of Whoism off the rails. *Rolling Stone* reviewer Tom Carson wrote: 'The music alternates between an up-tempo rock swagger that sounds imposed on the material and quietly filigreed melodic passages the band seems ill at ease playing.'

The work's greatest failure uncovered a deep chasm between lyrics and music. Of 'Cache Cache,' possibly the album's worst track, Carson observed: 'Townshend tries to patch compromises into the writing itself providing Daltrey and the band their due with passages of hard-driving rock bombast while stuffing his own version of sweetness and light into the cracks.'

Pete offered his own, legitimate reason for the debacle. Working on both his solo albums and the Who in the middle of a hectic touring schedule, something was bound to suffer. 'I went and wrote four songs while everybody else was resting,' he says. 'When I played them nobody said anything, not a dicky bird . . . I just picked up the tape and walked out. I thought, "I'm not breaking my back for these cunts!"'

'He could be brilliant on his own, and I mean brilliant,' said Roger. 'But he couldn't do that if he had to keep writing for the Who as well. To be totally good on your own is a selfish thing, and you can't be selfish in a band. I regret we went on after we learned Pete signed a contract for a solo career. That way we would have freed him to do his thing. I think he would have gotten bored and started up the Who again.'

In retrospect, Townshend agreed that his latest experimentation did not suit the Who. 'It was really with the best of intentions because I wanted the band to have material that was equally as varied as I would on a solo album. . . . Having enjoyed it as a solo performer, I thought, "Well, fuck it, why can't the band do it?" And the band can't do it because they're so wrapped up in their own tradition.'

Interestingly, the album's resulting single, 'You Better You Bet,' was a prime slice of sizzling Who heritage, a rousing rocker with a crisp hook and plenty of bite. Still, it remained the lone vestige of a once brilliant legacy.

Another concern was that the original four-piece unit had now been scrapped for a wider scope of more musicians, which Daltrey fought.

Townshend ultimately declared *Face Dances* an ineffective record that simply didn't work, and he was frustrated because he couldn't figure out why. 'I was hoping I was going to pursue two careers at once, not realizing they're irrevocably knotted together. I hadn't quite realized how much of what I did as an individual would affect the Who and vice versa.'

As if this wasn't enough, the Who's British tour – their longest, from January into March – was marked by both personal and technical problems. John and Kenney's marriages were on the rocks, and the pair commiserated by all-night clubbing. The effects showed on stage, with John playing too loudly while Kenney was unusually stiff and tentative behind the skins.

As for Pete, his savage binges were beginning to spiral way out of control. 'I'd often wake up in the morning with a roomful of girls I'd never seen before, simply because I had been so drunk the night before.'

There were technical glitches as well. The Who's elaborate sound system was not adaptable to many of the smaller venues, which one night caused a monitor to explode. It also didn't help the band's morale when audiences rejected the new material incorporated into their set.

It all came to an embarrassing climax during the Who's appearances on February 4 and 5 at London's Rainbow Theatre. An already thoroughly drunk Townshend consumed a monstrous four bottles of brandy onstage. Recalling that night, Townshend said, 'Basically I'd decided to go out and not play. I was just going to talk until somebody stopped me by knocking me out. I went out and started to talk, and the band began to play without me. I don't really remember a thing about it except I'm surprised I didn't kill myself.'

It was a show rife with Pete's freewheeling, extended codas. Lost in an anesthetized bliss, Townshend thought he was playing masterfully. But in fact, toward the end of the set, an enraged Daltrey slammed not one but two microphones down, nearly having it out with the guitarist right there and then. As he stormed off, Jones and Entwistle followed, refusing to do an encore. A dithering Pete remained, attempting to strike up a conversation with the audience, who responded with merciless heckling.

While the media played up the fireworks, including an alleged backstage row between Townshend and Daltrey, Pete insisted the voices raised were in passion, not violence. 'Far from kicking my head in,' he said at the time, 'Roger was worried I was killing myself. Roger's always said over the last year or so when I was going through a lot of shit . . ., "Listen, stop the band if it'll keep you alive. You're the important one to me." I think what I was doing at the Rainbow was testing that.'

At the end of the British leg, the rest of the tour was canceled. Townshend simply couldn't continue, and Roger, for one, was devastated. 'It ended it all for me. I was hurt. I thought we were the best rock band in the world till then. I thought we could change the world. What Pete did proved we couldn't.

'Ever since Keith died we were always trying to recreate what we'd been with him. So in that area it was a total failure. We didn't do anything new.'

Townshend agreed. 'The Who were sleepwalking along the edge of a cliff. The band had become a celebration of itself and was slowly grinding to a halt. But no one would make a decision to call it a day.'

Coming off the road, his very life crumbling, Pete was dealt another shattering blow: on April 7, 1981, Kit Lambert fell to his death down a narrow stairway at his mother's home. Rumor had it the former Who manager, who succumbed to a fatal brain haemorrhage, might have already been woozy from a beating he incurred at a gay nightclub earlier in the evening.

For the badly reeling Townshend the loss of his early mentor was a crushing blow. Kit, like Pete Meaden before him, and poor Moonie, gambled fate, overloading his system with drugs, money, success, and lost it all. At the end, Lambert lost his fame, fortune, his beloved palazzo in Venice, and was reduced to living with his mother at the age of forty-five.

Townshend remembered, 'He once turned to me in his declining years and said: "Pete, have I screwed you up?" And I said, "No, of course you haven't, Kit. You've helped me."'

His old friend's death increased the dissolution that had started with Keith Moon's death. 'I had even more license. . . . I felt I could get away with more.'

The aging rocker became part of the new club scene. He sported several bizarre haircuts, donned makeup. He even joined the New Romantics, whose primary hangout was the Club for Heroes run by Steve Strange. 'I'm really very weak when it comes to trends. I adore them and always get very drawn into them. I see myself wandering around looking for the latest thing.'

Pete's alcohol intake had reached the point that he literally couldn't stand being sober. His solution was to add to his vices. 'I just took anything I could lay my hands on as a way of passing the time, because I hated the sensation of *not* being drunk.' His trove of chemicals included an interesting combo, as reported by Al Beard, reception manager of the Rum Runner in Birmingham. Townshend hung out in the kitchen with some of the boys from a famous rock group of the day, who were steadily snorting several generous white lines. But, according to Beard, Pete had his ample nose in something else. 'Townshend was more interested in sniffing from a bottle. At first I thought he had a cold and was breathing in something to clear his nose. But what he had was amyl nitrate, which makes you feel very high and sexy. Townshend was passing the bottle to anyone who wanted it. Then he got out some cannabis and rolled a really strong joint.'

Pete's drugs and drink were causing increasingly bizarre behavior. One night after drinking with Mick Jagger and Charlie Watts in New York, Townshend zonked out in the cloakroom of Jagger's apartment. Another time at a club Pete disappeared, and his chauffeur, Paul Bonnick, after searching around, found the guitarist passed out high atop a heap of bricks and rubble. Another time, in Austria, he climbed into the bear pit at the local zoo (fortunately, it was empty) and was similarly discovered fast asleep the next morning. Townshend referred to both incidents in 'Cache Cache': 'Did you ever sleep in a bear pit/With apple cores and mice along/Did you ever lay on ice and grit/Or search for a place where the wind was gone.'

By mid-1981 Pete experienced a shock when he sought to purchase a £130,000 mixing board for his Boathouse studio. He was in debt for a staggering £1 million. It was the classic case of mismanagement, too many staff, and far too generous contracts to various authors.

A visit to the National Westminster Bank, at which he'd had an account since he was sixteen, was demoralizing. Townshend had gone from pampered star to just another rock 'n' roll bum. They were after his house, his recording contract, the lot. Pete admits he panicked. 'I had to go to Karen and say, "Can we raise money on the house? Can you sign this piece of paper which allows the bank to do this and that? Can we sell our country home?"'

Karen, though, used the leverage wisely. 'Before I sign this bit of paper maybe we could talk about us.'

For the time being, that was put on hold. Townshend seriously considered bankruptcy and going off to Paris in retirement. 'But in the end I thought, "No, I'll beat the bastards at their own game. I'll come back from the dead and make some money."'

He hired a tenacious accountant who pared down his employees by nearly half and sold off Magic Bus, his book-publishing firm, his Soho studio, and his PA hire company. 'That really hurt my pride. I don't like failing.' In the end Townshend managed to evade financial collapse, but just barely.

His money woes only fueled his excesses, leading to the first of two near fatal experiences. In early September Townshend was out for a night on the town at the Club for Heroes, drinking with Paul Weller and Steve Strange. While in the men's room someone gave him 'some terrible drug.' Unbeknownst to him, it turned out to be heroin. 'And I just went into a steep OD immediately.'

Believing that here was just another bloke who couldn't hold his liquor, the club's seven-foot bouncer slapped Pete over his shoulder and deposited him in his waiting car. Driver Bonnick, though, took one look at his boss and realized something was terribly wrong. Townshend's lips were blue, and he had a galloping, barely discernible pulse.

Racing to the nearest hospital, Bonnick screeched to a halt outside shouting, 'I've got somebody here; I think he's dying!'

It was no understatement. Townshend had stopped breathing; he was code blue. As he was rushed inside, a nurse began to pound on his chest. He was immediately connected to a life-support system.

Pete remembered he was wearing a suit 'in which every pocket had some weird drug. The woman who revived me studied with Meg Patterson. She said, "This guy lying in front of me helped finance the research at the Marie Curie Foundation?" For her it was a terrible irony I should turn up in front of her blue.'

'I think I actually drank so much brandy I gave myself alcohol poisoning. I just went black.'

Although badly shaken by the incident, Townshend nonetheless seemed determined to travel the road to self-destruction, even admitting to considerations of suicide.

During sessions for his second solo album, producer Chris Thomas observed that the heavy cocaine use was destroying his voice. After Townshend fell asleep over the recording console, Thomas ordered 'Get out of here, Pete, and come back when your head is in this.'

Townshend took the advice and commenced what would be a three-month leave of absence. He retreated to his cabin on the Thames, spending his time gardening, writing, even rowing, his doctor's tonic of 'violent exercise.' Within three weeks he disciplined himself enough to cut out his drug use and also significantly pare down the alcohol. But he soon drifted back to the reckless London lifestyle, as Richard Barnes put it, 'coked up to the eyeballs, twitching, shaking, and surrounded by the same old sycophants from the chic "living dead" of clubland.'

He then took his indulgences to New York, by this point only alive by the skin of his teeth. He'd hooked up with someone who was free-basing cocaine and was instantly reeled in, puffing on a waterpipe, unaware it had been laced with heroin. 'Someone would be freebasing, and you'd see them puff in a bit of burning junk through a straw. And that's it! A lot of people don't realize you are going to get addicted to heroin by smoking it. If you snort it, you don't get addicted instantly, but if you smoke it you do. It's not as dramatic as sitting at a party and drawing out a hypodermic needle and banging it in your arm, but it's the same thing.

'What was incredible to me was to watch the pushers come in and say I've got some nice stuff here, but it's not good enough for snorting, it's really for smoking.' And that was it. At least fifty people I know got addicted in the space of six months.'

Including Townshend. He quickly concluded that cocaine was nothing compared to smack. He related that all he felt from snorting a few lines was 'fucking awful,' alleging he could get a bigger kick ODing on aspirin. With heroin, 'Fuckin' hell! This works! This is a real drug.

'From the moment I touched smack, I felt as if I'd joined forces with the devil. I went from being unbeatably lucky to becoming a powerful foe, my own worst enemy. I had opted for self-destruction.'

Daria Schouvaloff, Kit Lambert's onetime business manager, pinpointed it to Kit's death. 'When Kit died, Pete went on a terrible heroin jag. He lacked any real confidence. A hundred people telling you you are wonderful is not the same as hearing it from the one person you really want to hear it from.'

By late October he'd gotten to the point where he was knocking off a drink in the morning just to feel normal. And when that didn't work he discovered it was making him feel terribly sick. 'In a brief period of panic,' he recalls, 'I tried just about everything in the world to feel normal again. And none of them worked. Nothing.'

At this point Pete packed up his parents plus an 'unbelievable woman' he called his 'temporary companion' to collaborate with Elton John in Paris on his latest album. Between five and seven in the morning he would raid the hotel's minibar and imbibe the entire contents: wine, brandy, beer, the lot. 'I don't think I have ever, ever been quite that bad, and yet I didn't feel any remorse about what I was doing. I didn't know that what I was doing was particularly exceptional.'

Furthermore, he made a fool of himself while dining at the very posh Parisian Hôtel Georges V. Downing a bottle of champagne, Pete promptly threw it all up into the ice bucket in full view of the establishment's upper-crust patrons.

Then, on Halloween night, following a flight back to London, he made a beeline for the nearest pub. Guzzling down five pints, Townshend felt wretchedly ill and began to suffer the D.T.s. Back at his country place, he consumed yet another two bottles of brandy, but the terrifying shakes continued. In a panic he warned his girlfriend, 'Get out of here. Abandon me. Just go back wherever you came from.'

'I was in a condition like a heroin addict, I needed so much alcohol to balance out the bad reaction, it would kill me if I drank it all.'

He phoned his physician, who advised him, 'Get out and row for three hours.'

'Are you crazy? I can't afford to spend three hours in a boat every day.'

'If you don't do it, you're going to die,' he told him gravely. 'Either that or don't drink.'

Faced with the alternative of rowing every day for three hours for the privilege of drinking his daily bottle of Rémy Martin, he decided to stop. In November he spent five days at a dry-out clinic, aided by hypnotherapy. As it happened, his mother had come to Oxfordshire to spend a few weeks (fresh from her own successful rehab program). Her presence provided Townshend with a new will to succeed. Not only would he show solidarity by quitting himself, but also he couldn't succumb to the genetic excuse, 'Oh, I'm a drunk because everybody in my family is a drunk.' Most significant, Betty served as his constant reality check. 'She was the person who made me think about starting to treat myself as an alcoholic.'

Townshend though did stop drinking, and another trip to Gotham found him freebasing coke and smoking heroin, in substantial quantities. He'd simply replaced one addiction with another. After returning to London after this spree, Pete returned to his doctor, who determined that his blood sugar was off the scales and prescribed a tranquillizer, Ativan, to subdue the alcohol craving. The parallels to Keith were now growing dangerously close.

Still out of control, Townshend began consuming the full prescription all at once, popping eight to ten of the tablets in one day. In addition, he managed to procure a supplemental supply from a dealer. On top of that he was still freebasing and smoking heroin in secret.

'Not living at home was very, very bad for me. I do find a family environment really valuable. Its security and stability is something which needs to be assured. So I was suffering badly from loneliness; I had an acute alcohol problem, a drug problem, and I was totally and completely broke with no immediate prospects. I just let go of a lot of the fundamental principles under pressure and lost the will to fight back.'

His downward spiral reached its nadir when he was given a heroin prescription simply to get off the far more dangerous Ativan. At Christmas Townshend visited his parents to declare his newfound sobriety. But the announcement backfired. Cliff Townshend looked hard at his son, haggard and thin, the ravages of narcotics edged in his face. 'You're on something, and it's a damn sight worse, in my opinion.' With that Cliff strode out of the room. 'He was the only person who seemed to know something was fatally wrong,' Pete remembers.

His father's brutal frankness gave him the courage to finally come clean with Karen. He was in for another surprise, this time a pleasant one. 'Why don't you come home for Christmas?' she asked.

'Do you mean it?' an elated Pete replied. 'Listen, I have to tell you I'm using smack at the moment. . . . Maybe I should come home for dinner and then go away.'

'Do you intend to get yourself sorted out?'

'Of course I do. Soon.'

'In that case, why don't you come and live here? Let's work out our problems.'

That, claims Townshend, triggered his decision to turn his life around. His wife, this beautiful, intelligent, spiritual, refined creature, was willing to accept him yet again. 'I was really in the abyss,' he says. 'In the end I reduced myself to a gibbering heap of rubble and then woke up in some venue [having] injected myself with whatever was available. I was literally just barely breathing, covered in blood, warts, slime, phlegm, and vomit.

'I was still surrounded by people who wanted to get close to me though. People did care about me, people did come to my rescue.'

The decision, he adds, was not the dramatic bottoming out complex of the typical addict. Rather, he compared it to walking out of a garden. 'And the garden was very rich, abundant and lush, but it had a wall around it. And you couldn't appear to escape.'

A lifeline was finally tossed by Margaret Patterson, the same doctor who had cured Eric Clapton of his habit. She urged Townshend to fly immediately to California, where she was now practicing. She started him on a month-long detox program under her highly innovative NET neuroelectric acupuncture therapy. Called the 'black box' cure, the technique removes addictive cravings within ten days with none of the usual nightmarish symptoms. Patterson claims a phenomenal 98 percent cure rate, although she admits about a fifth of the individuals relapse into addiction.

The system consists of a small black box resembling a tape recorder with attached wires that clip onto a patient's ears. Through the box a mild electric current is sent to stimulate and, in effect, reeducate the brain to produce natural endorphins, the body's own intoxicants.

Patterson says Townshend was devastated when he first came to her. 'He was so badly into drugs. He looked as if he had been in a concentration camp, but within a week he was totally changed.'

Like the final page of a Hollywood script, on the last day of his month-long program Townshend took a walk down the beach and came upon a small bottle washed up on shore. He picked it up and peered inside to its white powdery contents. Ferreting out a sample with his index finger, he brought it to his lips, confirming it was cocaine. With a wry grin he tossed it out to sea once more. On this, his day of reckoning, he knew he had kicked it for good.

'If I hadn't become a junkie,' Townshend stated in 1984, 'I would not have gone to Meg Patterson, and if I hadn't done that I would be dead. I would have crashed my car, gone back to alcohol combined with tranquillizers, all the standard ingredients of the drug alcohol cocktail story.'

Townshend might have successfully kicked his habit physically, but emotionally there was still much work to be done. Two years of intense psychotherapy followed. What he unlocked was intense anger at both the music industry and himself 'for not understanding that Keith's whole thing – "I am a crazy, wacky, wild rock star and I can do anything" – was, as they say, a cry for help, and he never got it. What he actually got was his disease fed and fed and fed until he finally died.

Rock 'n' roll is one of those professions that accommodates insanity.

'I'm talking about an industry that feeds on the frustration, the insecurity and desolation of the young. They don't care whether the stuff they sell is wholesome, whether it's true, helpful, or whether it has a function. All they care is if it sells. And there's no mechanism to help artists.

'I used to look at Keith and think, "This guy is gonna die," and I was afraid for him. And I still struggle with, as I think Roger does, our complicity in that. It was *useful* for us to have this crazy man in the band. It got us publicity.'

Pete also uncovered his inability to accept his own star status. 'It was my band, my responsibility. Roger is a very important figurehead in the Who, but he can't go on without me. I can go on without him. I could go out and do the Who without the Who. I realized I had become a megalomaniac, and I didn't like myself. I just wanted to be insignificant.'

By the late seventies Pete was no better, he claims melodramatically, than Manuel Noriega, Eva Peron, or even Adolf Hitler, delivering lip service to the masses from their own ivory towers. 'I'd created this new hierarchy of rock as something so powerful and important while at the same time I wasn't producing anything worthwhile. I suddenly realized, "Oh, God, you can't handle it!" This was my inheritance and I hated it, hated myself.'

He saw his band mates and friends as unwitting accomplices in his desperate escape from both the band and rock itself. 'The only way I could face work was by destroying myself. I didn't have the guts to stand up and say, "This is a bunch of shit. I've got to go." I didn't have the guts to do it the way Moon did it, to take a handful of elephant tranquillizers. I didn't have the guts to put a gun to my head. I had to make other people do it. I had to make other people responsible. I wasn't bent on self-destruction, but on having somebody else do the dirty work. That's what I think is so incredibly evil.'

At the core of it all was an old, still festering wound revisited: his belief in his own profound unattractiveness. His childhood illusion about physical beauty was still his biggest obstacle to overcome. 'It was one that was almost Freudian in character because it was very much looked in with the way I idealized my mother,' he candidly revealed. 'I've also come to sympathize with people who are born

beautiful and must struggle to achieve a sense of inner beauty . . .
I am truly able to say with my hand on my heart that I am now
able to look at beautiful women without being confused about their
value. That really makes me happy because my wife happens to be
beautiful, and I've finally realized that's just a lucky break for her.
What's lucky for me is that I'm now able to look past that and see
the great person she is.'

Even so, Pete had made a certain peace about his period of
infidelity. No longer did he think women were solely attracted
to him because he was a big-time rock star. 'These people who
I used to think were avaricious groupies,' he concluded, 'all they
were trying to do was make me happy . . . the kind of women who
see a wreck of a man and just say, "Oh, God, that poor guy, he
needs me."'

Pete also discovered another destructive aspect of his character:
propensity to sabotage his own success. Outside of the doomed
Lifehouse he'd never really experienced failure, nor had he ever
really had to struggle for achievement. Everything he set his sights
on he gained.

The problem, he said, was a dangerous feeling of omnipotence,
putting him in the category of a demigod. 'So what you start to do
is undermine that,' he explains. 'You say, "Let's see what happens
when you cut your arms and legs off. Let's see how effective you
are when you've got no brain."'

In that potentially volatile mindset Townshend followed the
pattern of Moonie, Lambert, and Meaden, filling up their space,
following his nose, he said, to wherever it led him. 'Even if that
was death.'

But still, Pete was always convinced of a higher power watching
over him and of the safety net below. 'In the depths of my depression, when I didn't know what the future held, one thing I was
absolutely one hundred percent sure of was that God wasn't going
to let me die. There was a tremendous prodigality to the feeling of
seeing how far I could go and still get back in the fold.'

Drugs, of course, were just the fallout of his inability to deal with
his real problem, alcoholism. It had began during those childhood
days on the road with Cliff and Betty, when handing musicians
beer from the crates made a gawky eight-year-old boy feel that he
belonged. Drinking became linked with the machismo of the Who
and a vehicle to smother shyness. But it insidiously escalated as

a crutch to bolster his self-image after his marital implosion and near bankruptcy.

Townshend recalls first being seriously confronted with his problem during the recording of *Who Are You*. He had tried to point Moon in the direction of many counselors, several belonging to AA. One of these approached Townshend in the studio and said, 'Keith's not really an alcoholic, you know. But you are. I could help you.'

He wasn't even aware he was putting away half a bottle of vodka after each session. It took engineer Glyn Johns to point it out to him.

Admitting he was an alcoholic was, of course, vital. Even just one drink would screw him up for months, the time it would take for the liquor to make him sick again. 'I'm now sober for life,' he proclaimed in 1982. 'I'm never going to drink again.'

Therapy also revealed why he had stuck with the Who. He needed it more than he'd ever realized. Within his fragmented personality, prone to free-falling excesses, the band provided him with an all-important structure. 'The Who [gave] me a platform and a set of restrictions, constraints, and limitations that are important,' he has said.

As had become his pattern whenever he came through a major crisis, Townshend bounced back filled with big ideas. He was ready to record again, and gathered the band together to see what they wanted him to write about. He was met by blank stares. The only topics they could agree on were the global concerns of nuclear war, hunger, and improved conditions for future generations.

His excitement undimmed, he proclaimed, 'The album the Who are working on is probably the most self-conscious and dangerous record we've ever set out on. Perhaps this one will open up a new door.' Once the work was released in August 1982, however, Townshend was saying just the opposite: 'We made it very unself-consciously. We were trying to get ourselves back into the old frame of mind.'

It's Hard was certainly an improvement over *Face Dances*, but it was also a fairly spotty work. For its supposed universal themes – nuclear holocaust explored on 'I've Known No War,' the destitute addressed on 'Cooks County,' shady politics on 'Eminence Front,' the central message seems to be that of growing up and the difficulty of casting off the past.

There are certainly some fine tracks. 'Athena,' the logical choice for a single, with its percolating rhythm guitar, performed reasonably well in the charts. 'Why Did I Fall for That' is an infectious rocker showcasing some nice guitar work backed by Rabbit's ever capable keyboards. And the album's anchor, 'Eminence Front,' has a jazz funk beat that harks back to the measured textured style of *Quadrophenia*. Yet overall the album was uneven once again.

Unfortunately, *It's Hard* sold poorly and Dave Marsh called it a failure. 'I think they're both equally inept; equally lifeless. They equally reflect the fact that the people who were making them didn't particularly want to be making a record together.'

Despite the project's failure, Daltrey insisted, 'When Pete does his thing for himself, it's not the same as when he writes for the band. Whatever he does on his own is not as strong as his writing for the Who.'

Meanwhile, an energized Townshend, still in the bloom of his drug-free honeymoon, was once again ready to hit the road. In mid-1982, during a meeting at Curbishley's home, Daltrey made a startling announcement: 'I don't want to tour anymore. I want to end the group in the right way, on top.'

In part, Daltrey's reaction was fueled by guilt, recalling how he badgered Pete into going on the road back in 1978. 'And after three tours of America he was a bloody junkie. I felt responsible for that . . . I mean, I think the world of that guy. I think enough of him to stop the Who.'

Townshend, however, convinced him otherwise. At this point he concocted an eighteen-month plan: one final tour, continue recording, maybe even add the odd concert here and there. After that, an open book. 'I don't intend to get off the road. . . . From my point of view I'm not prepared to just carry on doing albums. If the touring isn't there, then I'd rather go do my own thing which involves touring as well.'

The Who Farewell Tour, a four-month, forty-city trek of sold-out stadiums, began on September 22 and ended in Toronto December 17. Also, pay per view on December 16 grossed $40 million.

The supporting cast were unhappy, though. 'There was so much pressure the last time,' Kenney Jones admitted. 'Roger kept trying to explain my presence, but it always came out wrong.'

'Pete was going through his problems. He stopped talking about our generation and was trying to speak for a younger generation, which is a very dangerous game,' says Roger. 'When that happened we started to be about something else . . . It's a question of belief. I used to believe in this band in a way I don't now.'

Although reviews were generally positive, the old Who's spontaneity and passion were sorely missing. As Mikal Gilmore wrote in the *Los Angeles Herald Journal*, 'There was something in the spectacle of the event . . . that served to undermine its power. . . . Indeed, the guiding purpose of this tour seems not to be the defining of an audience so much as merely the possessing of one.'

As the tour wore on, Townshend's early upbeat chatter to the media about their upcoming album eroded into a fog of fatigue and bitterness. 'We seemed to be facing a fait accompli,' he said. 'We were a show business band. That's what we had become. We were out there to deliver. I think we forgot the essential premise of artistic entertainment, and this is that the people on the stage must genuinely be getting something from what they're doing as well.'

Nonetheless, there had been nights of real brilliance, when the magic seemed as powerful as ever. The overwhelmingly positive response by throngs of fans attested to the band's amazing endurance as a performing dynamo. Moreover, their single 'Athena' was doing reasonably well in the charts.

Daltrey, reflecting on all this, saw a new way to go. 'We've never, ever thought of quitting, not after Cincinnati, never. And I have the feeling we're only beginning to get to it. . . . Without having to go on the road we have so many more options.

We can experiment more, come up with a lot of ideas and throw 'em up against the wall to see what sticks. We can make an album with a 200-piece orchestra or vacuum cleaners. We could even do shows this way. We just wouldn't have to tour with them. . . . That doesn't mean an end to the Who. As long as Pete and John and I are involved together in something, there'll be the Who. It's as simple as that.'

But it wasn't that simple. Nothing about Pete Townshend or the Who was ever simple. Townshend was already dropping hints to the press regarding the band's 'final waltz.' At the tour's end, he was all but tolling the Who's death knell. 'They may not be as ready to make that radical change in their life, but that's tough. I've come too close to death, to really dying, to fool around anymore. I want control of my life, and I'm not in control of it in this band.'

Maybe Roger Daltrey wasn't listening. Or maybe he believed

the ever quixotic Townshend would change his mind, like always. This time, however, he was in for a shock. Pete Townshend was about to finally yank the rug out from under him for all time.

8

One-Man Band:
Townshend Alone

The Who is a bloody wild animal which has to be fed chunks of raw meat and Southern Comfort. It can't feed on anything less.

– Pete Townshend

Townshend's second solo effort demonstrated once and for all just how far he had distanced himself from the Who. Entitled *All the Best Cowboys Have Chinese Eyes*, the tightly knit, highly inventive album exhibited an artist no longer pigeonholed by his power-chord identity with the Who.

Pete was now a complete songwriter and vocalist, shifting styles at will from one highly original composition to the next. As *Empty Glass* was suffused with a kind of left-handed optimism, *Chinese Eyes*, written during one of his worst periods, spoke of the artist's pain, disillusionment, hopelessness, and brutal determination to survive.

Dedicating the album to Meg Patterson and all 'teenagers in love' – a reference to his reborn relationship with Karen – Townshend took a decidedly different approach from his last effort. '[I'll always remember] the ruthlessness I had to deal with from the Who and everything around me in order to get it made. It's actually a recognition of a set of principles I've debated over the past ten years: the importance of family, my role with my peers, the band and the importance of my freedom of expression. . . .

'I had this image,' he says, 'of the average American hero, somebody like Clint Eastwood or John Wayne. Somebody with eyes like slits who was basically capable of anything. Any kind of murderous act to get what was required, let's say, his people to safety. To those people he's a hero, a knight in shining armor, forget that he cut off fifty people's heads to get them home safely.'

On a personal level, Townshend labeled the album 'a study of the abuse of my position, power, and the inevitable damaging effects of money and decadence. . . . People spend most of their time looking for evil and identifying evil *outside* themselves. But the *potential* for evil is inside you.'

To make his point, in the liner notes Pete included a short story about the rise of Hollywood, which spawned 'dilettante pretenders' worshiped by the masses, a decadent lifestyle later adopted by rock's landed gentry. He then ends with a poem: 'I looked at the heroes/And the junkies in the billiard hall/All the best cowboys have Chinese eyes.'

Musician magazine ran this review: 'With its tangled imagery of mud, streams and rivers, [it] documents the painful, but necessary struggle to separate the fine from the coarse and forms a therapeutic chronicle of Townshend's recent dark night.'

What is generally acknowledged as the album's finest track, 'Slit Skirts,' was written at the depth of such pathos and resignation that Townshend claimed he didn't care if anyone ever heard it. It speaks eloquently about aging and a longing for the perennial romance of youth. 'Jeannie never wears those slit skirts/I don't ever wear no ripped shirts/Can't pretend that growing older never hurts.'

Being estranged from Karen around this time Townshend conceded, 'I was able to put a high value on what I *could* have had: a life where we grow old together and squabble, fight and collide. That's better than living in two different apartments on opposite sides of the planet. Which is what I was doing at the time. I was actually trying to celebrate that we *are* a couple of old farts, fair enough, but at least we're together. And when I wrote it, of course, we *weren't* together. So I was really able to see that it was important.'

The companion piece was the album's urgent opener, 'Stop Hurting People,' an open letter to Karen for reconciliation written over the turbulent summer of 1981. He apparently scribbled the words on a piece of paper in a moment of despair and only afterward realized it was actually a prayer. 'May I be matched with you again/I know the match is bad/But God help me/Without your match there is no flame.'

Lyrically Townshend took a break from his usual complex, multilayered phrasing for a more straightforward approach. 'One thing I was definitely trying to do was not worry about words being revered,' he recalled in 1986. 'At that time I remember thinking words were very, very cheap, and I really should be able to use them in whatever form I wanted. A lot of the thing was actually quite naive and simple like school poems. And a lot of it is actually quite blunt.'

This streamlined, literal approach was showcased in a trio of wonderful songs: 'Exquisitely Bored,' ostensibly about the nihilistic lifestyle of Southern California, but also strongly connected to the overall futility and shallowness of the material world itself; 'Stardom in Acton,' a concentrated, appealing 'be careful what you wish for' testament; and 'Communication,' all about how not to. In his clever, rat-a-tat-tat delivery, Townshend breaks up the syllables of the word communication and then spits them out. His intention was to demonstrate how people often only pretend to communicate.

Water, that eternal carrier of both spiritual gnosis and libido, comes flooding forth on the album's most brilliant gem, the sublime and soaring 'Sea Refuses No River.' Very much in the vein of 'Love Reign o'er Me' and 'Love Is Coming Down,' this is one of Townshend's finest ever. The theme operates on many planes, the highest being the spiritual realm of selfless love, unconditional acceptance, and ultimate forgiveness. In Townshend's emotional rendition, a deep trust worthy of humility shines through: 'The sea refuses no river/Whether starving or ill/Or strung on some pill/The river is where I am.'

According to its composer, the title had nothing to do with his love of the ocean, or indeed the elusive ocean of love, but rather the Townshend family motto. One day Pete's older daughter, Emma, looked it up in the book of Proverbs. 'Which I loved,' exudes Pete. 'It's what this family is all about, "The sea refuses no river." I got very involved with the idea and turned it into a song.'

Townshend also pointed out the tune's Bruce Springsteen feel was produced by the clever use of a glockenspiel, which the Boss frequently uses, most notably on 'Born to Run.'

The solo triumph signaled yet another step in Townshend's inevitable drift from the Who. As 1983 unfolded, he was experiencing significant problems writing for them. He spent ten months composing eighty songs, none, to his mind anyway, at all right for the Who.

'It's not for you to decide,' roared an ever indignant Daltrey. 'We might be able to make it happen.'

But still Pete simply didn't *want* to make it happen. Calling the group 'a band of middle-aged misfits,' he no longer wanted to be a party to what he labeled 'the perverted romanticism and posturing of rock; a fire that needs constant fuel . . . the ritual of sacrifice.'

By the summer of 1983 Townshend was freely telling the papers the Who were finished. By the reaction of the others – still talking publicly of future tours – something was terribly amiss. They didn't seem to be getting the message.

On December 16 the *Sun* carried his official statement. 'I will not be making any more records with the Who. It's already been stated that our tour of America in 1982 was our last. And I can now add that I will not perform live again anywhere in the world with the Who. In the first three months of this year I wrote songs for the next contracted Who album, and I realized after only a short time they weren't suitable for the Who. In March I informed the other members of the band and our manager that I was in difficulty. Several ideas were thrown around, but none helped. Therefore, in May I met with the band again to tell them I had decided to quit, leaving the Who with the ball in their court.

'I did nothing more until September, when I felt that out of courtesy I should explain my problem to the chairman of Warner Brothers USA, Mo Ostin. He was sympathetic and made several suggestions, none of which helped. On December 7 we received news of a Warner Brothers termination of contract. I feel badly that I cannot honor our commitment to Warner, and that many of our fans both old and new will be upset after being exposed to rumors that we were recording all this year. The fact is, we didn't even book studio time. My solo deal with ATCO will continue, and I hope to record an album next year. I wish Roger, John, and Kenney the best of luck with their future work and thank them for their patience.'

Shock and acrimony immediately whipped through the band. 'It was a wonderful Christmas present,' said Daltrey sarcastically. 'I don't know now whether the Who will ever work again. You can only take so much of being treated like a turd. It upset us the way he did it. I think he made a very big mistake. I can understand he is probably going through a period where he can't write, but that's not the point. The group may need for him *not* to write the next album. Maybe we need to sit in a room with each other and all write the next album. But he wouldn't do that; he wouldn't want to play with us. And that's the bit that upsets me and again, that's fine. He made the bed, he'll have to lie in it now.'

One could hardly blame Daltrey for his bitterness. Townshend's constant oscillating about the future of the band always kept him off balance. Even Pete admitted before the farewell tour, 'I really lammed into Roger, "You know we should think seriously before we make any rash moves." I also told him I didn't feel I could write for the band if it was just gonna go into a recording studio. I felt we *had* to perform *live*. I need that feedback as a writer.'

All this from the guitarist who'd vehemently resisted going on the road for some eight years, stating that he no longer *needed* to perform. One has to wonder if money may not have been a factor in his final decision. A seven-figure payoff had to sound pretty tempting to someone trying to recover from a million-dollar debt.

Though it wasn't a four-way, democratic decision, Pete declaring his abdication to the press was galling, especially to Daltrey, the group's founding member. Like it or not, Townshend was, in effect, saying *he* was the Who. As always Pete demanded, and got, the final word. Ironically, at the time of the breakup Daltrey was ready to release a solo work entitled *Parting Should Be Painless*.

The taciturn John Entwistle was perhaps the most profoundly affected, however, 'I was upset,' he commented, intense emotions smoldering beneath his laid-back tone. 'A third of the Who sound was me!'

Pete, of course, realized his old friend would mourn the Who more than anyone. 'He's losing a vehicle for his talent and passion he knows he'll never be able to find anywhere else.'

Afterward Townshend did express concern about emerging from

the fiasco a Judas figure. Despite the fallout, however, Pete termed the breakup 'the rightest decision of my life.' He would admit some seven years later, 'I felt dirtied, humiliated, locked in. We could have toured the world endlessly, stadium after stadium. We were really on a high, but it was all empty.'

Only through intense therapy was Pete able to work through the pain he described as like 'going through a divorce.' 'I was bitter during the last five years because I felt I couldn't get out. It seems very strange in retrospect because I now realize I could've gotten out any time. Why didn't I do it earlier? Instead of getting out, I became consumed by bitterness. I blamed record companies and even became angry at the fans. . . . People who are consumed by bitterness are trying to avoid acceptance of their own frailty by blaming others and the circumstances around them.'

In the meantime, Pete forged ahead on his own. In March 1983 Townshend celebrated his newly won independence with the release of *Scoop*, a twenty-five-track collection of demos from 1966 to 1982. Recorded at a variety of venues from home studios to friends' houses and professional facilities, from two mono Vortexion machines to the twenty-four-track sophistication of George Martin's deluxe Air Studios, the set includes both instrumental and vocals sprinkled with intense experimentation.

In the liner notes Pete writes, 'It emerges as being a fine example of how home recording produces moods, music, innocence, and naivety that could be arrived at in no other way. Music that was never intended to be heard by a wide audience. Away from sophisticated studio techniques and repeated soul-destroying takes, the real joy I get from playing comes through, and that joy is something I want to share.'

For devoted Townshend fans here was the ultimate treat. Unearthed was an intimate treasure of raw, unused material from *Lifehouse* and *Quadrophenia*, as well as songs targeted for his various solo albums. Now Townshend devotees could compare for themselves the demos to the finished product: 'Magic Bus,' 'Behind Blue Eyes,' and 'Squeezebox,' the latter recorded the very day Pete took up the accordion. Despite the often crude recording equipment, these musical first drafts match up admirably to the finished products, and sometimes even exceed them.

Of special interest is the startling vocal contrast between Townshend and Daltrey. A prime example is 'Behind Blue Eyes,' in which Pete's delicate melancholy turns the initially sympathetic lead character into the more enigmatic, shadowy figure he intended all along.

There are other revelations as well. A song called 'Popular,' a last-minute contribution to *It's Hard*, got such a lukewarm reception from the band that Townshend changed the chorus, which later became the album's title track. Another frenetic number, 'Dirty Water,' was recorded with Pete lying on his back on the studio floor. A Who reject, the inane 'Zelda,' ostensibly about Townshend's young niece, was so forgettable, even he had no idea what it was about.

Tasty too was *Scoop*'s rendition of 'Cache Cache.' The version on *Face Dances* was scrambled and dizzying, but here it is slowed down and more expressively delivered, resulting in a vastly improved, entirely different song. It also highlights how Townshend's more personal writing was often ill-advised for Daltrey's fire-and-ice interpretation.

Townshend would follow this up with *Another Scoop* in 1987. The double-disc compilation provided more of the same, highlighted by two songs, 'Cat Snatch' and 'Ask Yourself,' designated for the final aborted Who album he had intended to call *Siege*. 'It was rooted in the idea that each of us is a soul in siege,' Pete has recalled. '[It] was based musically on a series of five black note repetitions.'

In July 1983, Townshend showed yet another aspect of his multifaceted creativity. He stunned the music world by joining the publishing firm of Faber and Faber, a sixty-year-old institution in London's quietly regal Queen's Square, whose authors included Ezra Pound, W. H. Auden, and William Golding. Poet T. S. Eliot had worked there for thirty years as an editor.

The offer arose when Pete, searching for a buyer for Eel Pie Publishing, met with company chairman Matthew Evans. Evans found Townshend extremely literate and articulate. But it was the artist's interest in and criticism of British culture and societal troubles that made the publisher take a chance. 'I was keen to change Faber's reputation,' says Evans, 'make it more modern, get a more varied, unusual list.' Calling himself a failed rock 'n' roll star, Evans added, 'I grew up in the 1960s. I had all those early Who albums. Maybe that's my Achilles' heel. . . . I'd sit in those first meetings and think, "That's Pete Townshend sitting over there!"'

Not everyone at the venerable institution was impressed though.

'Perhaps we should rename the place Fabber and Fabber,' cracked one employee.

The retired rocker turned fledgling editor confessed it took him months just to learn the publishing jargon. An astute and determined student, he took home ten books a week, even though Faber poetry editor Craig Raine called him 'terrifically well read.'

'It's not a job,' said Townshend, 'it's a joy. It's something I do because I find it so enriching. Our job is to show them somebody somewhere still cares about good writing, about art, about their souls. A lot of people think it's just an intellectual, academic wank. Anybody that knows publishing will understand that literature and publishing are not something that go hand and hand.'

By all accounts, Townshend acquitted himself admirably. He sat on the editorial board, wrote publishing reports on five books per week, even did some line editing and proofreading. He also commissioned titles on a variety of subjects, from the Hell's Angels to John Lennon to Meg Patterson's innovative drug treatment.

'He introduced us to people who might otherwise have thought that Faber was just an up-market, prissy publisher,' explains Evans. Cases in point included *The Last Museum* by William Burroughs's secretary, Brion Gysin, and *The Life and Times of an Animal* by Eric Burdon. Another coup was Prince Charles's volume of his speeches on architecture, inner-city decay, and violent youth.

Townshend even produced his own collection of thirteen short stories, *Horse's Neck*, which Faber published in 1985. Although he wrote in the preface that the book was a journey to discover true beauty, he says, 'What I am in the book is not a pretty picture.' Written as part of his drug therapy, the sometimes graphic work is laced with surreal, twisted imagery.

Townshend was determined not to make the Keith Moon mistake of hiding his pressures beneath a veneer of calculated frivolity. 'What I've done in my life,' he assesses, 'is whined, complained, and been a victim. And it's kept me alive. No one's been in any doubt when I've been having a hard time or when I'm happy.'

In fact, the irrepressible Moonie turns up in the collection, along with Kit Lambert and even John Lennon in *Winston*, one of three stories exploring the often vacuous arena of rock music. 'Stars are attributed with intelligence they don't have, beauty they haven't worked for, loyalty and love they are incapable of reciprocating, and strength they do not possess,' notes Townshend.

John Moynihan wrote in the *Boston Herald*, 'The stories become interesting extensions of his songs. *Horse's Neck* is a curious hybrid that satisfies like rock 'n' roll. It tells its very personal tale in uninhibited English with disregard for convention or precedent. The emphasis is on what is being told.'

That inhibition is manifested in part in erotic images, providing a stereotypical view of women: prostitutes, groupies, one-night stands, mindless sex objects one and all. That, says the author, was on purpose. 'I tried to keep real women out of the book and to show how men of my generation have suffered because of the way they perceive women. We have to find a way of dealing with our inability to talk about our feelings.'

Townshend recounts how early on girls would shove him aside, zealously trying to get to Keith Moon. 'I used to bloody despise them because they didn't know how much it hurt. I was on a vengeance trip after that.'

Even today the more enlightened Townshend is still far more comfortable around men. 'The best fun are stag situations,' he once said. 'The bawdier the better.'

Karen was reportedly shocked by Pete's often explicit prose, saying, 'I didn't know you had it in you,' while his younger daughter, Minta, wouldn't even give it a peek. 'I know all about you and your hang-ups,' she told her father. 'I don't need to read that.'

His often gritty experience revealed that even the most tragic situations can sometimes encapsulate the sublime. One story, called 'The Plate,' had its genesis in a chance conversation. Townshend met a girl who disclosed that she had lost her boyfriend, her baby, had become a junkie, and, on top of that, had just been given the news she had cancer of the uterus due to working as a prostitute. 'Apart from that,' she told Pete, 'I'm really very happy.'

'I burst into tears,' revealed Townshend. 'She said, "What's wrong?" and I said, "I just can't say anything."'

The year 1985 proved a watershed period for the artist, who was now forty. *White City*, which Pete developed as a film, took a sharp turn from his last two efforts to concentrate on a deteriorating Shepherd's Bush neighborhood not far from where he grew up.

The idea was sparked by a visit to the World War II-era White City council estate. Townshend admits he was initially shocked at the marked disrepair of the area, shops boarded up, and street corners bearing stately names like Commonwealth and Crown now teeming with pimps and pushers. In this immigrant community of Jamaicans, Africans, Irish, and gypsies all living within an estate bordered by walls, making it, in effect, a fortress, Townshend found a seamy microcosm of postwar Britain, a tidy metaphor for the decline of the empire and an ideal topic for a musical film.

Sinking some three hundred thousand dollars into the forty-minute piece shot on 35mm film, Townshend focused on a married couple: Jim, an unemployed update of *Quadrophenia*'s Jimmy, and Alice, the estate's swim team coach. Jim's old mate, Pete (played with surprising ease by Townshend), is the local boy turned rock star who's come home to shoot a video. Jim and Alice's emotional and economic struggles are set against Townshend's theme: that evil is always lurking, but through hope one can endure.

In true Townshend form, hope is thematically expressed in the scenes at the White City indoor pool, the one element that unifies the entire community. 'I felt the people to be good, in essence, trying hard to live clean lives,' he noted. 'I found there was a sense of optimism and roots I was quite jealous of. Despite all my achievements and success, roots are one thing I don't feel I have.'

Musically the album projects a different feel: slick, shimmering, prismatic with his sixteen-piece Deep End band, a top-notch lineup of rock's finest highlighted by the incomparable drummer Simon Phillips, known for his stellar work with Jeff Beck and David Gilmour.

The thumping, resonating opener, 'Give Blood,' is a musical tour de force with multiple meanings. 'I felt it reflected the demands that were made of me as a young man, the demands which other people feel are being made of them all the time,' relayed Townshend. 'The idea that they have to give everything, that they can't be happy unless they've given everything, that they're not allowed to feel complete or fulfilled unless they've made the complete sacrifice.' The stirring antiwar anthem was also a call to revive the discarded idea of brotherhood. 'Blood has always been the coefficient of brotherhood,' Pete maintains. 'If you want to give blood, make it across two wrists on a back lot.'

Another song, 'Face the Face,' was ultimately released as a single and performed reasonably well. The inspiration was taken from T. S. Eliot's famous poem 'The Love Song of J. Alfred Prufrock' and, in particular, the line 'We must prepare a face to meet the face.'

Within the high-octane pace, though, the subtlety of the message was somewhat lost, lamented the composer. 'What I tried to do was write a song about facing up to the suppressed anger we all carry around. Once you face up to it, you don't have to act it out.'

The change-of-pace 'Hiding Out,' with its Afro-Caribbean rhythms, draws a strong comparison between the treatment of blacks in South Africa and on the White City estate. 'They give them their own territory and try to make sure they don't cause any trouble,' explains Pete.

Inevitably, through Townshend's eyes, the overriding message in this song, as well of the entire *White City* piece, is that even in futility there is still hope. 'Futility is optimism,' he suggests. While writing the piece he found himself gazing back over twenty years of interviews and his constant message: 'Rock is a symbol of hope and optimism.'

'The incredible thing is that nobody has to be hopeful or optimistic. The potential for happiness is actually bound up in the moment. . . . So many people don't believe in themselves. We underrate our own resilience.'

As Pete put it in 'White City Fighting,' co-written by Dave Gilmour, 'I finally grew up/To resist the temptation/The gutters all threw up.'

For all its bold strokes and creative risks the musical film tries to convey too much. 'I wanted to make a metaphor and I got a bit confused,' he confesses. 'To be honest, I wasn't sure of what it was I was trying to make a metaphor of. Whether . . . say, South Africa and apartheid out of what was happening in White City or vice versa. In the end I tried to create a kind of quantum symbol for the resistance. What's happening in Britain at the moment is a kind of French idea. That you can face changes by resisting them . . . refusing to let them affect your chosen way of life.'

Echoes of Townshend's uneven childhood appear all over both the video and album. An overt reference to his mother's hot and cold affections is presented in the aptly titled 'Secondhand Love,' a cool, bluesy wailer with a vocal reminiscent of Eric Clapton. In the film it signifies Jim's rejection of his mother's love, a woman whom he feels has long neglected him. 'His mother has almost seduced him,' relates Townshend, 'and yet she spends all of her time in the pub apparently giving lots of love and attention to the customers. I sang it with such pain and anger I realized I must feel something like that.'

A conversation in a pub scene, when Jim commiserates to his buddy, Pete, is culled directly from Townshend's past. 'I'll tell you a story of a boy who was always being sent away to his granny's for months on end,' Jim soberly recalls, 'just so [his mother] could get rid of him. The mother was always having affairs with people she met and the boy looked on in confusion until he grew up and met a girl. And he never knew how good it could be to be wanted by somebody.'

The highlight of the video is the poolside staging of the electric 'Face the Face,' in which director Richard Lowenstein effectively captures the excitement of a big-band performance and Townshend's joyous jitterbugging juxtaposed against the swimmers' synchronized movements. By cutting from Coach Alice to husband Jim, from the swimmers to Pete glimmering in a gold lamé, forties-style tuxedo, Lowenstein reveals more story line in these five minutes than the entire video.

But there is too little of this kind of intensity and drama. Too much time is focused on meaningless water shots, pummeling Townshend's overriding theme of 'water as the great equalizer.' This idea was taken from Ronnie Lane, whose debilitating illness placed him on a level playing field only in the pool. More focus could have been placed on the couple's relationship, along with the idea of the hometown boy who makes good contrasted with struggling Jim.

On the positive side, the venture indicated great promise, giving much to build on.

Despite high anticipation, the record and video, released on November 1, 1985, didn't really sell. Although it was critically well received on most fronts, Townshend admits it wasn't as good as his previous solo projects. As one journalist sighed, 'Pete Townshend in his postbinge mode became, to be frank, something of an old bore.' Even his own record company remarked, 'Well, you are a bit squeaky clean these days, aren't you?'

Seemingly overnight a controversy arose from his sharply changed public image. The raving nightclubbing, rock 'n' roll hellion had transformed into a priggish bookworm hopping on a new soapbox: trendy social worker and moral watchdog. A sarcastic Townshend defensively quipped, 'All I had to do to get the affection of the public again was to be found raving drunk with a needle in my arm coming out of the Town and Country with a carrot up my arse.

'Some say the fans want you to walk the tightrope. They lead boring, depressed lives and want their heroes to go crazy. It's a vicarious kick. To some extent I expect that's true, but nobody wants dead heroes. What good is a hero if he's dead? People build up heroes in order to examine them. There isn't much you can do with a corpse.'

Perhaps Daltrey's prognostications were coming to pass. 'Pete is one of the most mucked-up persons I know,' he once commented. 'I hope he never sorts himself out because then he'll stop being creative.'

Even Townshend expressed some worry that, now clean and sober, he had lost his edge. 'I've read lots of books on alcoholism in writers. . . . I suppose now I'm waiting to find out if what I write is any good.'

' "Rage, rage against the dying of the light," ' Dylan Thomas once said. 'I think one of the dangers of middle age in rock 'n' roll,' noted Townshend, 'is that it's very easy to take the easy way out. You have to be very angry in a sense to stay honest.'

Kathy points to another possibility in Pete's first real commercial failure. In his seventies bloom of devotion to Meher Baba, Townshend made gripping, emotional music that poured from his heart. As a result, she theorizes, 'Too many people were reading into his lyrics, and he was [forced] into saying, "No, no, *Quadrophenia* is all about Irish Jack." Bullshit, *Quadrophenia*'s about *him*.' Therefore, fearing the public was intruding, he recoiled, Kathy suggests, and took a more detached, distant approach.

Townshend himself almost admitted as much. 'A lot of Who fans feel that they know me very, very well, that they're getting another angle about the way I feel. That kind of interpretation is a shame. For instance, if I write a straightforward love song, they'll think, "Townshend's written a love song. What's going on? Is he in love?" rather than just accepting the music.'

Immersing himself in the social ills of *White City* was part of a larger evolution. Pete became a dedicated patron of charity: from Amnesty International to Prince's Trust, Rock Against Racism to Action Research into Multiple Sclerosis (ARMS), the latter inspired by Ronnie Lane's tragic plight.

Despite Pete's rough edges, compassion had long been a strong trait of this self-acknowledged sentimentalist who openly sobs at soap operas. During the mid-seventies, on a visit to Baba's tomb, Townshend took pity on a young man stricken with severe dysentery. 'He was small and fragile, his face was white and he was shaking like a leaf. . . . He brought out all my maternal instincts, if that's possible for a man. I just felt so much compassion for him and so much sorrow for him. And I saw him get down and put his head to the ground and tears began to stream down my face.'

Pete also became an ardent anti-drug crusader. He appeared in TV ads and wrote news articles. He even joined forces with the Tory Party, speaking at one of their conferences. 'It sexually sterilizes, it destroys ambition,' he told them. 'It alienates the user from family and friends. Worst of all, it instills a sense of utter worthlessness. We have to find a way to teach people to say no. . . . We have to grasp the snake by the neck.'

Pete's left-wing friends contended the self-coined 'closet Marxist' had lost all credibility by discussing the drug problem under a Conservative banner. 'Who gives a damn about banners?' he shot back quite rightly.

Townshend's relentless hammering helped push through the government's adoption of a six-point war on drugs, including life sentences for pushers, a drug squad on every police force, and grants for new rehab units and work programs for young offenders. His message hit home as well. 'I have never dabbled in drugs,' revealed daughter Emma. 'Happily my parents made sure I am not tempted by them.'

Pete's altruistic endeavors gained an international spotlight with the highly touted Who reunion for rock's most spectacular bicontinental party: Live Aid, to help rescue hunger-stricken Ethiopia. In typically explosive Who fashion the event sparked a flood of rumor. Initially a reunion wasn't supposed to happen; rather, the band planned to perform individually.

'We only got together for two fifteen-minute sessions, but I guess we'll battle through,' muttered Kenney Jones.

Townshend too reportedly moaned, 'I don't know nothing. I don't want to talk to the press.'

Behind the scenes, organizer Bob Geldof did some last-minute pleading. 'You can play for twenty minutes with your eyes closed, just show up!'

Their rustiness showed in the performance as the Who rocked out 'My Generation,' 'Pinball Wizard,' 'Love Reign o'er Me,' and 'Won't Get Fooled Again.' Entwistle pronounced it 'a disaster. I think the Who has become an albatross to us all. It feels like I'm trapped within the Who, and it doesn't even exist anymore. I think we were stupid to stop working.'

Daltrey, however, took a larger view. 'Look,' he clarified, 'we didn't row. We didn't want to go on as the Who. We wanted to do separate performances. But when Bob Geldof said it would mean a difference of between five and ten million pounds for Live Aid, we agreed.'

Something positive did come of it, however. Townshend and Daltrey, tempers cooled over the past three years, were laying their differences aside. Roger even accepted at last that the Who was indeed finished. This good feeling resulted in Townshend penning for Daltrey the moving 'After the Fire' for Roger's latest and best ever solo LP, *Under a Raging Moon* (the title track, a tribute to Keith).

For Townshend, Live Aid was a success on two levels. Rock was actually being a force for good, showing its great promise as he'd once hoped. 'The great thing about Live Aid was that suddenly the sweeping statements that had been made by rock 'n' roll weren't being kept, but they were at least being attended to. . . . It's acknowledging that when different factions of this industry unite, we have a kind of power.'

Second, it showed him just how much he missed performing live. In November 1985, Pete took his sixteen-piece Deep End band to impoverished Brixton for a pair of benefit concerts to aid his own Double O Charities. The set ranged from old Who material to his solo efforts and even songs by jazz greats Charlie Mingus and Miles Davis. This was Pete Townshend's public declaration that he was no longer shackled to the Who, that he was going to play his own music his own way.

The Brixton Academy performances, by everyone's account, were a tremendous sensation. Townshend played only acoustic guitar, and Bobby Pridden, his assistant engineer, praised his gutsy brilliance. 'He was taking a big, bloody chance taking a sixteen-piece band out. Pete is like Michelangelo; he matters more in the music scene than anyone other than John Lennon. That man is a bloody genius and a mad professor, which I love about him.'

In the wake of the concerts, Townshend came to an insight about his tours on the road with the Who. 'You know, just going into some small midwestern town and meeting a tall, willowy blonde and my marriage breaking up, or maybe the danger of going out and getting beaten up in a bar by rednecks. It did seem a very dangerous time. I found that exciting.'

Pete kept to his dictum of not touring. He was now leading a simpler, more structured life; he was changing, evolving, or maybe just growing up. Today he looks back on 'My Generation' and says with a sneer, 'I don't respect the snotty Herbert who wrote it. I was a fucking hypocrite really, I think at the time. My aim was to subvert, but at the same time infiltrate the establishment. I don't think I understood what the establishment was. . . . The establishment is not something you enter, it just suddenly appears around you. Suddenly you are a member of the fucking establishment, and there's nothing you can do about it. I have responsibilities now I just can't walk away from.'

Even Daltrey observed, 'Isn't it inevitable you become the establishment you once thumbed your nose at?'

Townshend now held a decidedly different view of freedom from that aired in the final story of *Horse's Neck*. In the story, he achieves ultimate liberation while riding a giant white horse – having conquered his greatest fears – into the ocean. 'That's how I felt for a while,' he later admitted. 'It's incredible, a sort of expansive freedom. But freedom is not important. That's the thing I realized. What's important is control so that *you* decide what you do.'

Rock's most famous rabble-rouser was now advising young people, 'Don't make a big deal about rebellion. Rebellion is just a token. It's like being stubborn. There's a bitterness about it.' This, indeed, was a giant step.

'I find the more I attack, the more respect and power I get', he said, 'When you actually confront the head of a record company and say, "I disapprove greatly of what you are doing," you immediately create a dialogue. You are immediately in a position to *effect* change. It's taken me a long, long time to realize that.' At another moment he declared, 'It's only by becoming part of the establishment you can actually do anything. That's why you find a lot of older musicians moving into the establishment infrastructure.'

Pete, firmly established in mid-life, no longer believed that rock 'n' roll would change the world. 'I've had it with rock,' he said in 1985. 'We were like the dumb shucks that sit in church who believe that because they believe, the world is going to change. We celebrated and we confronted, but we didn't deal with our own problems. We allowed our people to die, we allowed people to resort to drugs. We even acknowledged their decadence as being something we vicariously enjoyed.'

Townshend also pointed to the fact that white boys had taken over the rhythmic dance music rooted in the black slave experience and exploited it into their own 'church of the stadium,' as he calls it. 'Come to the church of the stadium . . . hear the music . . . look up and you'll see God, look down and you see hell!

'The message is still there,' he agreed, 'the uplift, the hope and optimism. But I've come to despise those words, they don't really interest me anymore. The only promise of rock is yet another power chord.'

To Townshend's mind the entire business needed a major reality check, a dismantling of its tacky, valueless Hollywood/rock star system. 'I'm glad I got out of all that. The realism I'm coming to grips with now is that I'm a nobody like anybody else. I'm only as good as my next trick.'

One who is convinced it's all blow and bluster is manager Bill Curbishley. 'Rock music is really a quest for Pete. He's always used rock to try to answer his own problems and questions. "I Can't Explain," "Substitute," all those songs were really him coming to terms with his own problems and by extension the problems of millions of others. I think that principle still holds true today. He really does believe rock 'n' roll has the capacity to change the world: that if enough people were to actually listen to what he and a few others have to say, then things might be a bit better.'

As a social activist, he began to speak out against nuclear arms and pornography, and even tackled the controversial National Front, Britain's neofascist political party. His anger on this issue was very personal. One of his musician friends in a reggae band had been involved in a riot against the fascist element, and some roughneck thrust an iron bar through his skull. 'I decided I was gonna stand up and be counted,' he affirmed. 'I think fascism stinks, and I'm gonna go up on stage and say so. I don't want to deny anybody their rights, but if the National Front can say, "Send the niggers back to wherever!" and "Send the Jews back to wherever," then I can say, "That attitude stinks!"

I'm a bit scared. Not for me, but for my family and the people around me.'

Those impassioned views are closely aligned with Pete's profound interest in the plight of young people everywhere, but especially Britain. The rise of fascism was connected with a violent gang mentality, a topic he explored in 'Uniforms,' off *Chinese Eyes*. 'The compartmentalizing of people's clothes,' he observed, 'of the way they look, into cults and ideologies and social sensibility, is what I find amazing. I know it's often said that just because somebody dresses like a skinhead, that doesn't mean they're going to kick you as soon as they get the chance. But it *does* start to affect the way they think. A lot of Oi-boys [Britain's skinhead bands] start off fairly innocuously, just interested in the look, and they end up believing they hate all Pakistanis.'

In a moment of heated frustration Townshend barked, 'Those people who say a spell in the army will stop street violence may well be right. The kids seem to want a license to wear uniforms and kick people's heads in.'

Yet philosophically Pete abhors any kind of violence, the most overt musical references manifesting in 'I've Known No War,' off *It's Hard*, and *White City's* wrenching 'Give Blood.' War, he feels, is a crass exploitation of working-class youth. 'We're very useful when there's a war on to go and tear people's guts out with a bayonet,' he charges. 'But as soon as some wanker with a striped suit tells us it's over, we're supposed to crawl back under our working-class stone on the dole and keep our mouths shut, just hide away on our housing estates.'

The blistering 'I've Known No War' was in itself a cry for boomers who'd never been called to combat: 'As soon as the battle was over/I was born in victorious clover/And I've never been shot at or gassed/Never been tortured or stabbed.'

'I've never been taught to fight,' proclaims Pete, 'I've never seen a gun fired'. These words are no doubt laced with guilt and probably a little confusion. Townshend's childhood view of war was its glamorous entertainment side, far away from the front lines. Yet he descended from a line of men who'd fought; in fact Pete was the first not to participate.

To compensate, perhaps, rock became his battlefield. 'The best thing that could have happened to me was to be called up, put in the army, and sent out to some battlefield. People might think that's sick, but I was brought up to do that and I respected people that did. My father did it, my grandfather did it, and I had to do it with rock 'n' roll.'

Perhaps more significantly, Townshend constantly battles with what he perceives to be evil forces whether it's complacency, human suffering, or his own private demons. He desperately wants to wear the white hat, a quest complicated by the modern day ambiguity that the guys in white are not always what they appear. His solace lies in his one shining absolute, that there is only one true, constant good and that is God.

Infusing all of his social endeavors was his his devotion to Meher Baba. When asked if he still considered himself a disciple of the avatar, Pete would enthusiastically reply, 'Very much so!' But as the eighties wore on, he grew cagey, replying, 'I don't think it really matters.' In fact, he even theorized he wasn't certain if his life would have been any different without Baba. 'I can't say I'm a better person because of him or otherwise.'

'He became disillusioned,' thought Kathy. 'I think he realized he had to find what he was looking for within himself, not an avatar or icon.'

Throughout his tumultuous ups and downs he feels that a core inner light has remained. 'The very real feeling of God's presence is what's enabled me to retain a sense of humility. It's not a pose I've adopted and have difficulty keeping up. If I wanna behave like a flash bastard, that's when I'm posing.'

Rocker Patti Smith once asked, 'How can somebody like Townshend follow Meher Baba and be such a miserable bastard?' It is a question he has often asked himself.

'Could it be I'm actually happy when I'm depressed?' he conjectured. Later he put it more poetically in *Horse's Neck*: 'I live in a paradox. I feel comfortable with this unhappiness. I am content with misery.'

Suffering, in fact, is something that Townshend openly welcomes and that has paid him handsome dividends through his work along the way. 'I pray for suffering,' he has said on a number of occasions. 'I think it's important to realize the darker side of life, that suffering and indecision are a fundamental and valuable part of life. Without them there'd be nothing to write about.' In a wry aside he adds, 'The emotional conflict game has been very profitable for me. I put it into words and make millions of dollars out of it.'

During his collapse from 1980 to 1982, he concedes, he took things a bit too far. 'At a point of extreme overconfidence I said, "Listen, God, I've had more than my fair share. I feel like a really lucky guy. I've got a lot of money, lots of friends, lots of talent, a beautiful wife, two beautiful kids. If I can be useful to you in any way, don't spare me. Put me through it. I can take it."

'I soon found out, though, I couldn't handle what I'd asked for. So I've decided now I'm not a soldier for God. I'm a servant as much as I can be with his grace, but no soldier.'

In a final note, his view of the power of prayer is illuminating. 'It's incredible what a last resort it is to a lot of people and how often it also helps in that last resort. . . . This modern attitude that man needs nothing, that he's got to stand alone, that his strength is in his mere existence, is obnoxious to me. It's an indication of the nastiest medico-pyscho bullshit I've ever come across.'

On a more earthly plane, Pete was delighted when he was asked to introduce the Rolling Stones into the Rock 'n' Roll Hall of Fame in 1989. 'I can't analyze what I feel about the Stones because I'm really an absolute fan. The Rolling Stones were just shocking, absolutely riveting, stunning, moving; I mean, they changed my life completely. . . . Guys, whatever you do, don't try to grow old gracefully. It wouldn't suit you.'

Among his close mates, Townshend counts the Stones' Charlie Watts, Keith Richards, and Mick Jagger, to whom he remains the closest. Mick's studio is plastered with vintage Who photographs; it was Townshend's advice he asked on the replacement of Brian Jones just a week after his mysterious, murderous death. Townshend penned a full-page birthday tribute to his mate in the London *Times* on Mick's fortieth birthday in July 1983. 'Jagger wrote the blues before I did, played it before I did, made a million before I did, went to America . . . tried LSD, DMT, cocaine and marijuana before I did.'

With Pete, though, there is a tendency to rub friends up the wrong way. When both the Stones and the Who were on tour that same year, a reporter asked Jagger if the band was doing it for the money. 'No,' sniped Mick. 'That's the Who!'

Townshend snapped back, 'I can assure you Mick Jagger needs money more than I do. I know more about his financial situation than he does about mine. His last album was a flop, and if we want to get really bitchy he's surrounded by a lot of people he presumably loves who also need money.'

Professional jealousy has often led to acerbic comments from Pete. He calls Paul McCartney a friend, but thinks nothing of trashing his music publicly, calling it 'commercial goo production.' Of McCartney's blockbuster 'Ebony and Ivory,' Townshend cracked, 'He's actually taken black and white, put a bit of tinsel around it [and], by hook or crook, managed to get Stevie Wonder to sing on it.'

His penchant for speaking out of turn has even rattled Eric Clapton, his best friend in the business. In one unhappy incident Townshend told the rock press that the blues guitarist was upset when he didn't win the Best Guitar Player Award one year and called Clapton's reaction 'shallow.' Eric, whom Townshend and others have labeled as 'very sensitive,' lashed out at his colleague. 'I ticked him off and said if he felt that way about me, why didn't he tell me face-to-face or on the phone instead of blabbing to the papers?'

Townshend's response was that he was only trying to 'feed the creative machine, and besides, our relationship should be strong enough to take a knock now and then.'

The way Kathy sees it, however, Pete has few intimate friends. 'Of the people in the rock world, Eric's probably one of his best friends. I don't think Pete has a lot of friends. I think that's one of his biggest problems. That's always been a void in his life.'

A case in point is his longtime band. Even though he speaks of the Who as family and once said, 'If I had to choose three friends, I'd start with them,' relations have always been very much up and down. A prime example is Roger Daltrey. The first thing he asks anyone connected with his old mate is, 'How's Pete doing?' and then pumps them for information. 'This is very sad,' sighed one Townshend observer. 'Roger can't just call up Pete and ask, "What are you up to?"'

Even Townshend himself acknowledged that 'rock stars are not the kind of people you can really get close to. In fact, you feel much closer to them on stage than you do when you meet them. There's no village in the rock business. Relationships are competitive and shallow, and real friendships are hard to find.'

Insiders say Townshend's true friendships come from those unafraid to take any guff from the superstar and who have the nerve to call him an asshole when the word applies. A prime example is cited by a Townshend pal we'll call Terri, who was a guest at the wedding of Pete's brother Paul. As Terri strolled over to greet the groom, Townshend's reaction was an inexplicable cold stare as if to say, 'Fuck you, I don't want you here.' The musician then proceeded to rudely ignore her for the rest of the afternoon.

Terri promptly fired off a letter in response to the artist's boorish behavior. 'Listen, I don't know who the fuck you think you are, and if you don't like me, fine, just don't go being nice to me when I see you at a charity function and then ignore me around your family. Sorry, Pete, but that doesn't wash in my book!'

Townshend replied with a less than convincing excuse of not wishing to detract from his brother's big day. And at the next family function Pete atoned for his churlish conduct. 'He literally leapt over a table to give me a huge hug,' recalls Terri. 'I know he felt really badly about what he did, and didn't understand he was being rude to me. The thing is, he knows when he does wrong and cares enough to rectify it.'

Another explanation is that he has bouts of acute shyness. One Townshend acquaintance tells of being invited to lunch by the artist only to endure a bizarre conversation whereby her host was nervously spouting trivialities such as how *Scoop* outsold *Chinese Eyes*. It turned out the nervous musician had written out a list of questions and memorized them just to avoid any uncomfortable lapses in conversation.

Given such insecurity, it is obvious why his marriage is so important to him. On the face of it an odd couple, he and Karen actually have much in common, including their regard for Meher Baba, a keen love of the arts, plus a high value on education, Karen having pursued a teaching degree.

As outspoken and public as is her famous husband, Karen is precisely the opposite, maintaining a low profile and virtually *never* speaking to the press. When approached in 1985 about participating in a book on celebrity wives, her incredulous response was 'That's not me at all.'

Part of the reason, according to Kathy, is her almost complete disdain for the Who and, more pointedly, their fans. 'Karen doesn't like the fans and never wanted anything to do with the Who. With Pete, that's his life. I think it was one of the biggest problems in their relationship.

'She's aristocracy and Pete's totally working class. He wants everybody to love him while Karen might be classed a snob. So, where Pete wouldn't mind hanging out in the pub with Who fans that were garbage collectors and mailmen, Karen wouldn't especially want him to. Karen would never go to a show or Who functions.'

What did finally lure her into the spotlight, if only for a moment, was her involvement with the Chiswick Family Rescue, an independent London organization that oversees three refuge houses for victims of domestic violence. As chairperson of the Committee of Management, which she joined in 1983, Karen's main focus centered on fund-raising. 'There was one woman I used to see with bruises on her face, but it was a subject I hadn't really heard much about,' she says. 'I was absorbed with my kids. . . .

'I must admit, there comes a time when I speak to people and I have to say, "You know, I'm Pete's wife," and it can be extremely awkward. I still don't particularly like doing it, but it does help, and we do need the money.'

In fact, it was through her husband and his concerts for the program that Karen first became involved. Townshend had learned of the cause from Keith Moon, whose initial visit to the first refuge reduced him to tears. Calling wife battering 'an appalling problem,' Karen explained that 'too many people still believe the old clichés that women either like to be beaten, that they ask for it, or somehow deserve it. Old attitudes die hard.'

Despite her own deep commitment, according to a British newspaper report in early 1988 she influenced Pete to shut down his own Double O Charity. Townshend's then personal manager Sally Arnold speculated, 'I don't think he expected Double O to get so big, or so popular. He prefers to remain more low key.'

Townshend himself was unpredictably quiet on the subject. Given Karen's ardent aversion to show business, perhaps she felt the cause had been overshadowed by all the star-studded fund-raising parties and concerts. 'Other stars have given generously to the rescue in the past; Bruce Springsteen gave us money when he was over here for his concerts, and so has George Harrison. . . .

'It's very easy to say, "Oh, let's have a concert and raise some money." That might work for the short term, but it's not doing anything for the long-term public awareness. It's hard work raising money, and at the moment so much of our energies go into that, simply to keep going.

'We need more premises, more staff, and above all, money for a massive education and publicity campaign for the authorities and the general public about battered wives.'

On the home front, there has never been any question of her loyalty and determination to keep her marriage together under the most tumultuous situations. Not only has she fought the fallout of mega stardom, Pete's drug and alcohol abuse, numerous infidelities (all played out very publicly), but also the many idiosyncracies of a very complex and quixotic personality. Pete, however, sums it up by saying, 'My wife knew I was an asshole when she married me.'

As for Townshend's ultimate victory over drugs and alcohol, according to Daria Schouvaloff it was Karen's tough love that pulled him through. 'The reason Pete didn't go down,' she discloses, 'is that he has a very loving wife. Karen left him when he went into his heroin jag, which is precisely what you have to do if you love someone.'

Townshend echoed very much the same sentiments. 'I have always underestimated my wife's importance and the value of not just her affection or love for me, but her ability to adapt to problems I feel have been very much a part of my working life. I got great strength from her, and that's the single thing that turned me around.'

Despite nearly continuous turmoil, something has made this extraordinary marriage work. That is a seemingly indestructible love coupled with an iron-willed dedication on both sides. 'Karen's the most stabilizing force in Pete's life,' affirms Kathy, while Townshend added, 'If she hadn't been so stable, maybe I wouldn't have allowed myself so much personal license.'

Pete admits to a sense of worthlessness during their many separations. 'I felt devalued by not being able to make the contract work because I despise men who run away from marriage.'

He gained that sense from viewing his parents' rocky union. 'Listen,' he once told his mother, 'you know, it's great you've stuck together. What makes it even greater is that you obviously don't really belong together. That's helped me to value sticking with people you don't necessarily fit with.'

To his critics, he responds, 'All I can say is I'm still married to the same woman, and I'm the only man in rock 'n' roll who is. Show me another.'*

When Townshend was in the suicidal throes of his addiction, what also kept him from plummeting over the edge were his beloved children. 'When you have kids,' he wisely observed, 'you are constantly reminded of your duty to live.'

Daughters Emma and Aminta, now twenty-six and twenty-four, Kathy describes as 'really nice girls whom [Pete] loves to death.' Their growing up was not without its problems. 'There was a time when they suffered a certain amount of fear and deprivation as a direct result of my behavior,' he soberly discloses. 'I've never beaten them up, but I've scared the shit out of them when I was arguing with my wife or even myself.'

On the brighter side, the girls inherited their parents' intense love of learning. Emma earned a Ph. D. in economics from Cambridge, and Minta recently graduated from Exeter University with a degree in modern languages. 'She's a real free spirit,' says Kathy. 'Minta's a Townshend with Pete's photographic memory while Emma's very much an Astley.' Yet it's the more scholarly-minded Emma who may yet follow in her father's footsteps. At thirteen she formed her own all-girl band, Emma and the Laundrettes, whom proud papa Pete recorded at Oceanic. Emma also sang backup on the *White City* disc and film. She reportedly had a record contract waiting for her as soon as she finished her schooling, but thus far no Emma Townshend records have appeared in the shops.

For all his many public declarations, Townshend has not revealed a great deal about his relationship with his father. Both shared a rare appearance in 1981 on the BBC's Michael Parkinson chat show, where Cliff was a member of the house band. The pair exchanged barbs before performing together for the first time anywhere.

'If I take my guitar and smash it to the ground,' Pete explained to the audience, 'I bring the house down.'

'Hey, if he cracks any more, he'll be put to bloody bed!' bellowed Cliff jokingly.

'And you won't get no tea,' Pete shot back, mischievously

---

* Pete's well-documented generosity has extended to Karen's large family. He brought in Karen's brother Jon to be Glyn John's assistant engineer on *Who Are You* and *Rough Mix*. His father-in-law, Edwin, conducted the superb arrangement on 'Street in the City.' His beautiful sister-in-law, Virginia Astley, a pianist, participated on *Chinese Eyes*.

adding, 'If you look closely at his saxophone, you'll notice it's badly bent.'

Back in the seventies, Pete recalled, his father tossed away his lifelong proper British mannerisms and abruptly declared, 'We are going to be an Italian family! When my sons come into the house, they must kiss their father and that's it!' Pete and his brothers, while stunned, good naturedly accepted his sudden about-face.

The story moves forward to late 1985, when Cliff Townshend became ill with cancer of the colon. Upon a visit to the hospital, Pete saw his father after a bout of chemotherapy. When it was time to say good-bye, Pete gave him a kiss. 'And the thing was,' says Pete, 'at the time he wasn't my father anymore; he was this person who needed me to be strong. If anything, the roles sometimes reversed, where I was the caring one and he was the helpless one.'

He rushed back home to the piano to write a song, 'We Kissed for the First Time.' 'It did feel like the first time I'd ever really kissed a man,' he noted. 'If you didn't know the story behind it, you could come up with all kinds of ideas. And there's quite possibly a lot of Freudian bullshit sexuality behind it as well, but the point is that it was an amazingly pure moment and unbelievably important to me. That moment resonates for me and completely changed the way I feel about my father.'

In early June 1986 U2 lead singer Bono asked Pete to participate in an Amnesty International concert in New York. He agreed despite his father being near death. He'd no sooner landed in New York, though, when he received an urgent message that Cliff had taken a serious turn for the worse. 'I got back on a plane and eight hours later found him completely alone on a stretcher in the hospital corridor.' A few weeks later Cliff Townshend quietly passed away.

'I had a terrible time because Cliff refused to be treated at hospital and wanted to die in his bed,' Betty Townshend remembers.

'At Cliff's funeral we all got steaming drunk, and Peter and I made a pact to go on the wagon. I was doing great for two years and didn't touch a drop, and then a very dear friend of mine died. I went to pieces and hit the bottle again. But Peter has managed to keep off it. He is a very strong person and just has the occasional glass of champagne.'

It's just the high life, she protests. 'I'm not an alcoholic. I like a good drink and I love to have a good time, but only when I'm in good company. . . . I never drink alone, which is the real sign of an alcoholic.

'But Peter doesn't try to stop me drinking anymore. He has given up all hope of ever calming me down.'

Although Betty claims she didn't hit the bottle again for some time, in November 1986, still emotionally unable to cope with Cliff's passing, she was admitted for a six week dry-out to Plymouth's Broadreach House, one of the centers served by Pete's Double O Charity.

Of the lifelong combustible relationship between Townshend and his mother, Kathy maintains it's probably easier for him now that he's got his own family, but added that Pete and Betty are really too much alike ever to be truly close.

'Betty idealizes Pete,' reveals Kathy, 'but she can't really communicate with him because she feels he's so far above her. Pete doesn't realize that. He thinks she just doesn't love him. When you've got two people with the same personality dealing with each other, wanting the same things and no one's giving, it's going to cause problems.'

First introduced to Mrs Townshend at a London pub, Kathy remembers a drunken Betty accusing her of being a Who fan and trying to get to Pete. She was 'slagging me off bigtime,' says Kathy. Betty's attitude, however, dramatically changed a few months later over a Townshend family barbecue when she observed the warm and friendly exchanges between her son and this so-called fan. The next morning Kathy, to her astonishment, received an invitation for tea from a completely transformed Betty.

'Suddenly, she'd totally fallen in love with me because Pete liked me.'

An avowed free spirit even now, Betty still frequents nightclubs, singing and dancing and on at least one occasion performing a striptease.

In recent years Mrs Townshend has taken up with reputed toy-boy Juan Justicia, some forty years her junior. After employing the former waiter to be a handyman around the Mediterranean villa on the Spanish island of Minorca (which Townshend purchased for his parents in the early seventies), Betty asked him to move in. 'Of course, Peter was worried about the age difference, but he even promised to buy Juan a car as a thank-you for everything he's done for me,' she said in 1993.

'He is happy with me and I love him dearly. The first time I set eyes on him I thought, "God, you're beautiful and I'm going to have you."

'We got talking and I asked him to do some work for me around the house. Within weeks we had fallen in love and he moved into the villa.'

For his part, Pete apparently takes it all in his stride, saying that he's well used to his mother's incorrigible behavior. 'Dad used to say that whatever it was like with Mum through all the ranting and raving, it was never boring. People ask if I'm embarrassed by Mum's antics. Well, imagine what it was like being Pete Townshend's mum!'

Pete's relationships with his brothers Paul and Simon have been noticeably calmer, despite spates of jealousy on all sides. Simon remembers being backstage at the Young Vic during one of the Who's first tours. 'I used to run in and Roger would cuddle me. He always used to do that. While I was growing up, Pete was getting more and more popular all the time. I thought he was famous since I was a little kid, but he probably wasn't anywhere near as famous as after *Tommy*, but I always thought he was.'

Due to the age difference between them, Pete has only recently really gotten to know the pair, both now married. Simon and Paul recently threw a birthday spread for big brother.

Simon has carved himself a small but comfortable niche in the music world. He did some backing vocals on both the *Tommy* album and the film soundtrack as well as appearing briefly in the Ken Russell movie. In 1983 Townshend produced his brother's LP, *Sweet Sound*, which included the single, 'I'm the Answer,' complete with a video aired by MTV. 'Working with Simon was very interesting,' noted Pete. 'Working with him on the record was like getting to know him, really. He's a good kid.'

Once again, however, Townshend's professional jealousy flared. In the aftermath of producing *Sweet Sound* Townshend confided to his friend Terri, 'I don't know if I can handle Simon being famous.'

'Why, are you jealous of him?'

'Well, yeah,' he replied sheepishly.

Terri explains that Pete has always enjoyed his Who prestige and favored position within the family. 'He's afraid that if somebody else gains the same stature, it will take away from him and he won't get the love. He feels he's loved through his fame, not for who he really is.'

Simon, however, has always lived in the giant shadow of his famous brother. The problem is exacerbated by the fact that the two look and sound very much alike. As Simon puts it, 'I could be his twin.' Clearly, any comparison grates on him, especially since he has toured with such groups as Duran Duran and the Pretenders. 'People come out [to shows] because I'm Pete's brother ... but when they've seen the gig it's *Simon* Townshend.'

According to Simon the two really got to know each other through a quasi-psychic link. 'We sort of thought into each other. . . . He can say something to me and I give him an answer before he says it. That happened a lot when we were recording. It's a very strange thing between Pete and me.'

An affinity for the paranormal, specifically astral projection, is a trait of the Townshend men, or so they contend. Simon recounts a story about the Who, who were once booked on the twelfth floor of a hotel. In the middle of the night Pete insisted he was awakened by a policeman collecting for 'a fund for the people that died.' The next morning he told Richard Barnes about it. An incredulous Barnes told Pete, 'Christ, that's amazing. I've just found out twelve people died on this floor from a strange disease.' Cliff Townshend too claimed to astral travel via self-hypnosis, as does Simon.

As for Paul, insiders say he is somewhat intimidated by his famous older brother. 'He's a Who fan, overawed by Pete's phenomenal achievements and position,' observes Terri. 'Paul looks at Pete and thinks, "I could never do what he did and therefore I'm nothing." He's afraid to even talk with him.'

Paul tried his hand as a musician and journeyed through his share of bands. He and Simon had a group called Clear Peace, and in 1983 Paul toured with Simon solo. 'He's a wonderful character,' says Simon. 'He was into music [but] sort of went in and out of it . . . I don't know. . . . Everyone's told him to keep at it. He really needs encouragement.'

Betty said, 'he's an amazing performer. I think he leaves Peter and Simon streets behind. He's absolutely brilliant.' But as Kathy noted, 'Although Paul's a great musician, he has no real motivation.'

Paul has since gone on to become an interior decorator. This career change stemmed, Kathy remembers, from a troubled letter from his wife, Sandy, explaining that the couple were ten thousand pounds in debt. They had no prospects in sight, and creditors were threatening to repossess a flat they had only just purchased. Kathy, stirred by the desperate tone of the note, immediately forwarded it to Pete.

'I said, "Look, Pete, it's none of my business, hate me for the rest of your life, but these are my friends and this is your brother. He loves you, he looks up to you, and if there's anything you can do to help him find work, please do what you can."'

A few weeks later Kathy got a call from an elated Sandy. 'Guess what! Pete gave Paul a job. He's redoing the whole Boathouse.'

'He's a real brother to them,' Kathy affirms. 'They might not be close, like they call each other up and cry on each other's shoulder, but how many brothers really do that?'

Neither family nor friends, however, can account for the most enigmatic facet of Townsend's personality: his baffling and sometimes contradictory nature.

'There's obviously two sides to my personality,' he has said. '[They're] either toward excess or total rejection. I either let go completely and become the person whom the public sees as the successful performing Pete Townshend, or I go into a mood and don't communicate at all.'

The poet Byron deemed it the black dog syndrome, bouts of depression many artists struggle with. Most artists, contends the poet, are manic-depressive and obsessed by their art. Every artist has to battle depression, an almost obligatory component of creativity.

Townshend admits he fits the bill. 'I have this idea of myself as being a classic English poet, which is bullshit really, but I carry the idea around and wear it like a hat.'

Once Pete Townshend remarked, 'I enjoy depression.' These days, though, tumult does not hold the same thrill. 'I would prefer to be balanced and gently happy with occasional moments of euphoria and depression and write nothing again, rather than ending up where I nearly did and having people tell me I'm a genius.'

As the eighties came to an end, though, Pete was already spinning in yet another new direction, one that would prove he could never really escape the Who, and in the process would bring him full circle in his first half century.

9

The Prisoner: *Passion, Power, and Middle Age*

I'd like to be a reed. You get blown backward and forward by the ebbs and flows of what is happening in the world. But you don't break. I have never broken, and I will never break.

– Pete Townshend

From the beginning of his career Townshend always believed that his true home was the theater. Spectacle was always a key ingredient of the Who. So his next creative foray seemed natural. 'I think musical theater is where I belong as a songwriter. It feels exactly what I should be doing at the moment,' he commented in 1993. 'It combines all the elements of the show business I grew up with, even from childhood, before I got into rock 'n' roll.'

Pete would like nothing better than to infiltrate the current theatrical scene dominated by his countryman, the prolific Andrew Lloyd Webber. 'I hate Webber's success,' he frankly stated. 'It's extraordinary theater, but the music is dreadful. Most of it is garbage and none of it modern.'

The former rock star's entry into musical theater actually began as a project for Roger Daltrey. Following his renewed accord with his old band mate in the wake of 1985's Live Aid, Pete set out to find a vehicle for the now bandless actor-singer. He remembered a book given to him when he was getting Eel Pie Publishing off the ground in 1976, the enormously popular children's classic *Iron Man*, written in 1968 by Ted Hughes, now Britain's poet laureate.

'I thought, "What does Roger represent in rock 'n' roll [but] this kind of Iron Man?"' reasoned Townshend. 'Then I went back and read the book and realized there was more to it than that. The real essence of the story came through, and I decided to use it as a project for me.'

The basic story concerns a boy named Hogarth, who befriends a menacing metal-eating giant who subsequently becomes a hero by defeating a horrific space dragon. The story, bearing elements of *Tommy* and *Quadrophenia*, is a rock fairy tale, Townshend says, about fear, deprivation, and the isolation of children. 'We're going back to a time where we need fairy tales,' he contended. 'At least I need them.'

Pete refused to categorize it as a children's tale, but rather a fable similar to those of ancient times, when such stories helped people learn about the mysterious world around them.

Ted Hughes gave Townshend the go-ahead for a musical adaptation after the pair hit it off while meeting at Faber and Faber. Since then Townshend has been a regular guest at Hughes's Devon home. 'He's an enormously imaginative fellow,' praises the poet. 'He has an unpredictable fantasy life which ranges across a whole set of barriers and limitations that restrict most other people. It's a very free imagination.'

Pete set to work in 1986 writing a twenty-song cycle in the tradition of *Tommy*, along with a libretto, an overture, and recitatives. The project also marked a couple of firsts, notably Townshend's adaptation of an existing piece. 'I had written myself out,' he acknowledged, 'and I wanted to tackle something that might make me start feeling things again and I knew it wasn't going to come from me.'

Second, the composer who had long resisted the collaborative process suddenly found himself comfortable working with others. 'I've been a loner for too long,' he concluded. 'Having written for Roger Daltrey all my life it's invigorating writing for other voices.' Those other voices included pop singer Nina Simone as the Space Dragon, Australian belter Deborah Conway playing the Vixen (who acts as Hogarth's conscience), and the venerable bluesman John Lee Hooker as the perfectly cast Iron Man himself.

Several of Hughes's original ideas were judiciously amended. Although Townshend relayed the essential theme of the original story, that of man's preoccupation with war machinery, Pete updated the World War I setting to modern times, envisioning the Iron Man not as a lumbering, oversized tin man, but a 'robot programmed to destroy any other machinery.' He also infused a politically correct ecology theme by redirecting the Iron Man's indiscriminate eating habits to a scrapyard, whereby he could aid in cleaning up the environment. In addition, Townshend conceived a cast of gentle Woodland Creatures for the purpose of instructing the young protagonist. One of these, the Owl, is played with great effectiveness by Simon Townshend, who sings the moving war indictment 'Man Machines.'

The key alteration from Hughes's parable was Townshend's decision to portray the main characters, Iron Man and the Space Dragon, as distinctive father and mother figures to underscore Hogarth's rite of passage into adulthood. 'He's been a child in a world of nightmares too long,' Pete reveals, 'and he finally has to realize he controls his destiny.' This was something its composer took some forty plus years to learn.

Iron Man may be Ted Hughes's story, but it is certainly Pete Townshend's musical. Those expecting thundering Who power chords might be disappointed. But within the realm of a fairy tale and the more understated approach required, Pete has left his mark with stunning brilliance. Sharp and clear, with a crystalline buoyancy throughout, the mix is impeccable, bringing out each distinctive contribution by Townshend himself and a crackling chorus of superior vocalists.

One of the most outstanding tracks, 'I Won't Run Anymore,' depicts the protagonist's first bold steps to adulthood. When Hogarth first spots the Iron Man, instead of running as one might expect, he valiantly decides to confront the beast that represents the nightmares and fears of his childhood. 'He's afraid of the responsibilities that [growing up] will bring, of the things he's got to face,' explains Pete. 'It's about the moment when a child balances those symbols of fear and smashes them against one another and grows up.'

Critics and listeners alike generally rank as the finest song a Townshend anthem of a very different kind, the gospel-like 'All

Shall Be Well.' The momentum builds from beginning to end, heightened by a rapid-fire chorus with its impassioned, near delirious delivery by vocalists Conway and Chyna. Townshend drew the song's inspiration from a phrase by a canonized English nun, Mother Julian of Norwich, who stated, 'All shall be well and all manner of things shall be well.'

As Pete divulged, 'It bridges the last five or six years of my life. I was deeply struck by that and felt it was a great dictum for living.'

An element lacking in Townshend's material throughout his long career is humor, but he effectively draws it out here in two numbers. One is John Lee Hooker's superbly dry-witted rendition of the bluesy 'I Eat Heavy Metal.' Yesker's gruff, mumbled delivery alone conjures up a metallic behemoth scouring the landscape for hubcaps and aluminum siding. 'I eat heavy metal/Gargle premium gas/I drink heavy water/Nitro demitasse.'

Said Hooker of working with Townshend: 'I never thought I could do that. I never dreamed . . . that was so far out of my territory in music. The lyrics he wrote for me to do, I never heard such lyrics. "I'm the Iron Man, I eat barbed wire," something like that. I said, "I can't do that Pete." He said, "Yes, you can. You've been my idol all my life; now you tell me you ain't gonna do it?" Now I never say I can't do it anymore.'

In what would be a prophetic move, the Who rejoin Townshend on two tracks. The first is the infectious, toe-tapping 'Dig,' with a crisp, controlled lead by Daltrey, displaying his more mature vocal talents. Within the story's context, the words refer to a frightened community attempting to dig a pit to trap the Iron Man. In true fable form, however, the lyric delivers a sly double meaning, the misguided notion that hard work is man's salvation. 'That we can dig our way out of this,' says Townshend, 'that we can dig trenches, we can dig down, we can find treasure; there's more oil down there, more coal. We just have to dig! And, of course, it's futile!'

'Fire,' which accompanies the climactic duel between the Iron Man and Space Dragon, proves the Who and the Crazy World of Arthur Brown just don't mix. A cover of the original sixties hit, this track was the one real downer in an otherwise sterling score. Heavy, grinding, almost dirgelike compared to the original, it lowers the overall vitality of the work considerably.

Townshend's twist on the theme of good versus evil continued what he began in *White City* with the notion that white and black are not all what they seem at first glance. The Iron Man, for example, is perceived as a threat, yet once his true purpose is understood, he becomes a productive member of society. The even more menacing Space Dragon is essentially a benign entity created to spin celestial music, but is lured to earth by the horrendous events on the planet.

Hughes's original happy ending is one Pete clings to; the Space Dragon is conquered and sent back to the stars to once again weave heavenly music. Townshend appropriately ends the musical on a lingering crescendo. What else could this be but the universal lost chord, for which he has been searching all his life.

Bringing *Iron Man* to the stage would take several years, but linking up with his former band mates had an immediate result. They decided to reunite the Who for their twenty-fifth anniversary.

Yet again Townshend had reversed his stand on touring. The turning point, he claims, was attending the 1989 Rock 'n' Roll Hall of Fame induction ceremony. 'I realized that this undeniable American art form of rock 'n' roll had given me a reason for being, a focus, a destiny, a past, a present, and a future,' he said. 'And I thought if these guys want to honor the Who next year, if the audience wants to come to our twenty-fifth anniversary party, who am I to stand in the way?'

As the plans unfolded, however, Pete confessed to more worldly motives. Since the *Iron Man* soundtrack was being released in June, he figured why not piggyback some free publicity on the more than capable shoulders of the Who? It seemed a brilliant plan. Insert a few numbers in the show, play a video on the large screen during the intermission, and capitalize on the Who hysteria that was once more about to erupt.

Ultimately, the decision to hit the road was whittled down to dollars, and plenty of them. The tour was anticipated to gross over $50 million, a sum Townshend simply couldn't refuse. 'With money like that we could solve the Ethiopian drought problem. When you earn that much money and keep 142 people employed full-time on the road for nearly twenty weeks and you can also generate large amounts for charity, there comes a point when you can't say no.'

His fellow Who cohorts were keen to jump on board as well. Roger, despite his earlier concerns about the band performing past their prime – 'You wouldn't want to see the Who like that, would you?' – was now eagerly embracing the prospect. 'I just want to play,' he exuded. 'Whether there's an audience or not doesn't really matter.' John was equally game, not exactly having made a huge splash on his own, lamenting, 'They won't let me do fuck all else. The only way I can play in front of a big audience is with the Who.'

The question of the drummer though produced some animosity. Pete ultimately decided to bring Simon Phillips on board, whom he pronounced 'the greatest rock drummer alive,' a musician more capable of approaching Keith's freewheeling style than Kenney Jones. While it was reported that the band gave Jones his walking papers, Kenney says he quit to join Paul Rodgers, tired of waiting for the Who to re-form. In closing, he accused Townshend of ferreting away the best material for himself, and then added the ultimate stinger: 'I was constantly being compared to Keith Moon, and Keith was such an opposite to me.' John Entwistle later saw that it 'got to the point where there wouldn't have been a Who with Kenney Jones. Roger would not have come back if Kenney were here.'

As could be expected, Townshend had his own view. 'That is not a conflict. Kenney isn't here. I chose the new drummer. You could go down the rest of the band, and I think you'll find I chose most of them [the touring band had fifteen members]. In fact, I chose the whole fucking lot of them. There's no conflict. This is my band. The only potential conflict is based on how John and Roger feel about working in that environment and calling it the Who. Maybe they would prefer going out as a four-piece, and we thrash away like we did in the sixties. I don't know what's on their minds. They're not entirely honest with me all the time. They treat me like a lunatic sometimes.'

Pete was painfully aware of his mid-forties limitations, clearly evidenced by a Perspex screen that shielded his side of the stage from the higher decibels, and his decision to play electric guitar through only half the show. Still, he broached the situation with humor: 'Imagine an eighty-year-old grandfather at a party filled with pretty girls and young nephews and nieces. Someone stands up to make a speech and says, "Here's someone we all love. Come on, Grandad, dance!" Then everyone stands back and watches the old guy dance an arcane little pagan dance that isn't done anymore and looks a little ridiculous. That's kind of the way the Who feel.'

The Kids Are Alright tour kicked off in Glens Falls, New York, on June 21, 1989, and rolled across North America and Britain for fifty-three shows, climaxing November 2 at London's Royal Albert Hall. The three-and-a-half-hour concerts included special all-star performances of *Tommy*, featuring Elton John, Patti LaBelle, and Phil Collins, at Radio City Music Hall, L.A.'s Universal Amphitheater, and the Royal Albert Hall.

The tour, however, wasn't without trials. The corporate sponsorship of Miller Brewing and Anheuser-Busch unleashed a swirl of controversy. Paul McGuinness, manager of U2, brandished Townshend for 'selling out' by accepting the assistance in light of his own drinking problems. 'Pete is a recovered alcoholic,' leveled McGuinness, 'and I really think he ignored rather than was unaware of the contradictions contained in his position. It is this kind of greedy sponsorship that makes me uncomfortable.'

Townshend, however, claimed it was absurd to equate a few beers with alcoholism. 'Since I stopped drinking in 1981, I've done so much work in rehab and talking to people, people who are writing books on the subject of alcohol. [But] banning alcohol tomorrow would not stop alcoholism; it's been tried before.' As for accepting sponsorship, Pete pointed out that nearly every cent went to charity: the Texas Special Olympics and the Nordoff Robbins Foundation, which uses music therapy to help autistic children.

There was also a nearly disastrous accident. In Tacoma, Washington, on August 16, Pete, in the middle of his famous windmill, impaled his hand on the whammy bar of his guitar, tearing off several fingernails and sending the guitarist running off stage in excruciating pain. He came within a hairsbreath of severing a tendon.

During the British leg, an unsavory incident soured a performance before twelve thousand at London's Wembley Arena. After the band left the stage to roaring applause, Townshend remained behind taking the microphone to launch into a derisive mock apology to the crowd, telling them, 'This wasn't really the Who.'

'That's just him, isn't it?' responded a piqued Daltrey. 'We all know the guy's a writing genius, but he has got a problem. He thinks *he* was the Who. . . . It's weird when he does that shit, putting down audiences and that. He does it to us too! Sometimes all I want in the world is to play with him, make that music; other times when he starts all that, I wonder if I really wanna know the bloke.'

In general, though, the tour was a booming triumph. Fan reaction was enthusiastic, and the band seemed more relaxed. The concerts were more uniform, unlike the gritty highs and lows back in 1982. Phillips proved himself a vast improvement over Jones, and the fifteen-piece band, especially the Kick Horns brass section, was a welcome addition. Some critics, however, saw it differently. *New York Post* writer Rob Tannenbaum called it 'diluted and predictable, a tepid simulation of the band's spirit that calls to mind the mirage of Beatlemania. . . . The extra dozen musicians were a cushion to protect the Who from the unpleasant truth of its fossilization.'

Despite the detractors, however, Pete thoroughly enjoyed himself. 'The pressure wasn't on. There was no creative role to play. What I was enjoying was just getting on stage and playing the guitar.'

The rigors of the road did exact a toll on Daltrey, who, according to Townshend, was stressed from handling three plus hours of vocals and often came croaking back to the hotel. 'I had terrible trouble,' he admitted, 'and I am very fit. I was losing about seven pounds a night. I got to a point in Miami where I was almost seriously ill. We would sometimes give four-hour shows, and when you're forty-five years old that's pushing it.'

Moreover, the entire experience, which one broadcast journalist appropriately stamped 'a memory on tour,' acted as a cruel reminder of what could no longer be. 'It was horrific for Roger because what he really wanted was his past back,' surmised Townshend. 'If he were left to his own devices, he'd be like Jagger and Richards and keep the band going, keep fighting the good fight.'

The 1989 tour appeared to draw the final curtain on the Who. Any hope to the contrary was snuffed out when the band's thirtieth anniversary quietly passed without fanfare in 1994. 'I'll never outgrow the Who,' Pete affirmed. 'It's been my life. The Who is me. What's exciting is that the group offered a mechanism by which all of us could find ourselves, find a role and do a job. What's interesting about the Who is that we were successful because we were very much the same as other people.'

For Townshend, 1989 may have been called the Year of the Child. In addition to the children's fable *Iron Man*, there were rumblings of taking his talented tot *Tommy* to the theatrical stage. Then on November 21, eighteen years after the birth of their youngest

Above: The Who in full, super-sonic flight in 1970. (© *The JoAnn Newburg Agency*)

Right: Nine-year-old Simon Townshend rehearsing with a little brotherly backing from Pete and Paul (on drums) at Townshend's makeshift London studio in 1970. (© *The JoAnn Newburg Agency*)

Left: Avatar Meher Baba, the inscrutable spiritual master who captured Townshend's heart for a time.

Below: Keith Moon and his lovely young wife, Annette, near the end of his unparalleled explosive lifetime. *(© The JoAnn Newburg Agency)*

Townshend strums away passively during Paul McCartney's lukewarm Concert for The People of Kampuchea. (© The JoAnn Newburg Agency)

Townshend undone, hanging on old buddy Mick Jagger in 1981. (© David McGough/ DMI)

Pete and Roger performing in Worcester, Massachusetts, during The Who's 1982 Farewell tour. *(© David Atlas)*

Below: **Townshend makes an appearance at a fan club party in the late 80s.** *(© The Who Fan Club of America)*

Pete performing in New York during the band's 'Tommy' tour of 1989.
(© David Atlas)

daughter, he and wife Karen became the proud parents of a boy, Joseph. 'I remember I sat down with Karen, and we talked about whether we were going to have more children. We've got so many people around us who are older and have quite young kids that it made the pair of us very broody. Then just as we were thinking about adopting, Karen found she was pregnant, which is apparently a very common story.'

The grapevine had it Pete wanted to name his son Tommy or Mick after Jagger. His third chance at fatherhood, however, was tempered by old ghosts. 'You kind of make a contract with kids; you're going to get my time twelve hours a day. [But] I wonder if I've really learned. I feel the things I'm doing wrong more acutely, the time I spent away. The excuse I had when I was young was that I had to make money.'

'He absolutely adores Joseph,' notes Kathy. 'He's very doting. He takes him to school every day. With Joseph I think he's really settled down a lot in the last few years.'

Pete's good fortune continued to hold as the Who were inducted into the Rock 'n' Roll Hall of Fame on January 20, 1990, playing 'Pinball Wizard,' 'Won't Get Fooled Again,' and 'Substitute.' U2's Bono provided the witty introduction: 'It's written in rock 'n' roll that all you need is love. . . . But I think much more than that you need a great nose. The Beatles, I mean, they had Ringo. The Faces, they had two, so they gave Ron Wood to the Rolling Stones, who didn't have any. Some people have 'em and they chop 'em off. We call those people "pop stars." The Who are rock 'n' roll stars!'

Of this tidy corner of pop immortality Townshend remarked, 'It's the only reward that we've ever had that really touched the spot with me. I really take it very seriously.' At the podium Pete warded off tears with cynical remarks by affectionately referring to the Who as 'an irritant' and praised rap as a quasi second coming of rock: 'It's not up to us to try to understand it. 'It's not even up to us to buy it. We just have to get the fuck out of the way.'

But as time has proven, controversy never trails too far behind Mr Townshend. In November 1990 some very unwelcome headlines erupted in every major British tabloid: MY GAY SECRET, OUT OF THE CLOSET, and I AM WOMAN. A media feeding frenzy broke out in reaction to an interview by New York journalist Timothy White, for his book *Rock Lives*, in which Pete discussed his sexuality. White digressed ten years to the song 'Rough Boys,' off *Empty Glass*, which triggered the initial hoopla from the gay community. Townshend gave it plenty of renewed firepower.

'How could "Rough Boys" be written for the Who?' he snapped to White. 'It's about homosexuality. [It] was almost a coming out, an acknowledgment of the fact that I'd had a gay life and that I understood what gay sex was about; it was not about faggery at all. It was about violence in a lot of senses. It leans very heavily into the kind of violence men carry in them.

'So in a way, it's like me saying, Listen, one of the things I'm gonna do in the first track, you're gonna hear from Pete Townshend as a solo artist is say, "I know what's happening, and I am not that kind of macho rock star." It was really important to me because eighty percent of the Who's audience is men.'

He then moved on to the song 'And I Moved,' noting that he had discovered a new female audience just by being candid. 'Not necessarily by saying, "I am gay, I am gay." But just by being honest about the fact that I understand how gay people feel and I identify. I know how it feels to be a woman because I am a woman. And I won't be classified as just a man.'

An utterly shocked Roger Daltrey raced to exercise some damage control. 'First of all, although it is untrue, who gives a shit if he's gay anyway? . . . But if you read what he says, he never, ever says he's had a gay experience. . . . He has three lovely kids. I've never seen him with a man, or making eyes at a man or anything.'

Even Kenney Jones came to his former colleague's defense. 'He was always strange, but he's not a poof. He was totally misunderstood. What he said was there's a feminine feeling in all of us just as I'm sure there's a male feeling in women. That's all he was saying. . . . It was a sensationalized comment.'

The explosive revelations however were not completely new. In a 1980 article Pete had revealed about how shattered Karen was over his unveiling of an affair he'd had with a man before the couple were married. 'I couldn't make her understand I talked about it because it's my way of reaching out and letting people know about me,' he said in frustration.

In 1986 Townshend further admitted in a print interview that during his downspiral of the early eighties, 'I even went through a gay period.'

In the wake of the fiasco he sought to clarify his remarks about the controversial pair of songs. 'These songs were welcomed by my gay fans, but you have to listen to them to understand what I am really saying. I don't want to betray my gay fans' feelings of solidarity with me by saying any more.'

But his addendum only darkened the picture. It was clear he had done some experimenting in the past, but beyond that he was being deliberately cryptic.

Kathy adds this insight: 'It's not something that's partial to Pete Townshend alone, it's part of the artist's lifestyle. Most artists do not specify the gender of a human being. If they're attracted to a person, they're not concerned whether they're male or female. It does not mean they're gay.'

The media was still making waves in 1993 when London's tabloid *Sun* dubbed him a 'self-confessed transvestite.' Townshend further muddied the waters with this response: 'What is interesting is I won't trivialize my sexuality in that way. If only I was just a transvestite. But I think I'm much more interesting than that. And much more complicated. And more honorable. I would never ever betray any relationship I'd had out of any kind of degree of sexuality or perversion. I would never ever comment on its value to me by inferring that I have had or have not had a homosexual or a heterosexual or a whipping thing or an enema thing.'

An entirely different sensation was in the making. On a professional level, Pete was close to realizing a twenty-year dream. His landmark rock opera, *Tommy*, had appeared in every configuration except for the theatrical presentation he'd initially envisioned from its inception. True, the work had a brief eight-week stint in early 1979 at London's Queen's Theatre, but it had been a more abstract, flashy production, bearing little of Townshend's input.

Broadway director Des McAnuff wanted to go big-time. 'The Who's concept album *Tommy* was the first time a rock 'n' roll band had created a piece of music theater,' he stated. 'We all created images to accompany us while we listened to *Tommy*; that music and those images combine in a very powerful theater of the imagination. They were powerful enough to make me wonder why there had not been a significant stage production of *Tommy*. They made me want to talk with Pete about exploring the possibilities of a collaboration.'

Townshend readily agreed. 'I've waited, sitting on the rights like a mother hen, until the public was ready to go to the legitimate theater instead of some impersonal stadium to see the Who.'

The lazy oceanside hamlet of La Jolla, California, where McAnuff was director of the local playhouse, became the launching site. McAnuff and Townshend, having become fast friends, hunkered down in 1991 for a six-week rewriting of the script. While Des essentially remained faithful to Pete's vision, several substantial changes were made: a strengthening of parental characterizations, a reordering of the songs to make for more seamless transitions and concentration on Tommy's rise to stardom.

Overall, the rock opera's retooling exchanged ambiguity for a more nineties realism and accessibility, stemming in part from Townshend's retreat from his earlier ties to Meher Baba. As McAnuff observed, 'I think his beliefs have evolved and changed.'

Townshend further clarified: 'The spiritual metaphor I used, being deaf, dumb, and blind, equating to our spiritual ignorance, also equates to the social isolation of young people crawling out of adolescence. That gave me a new way of looking at the story of Tommy. I was able to look at Tommy as a real person, rather than a figment of my Meher Baba-Sufi spiritual inclinations at the time.'

The one element of the show that caused controversy, for fans and critics alike, was the dramatic change of the play's finale. Instead of the quasi-mystical ending of the original, the play's ends were neatly tied up: Tommy returns to his family to work things out.

Townshend had long been bothered by his original, too nebulous, finish, which he said was directionless. 'You didn't know whether you were supposed to side with the audience who had been used and abused and were obviously by-products of organized religion or with the benefactor, Tommy, who was the engine of it all.'

Brett Easton Ellis, writing in *Vanity Fair*, called it 'a Nancy Reagan ending,' sending Pete into a fury. 'Nobody's thinking very much about this at all, and it enrages me,' he fired. 'I was going to get on a plane, find Ellis and smash his teeth in and show him what the dark life can really be about. I've been there, you know. You don't just shove it up your nose.'

Seen another way, the ending mirrors Townshend's coming to terms with his past, focusing on his own parents' reconciliation after their separation when he was a child. Pete revealed the ever fiery Betty was set to split with a lover who was to spirit her off to an oil country. 'My father didn't want me to go, so he took her back,' says Pete. 'My mother's side of the story is that she took him back, you know, for my sake.'

Townshend says their reunion resulted in a fairly normal life from that point. But it was only when he made peace with his mother that he compared his own shortcomings as a husband and parent. 'I realized I had made as many mistakes as her in being a parent, if not more. I'm in a failing family. . . . I don't see myself as a good father or even a decent man. When I talk about the importance of family, I'm just saying I wish I could do that.'

Therefore, says Pete, the revised *Tommy* ending reflects a reconciliation with the generation that preceded his own. 'I feel tremendous sympathy for people of that time. I began to manifest this sympathy in *Tommy* because I actually looked at what the people of my parents' generation had done.'

When Tommy returns to the Walkers, it's a celebration of the potency of family, he explains, as well as redemption and forgiveness. 'In the end the whole story turns to face God,' he says. 'When the people stand up and cheer, even though they may not know it, they're actually praying.'

The restructured *Tommy* debuted at the La Jolla Playhouse on July 9, 1992, to spectacular reviews. McAnuff's high-energy direction seemed based on continual MTV-like motion, complete with a nineteen-minute overture, flying props, video projections, and choreographed movement rather than pure dancing. The latter was Townshead's decision. 'No fuckin' dancin'!' he had barked to choreographer Wayne Cilento right from the very start.

The show-stopping 'Pinball Wizard' pulls out every stage gimmick ever conceived. Tommy is whipped and tossed about in a giant gyrating pinball machine that explodes into flames, pitching the entire theater into a frenzied kaleidoscope of light and color.

Aside from the problematic 'icky new feel-good finale,' as one critic dubbed it, Townshend also drew ire for his added song, 'I Believe in My Own Eyes.' It's not a bad tune, but within the context of Townshend's rock opera, written twenty-five years previously, it seems showy. As Jim Farmer in the *New York Daily News* cracked, 'Unfortunately, it seems to have parachuted in from another play.' John Entwistle echoed the same sentiment. 'It sounds a bit Broadway, doesn't it? The Who would never have done it.'

But Pete was no longer part of the Who, and his call to the Great

White Way had clipped any lingering ties to his old obsession. Even as his success in the theater capital was all but assured, Townshend had doubts about mounting the production on the world's most famous musical avenue, fearing it would mean a radical change in his life.

'I was excited that if the show did well, it could feed my future creative life, but I was also frightened that maybe I should be retiring. Maybe I should just be taking the money I already have, slowing down and getting out of show business.'

The $6 million venture, debuting on April 22, 1993, at the St. James, was a smash. Once again critics raved, led by Frank Rich of the *New York Times*: 'The show is not merely an entertainment juggernaut riding at full tilt on the visual and musical highs of its legendary pinball iconography and irresistible tunes, but also a surprisingly moving resuscitation of the disturbing passions that made *Tommy* an emblem of its era.'

In the wake of his triumph, Pete related a story about meeting up with a street person in Times Square. 'Ain't you Pete Townshend?' slurred the man. 'Hey, I love that "My Generation" thing; I love that *Tommy* thing. Hey, ain't that *Tommy* thing on Broadway now? That's great, man. You're on your way, baby!'

Pete paused and then generously prompted, 'Isn't there something I can do for you?' and gave him a hundred-dollar bill. To his amazement the very next day he was accosted by a second individual, who eloquently reenacted the same routine. Pete was impressed. 'Hey, this is New York,' he said. 'What professionalism. Even the panhandlers do their research.'

Two months after its premiere, the musical won five of eleven nominated Tony Awards, including one for Best Director. At the televised ceremonies on June 7, 1993, Townshend himself was called to the podium to receive his honor for Best Original Score. The working-class rocker from West London had become the toast of Broadway. His brief acceptance speech offered his usual sardonic wit: 'I saw *Kiss of the Spider Woman* twice and I loved it. I saw my show one hundred times, and I hate it.' Later he admitted with all humility, 'The Tony is the first artistic award I've ever had. . . . I've never won a Grammy or anything for my creative work. At this time in my life it's like getting a knighthood.'

Underlying the celebration, the edges of Townshend's personal life were once again beginning to fray. Success and New York, that strange, potentially deadly combo, were about to do him in. In a conversation with Des McAnuff before the show opened, the director assured him, 'Don't worry, it's going to be successful.'

To which Pete responded, '"But, Des, that's what I'm worried about." The thing I had to worry about was not that the show was going to flop, but that it would be too much of a success. I was worried I would get drawn into a kind of ecstasy and it could destroy me.'

Sure enough, at the preview Townshend once again indulged his old habits. According to several guests on hand during a party at the Hard Rock Cafe, several cast members, fully aware of Townshend's status as a recovered alcoholic, nonetheless plied the artist with shots of brandy the entire evening. Eventually a hopelessly inebriated Pete had stumbled out of the establishment and into his waiting limo. As one Townshend friend noted, '[When he's drunk] he's funny, he's friendly and loves everyone. One thing about Pete Townshend, you never know if he likes you unless he's nice to you when he's sober.'

Once more he seemed headed for disaster, announcing, 'My wife says what's so awful about living with me is that when things are going well, it is a signal for a manic self-destructive act.'

Now that he had scored a major hit, investors were at his door waiting to sign him up for future ventures, all pulling him back to his doomed Garden of Eden, the Big bad Apple, where he now had his own apartment. 'I pulled out of,' he adds, 'a rather unsatisfactory life at home where for twenty-five years I've been married to somebody who doesn't like show business very much. It's quite a good thing my wife doesn't like the business, but it does make it difficult. I've got a young son and I don't like to be away from him, but I feel dragged into the excitement and vigor of New York.'

In the meantime, back home in London the curtain opened on the long-awaited staging of *Iron Man* at the Young Vic on November 25, 1993. Townshend's 1989 album had fared poorly, only charting as high as fifty-eight in *Billboard*, a result of a poor marketing strategy with the Who tour, he felt in hindsight. Pete was confident, however, of reaching a wider audience via the stage.

But despite his roaring success with *Tommy*, it appeared Pete did not have the Midas touch after all. Although not all reviews were negative, the difficulty in presenting a rock fairy tale was apparent.

The multiple meanings proved too sophisticated for children, yet not quite satisfactory for adults.

As fine as the music itself is, the production doesn't quite achieve its lofty goal. Even more than *Tommy*, the storyline can't really stand without explanation. Townshend conceded the work's tricky lyrics are not conducive to the rock medium.

Another major problem is Hogarth's strong identification with Iron Man as his father and Space Dragon as his mother, confusing the role of his real parents, especially the father played by Daltrey. Furthermore, the underlying erotic tensions are too overt in the innocent realm of a ten-year-old hero.

London's *Evening Standard* critic Nicholas de Jongh said, 'Townshend's adaptation misses out on Hughes's great set-piece duels between the Iron Man and Dragon Star. And the euphoric ending is imposed rather than won through struggle.' After a short run the show closed.

A devastated Townshend groped for consolation; the white wine he'd been sipping at meals now turned into semi regular brandy binges. It was the same old story, 'a nightmare year' of professional pressures, on the road away from the stability of his family, and the inviting terror of New York. 'Once in America I tend to socialize extremely hard, partying every night. My problem is I love New York. The Who always considered it a spiritual home. I was feted there and loved the social life. I developed a close group of friends and spent as much time as possible with them.

'I needed to liberate myself from the dark place I'd put myself into, saying no to everything. I got into trouble saying yes, but had taken control too far. I wanted to become a human being again. And that meant brandy.'

Back home, Karen had put up with these antics one time too many and so banished her errant husband to sleeping quarters in a cottage at the end of the garden. According to those inside Townshend's family circle, he came very close to leaving London and Karen and permanently moving to New York, and rumors abounded about possible infidelities.

But in the end, another dose of detox and rehab and the emotional support of Eric Clapton staved off a breakup. By early December the couple were communicating once more. 'We have some way to go yet, but I hope and pray I can sort my brain out and keep my family together,' said a fragile Townshend. 'I've been dry now for thirteen days and with the help of friends and colleagues (many in show business) I will sort this problem out.

'The main thing we're agreed on is the importance of preserving a proper environment for Joseph. Despite all my neglect I firmly believe that a family with a mum and dad is the best thing any child can have.'

This binge seems to have brought home another truth as well. His graying, receding hair and complaints of arthritis and hearing loss were outward signs he was no longer a young man. 'Rock 'n' roll doesn't age you in time,' he wryly observed, 'it ages you quicker than time.'

Throughout the eighties he had always regarded his contemporaries as barometers, warning that the public was waiting to see the fall of rock icons such as David Bowie, Rod Stewart, and even Roger Daltrey. 'Mick Jagger,' he noted in particular, 'will eventually become the Chuck Berry of the sixties, constantly parodying himself on stage.'

Recently he commented, 'You know what happens to the likes of Bowie, Jagger, and me? Our teenage kids turn around and say, "You look like mutton dressed as lamb. How can I possibly have my friends round? You look fucking ridiculous. Why are you suddenly wearing an earring?"'

Pete inevitably found himself facing the consequences of that notorious line, 'Hope I die before I get old.' In 1989 he reversed his brash stance on youth, declaring, 'Now that I am older I very much hope I will get old. It's quite perverse really because it's the one thing I've been longing to experience all my life. I never much enjoyed being young. I always knew there was something else.'

Townshend notes that while Jagger says his fans want him to preserve their own youth to avoid confronting mortality, he stands firmly on the other side, reminding his followers no one lives forever. The media quickly got on the case, launching silly headlines like PETE'S DEATH WISH. 'People think it's sick, but I want to die because I have a feeling about life that it is a responsibility given to you by somebody else. Death means freedom from that responsibility. But that doesn't mean I run around trying to kill myself. I hope to be forgotten in my lifetime rather than remembered after death.'

Despite all the verbal posturing, Kathy put it more bluntly: 'The man can't stand a birthday.' A case in point was Pete's all-important fortieth. One Townshend fan remembers being among a band of obsessed Who fans who tramped down to the Boathouse in the early hours of May 19, 1985. To mark the milestone they raised a fifty-foot computer banner proclaiming, 'HAPPY FORTIETH BIRTHDAY, PETE TOWNSHEND!' rimmed with a host of multicolored balloons and streamers. The early-morning festivities attracted passersby honking, laughing, yelling, 'Way to go Pete!'

In the midst of this joyous revelry, the door to Townshend's office suddenly burst open, and minder Paul Bonnick stepped out with a decidedly uncelebratory look on his face. 'I'm sorry, but Pete got me out of bed and said to get this stuff down and get it down now.'

'He's fifty years old; he's not a rock star anymore,' declares Kathy. 'Pete Townshend isn't Keith Richards or Mick Jagger. Roger Daltrey is and that's a problem the band had. Pete doesn't want to be a fool on stage. He can't do what he used to and doesn't want to. He doesn't really have the interest anymore.'

Pete has pondered the coming years. 'There are a few people from the old guard left, and everybody's watching: how are they going to grow old? Elegantly, stupidly, or what? The way I see it, David Bowie's got a shock of blond hair, Mick Jagger's got a flat tummy, and I've got a brain . . . and Ray [Davies] is neurotic. How we're gonna go into our middle fifties I don't know.'

He proceeded to explore this brave new world of aging rockers in his most recent solo project, *PsychoDerelict*. It was a telling coincidence that the album was released in June 1993, the same month Pete was reaping accolades for the success of *Tommy*. He was continuing to explore a new frontier.

In his latest venture Townshend tackles a new format: songs threaded within a radio play. The plot revolves around Ray Highstreet (professionally known as Ray High), a sixties rock star turned nineties recluse whose return to the limelight is manipulated by his irascible manager, Rastus Knight, and muckraking broadcaster Ruth 'Life's a bitch and so am I' Streeting. The scam involves Ruth inventing a persona as Roz Nathan, High's precocious fourteen-year-old pen pal and an aspiring singer. A flattered Ray takes the bait and writes a song for this ingenue, initially unaware of the conspiracy to engineer a rejuvenation of his career. Interspersed throughout is a techno, sci-fi subplot lifted from Townshend's aborted *Lifehouse* project in which Ray is writing a concept called *Grid Life*, a virtual-reality concept that espouses the lost dream of the sixties anchored by the familiar search for universal harmony through music.

If Townshend's Ray High is mired in a middle-age funk, Pete is anything but. The music is as potent, dynamic, and liberating as Townshend has delivered in more than a decade. Back to guitar-based melodies, his songs are interspersed with familiar synthesizer interludes culled from *Who Are You*. All his familiar band mates are here: Simon Phillips, Rabbit, the Kick Horns. This time around, however, Townshend drops the big-band sound for more rhythmic arrangements and, more important, offers an intuitive and emotive lyricism not seen in quite a while.

The album kicks off with the blistering 'English Boy,' seemingly about the emergence of modern punk. The anchor of the work, it is a scathing indictment of society's using youth as a convenient scapegoat for its problems.

As always, Townshend meets issues head-on, but this time with a new attitude, not self-indulgent or contentious but one born of honest self-appraisal. None is more candid than the self-explanatory 'Let's Get Pretentious.' It's precisely this posture for which he's been criticized over the years, sometimes unfairly he contends, simply because of the position he's in.

'I am frightened of being thought pretentious,' he admitted. 'It's not insecurity, it comes from being badly educated. That's what was difficult about the editorial committees at Faber. Even the secretaries on five grand a year had degrees and were better read than me. But I'm more careful now about expounding on subjects on which I know nothing.'

On the nicely understated, 'Outlive the Dinosaur,' with its flickering shades of jazz, Pete examines aging from a different perspective, that of humans beings, the only animals who live by a calendar and watch. 'When you look in the mirror as you grow older, you see this person you regard as yourself growing old, but you start to move away, to subtract yourself from that person. Nonetheless, one day you look in the mirror and you see this decaying individual and you cry. And the person sitting next to you says, "That's self-pity." You're as young as you feel. You've got to hang on to the end. You've got to believe. My belief is that you're not crying for yourself, but for the child you once were, and you're crying for youth, which is indeterminate and something you can't have.'

This is precisely what Pete's alter ego Ray High is doing in the play. Unlike his failures with *Iron Man* and *White City*, Townshend finally weaves his songs effectively within the framework of the dialogue. No longer just isolated tunes, they are firmly engraved within the context of the piece.

'Fake It,' conversely, is the response to that. 'I'm going to ask you to act it/Don't let me see if you're bored/If you use the right antic/You will hear me applaud.'

Together the tunes suggest a complicity between fan and star, a willingness on the fan's part to believe in a larger-than-life fantasy, and on the performer's to control and perpetuate that fantasy by being submissive to his audience. 'It's a really perverse idea,' confirms Pete. 'And where do you learn that trick? You learn it as a child, if you're submissive and do as the adults tell you, you can get by and have a quiet life.'

The songs also confront the cautious, potentially explosive relationship between performer and critic, as personified by Ray and Ruth. It's a subject he's laid low on over the years, except for a brief discharge on 'Jools and Jim,' but one that has obviously festered in the artist. 'There will always be a war between the artist and critic,' he maintains, 'because the critic is necessary and the artist would like to think they weren't. . . . The power of the critic to destroy is underestimated. Not to destroy the work, not destroy the relationship of the artist to the audience. But to destroy the artist's enthusiasm to work.'

A line in the play that brings this home has the opportunistic and greedy manager Rastus cackling, 'I'm running out of *your* money!'

'Now and Then' and 'I am Afraid,' address Ray's incredulous love for the rapier-tongued Ruth, and represent a pair of the most emotionally impacting songs in the Townshend catalog. Both spin delicate, vulnerable webs of those initial helpless moments of love. 'Now and Then' represents the staggering realization and futility of losing one's heart: 'Now and then you see a soul and you fall in love/You can't do a thing about it/For though you knew that I was twice your age/To make you laugh seemed youth enough.'

Townshend impacts a feeling we can all identify with, which has always been his unique strength as a composer and performer.

'I'm Afraid' subsequently explores the perilous ramifications of 'Now and Then.' 'As I stand beside you I have denied you/I am afraid.' Lyrically it quivers with a raw grace born of not only physical, but spiritual love, and is perhaps Townshend's truest, most intimately revealing treatise since 'Time Is Passing' off *Who Came First*. 'By my religion I stand here naked/I cannot fake it with God as witness/My little children who wait for feedin'/I watch you bleeding I am afraid.'

Within Townshend's exquisite, haunting delivery there lies a new fragility, his voice rimmed with textures and vulnerable crevices never before captured on record. Stripped bare, at the mercy of the listener, of his God, it stands as one of the artist's most potent moments on record.

Yet all this pathos is considerably weakened within the context of the radio drama. Out of the blue Ray High announces his love for the backstabbing Streeting, who is anything but lovable. First she seduces the rock star under the guise of an imaginary teenager (all the while having a kinky affair with his manager), then betrays him with a manufactured high-profile sex scandal, ultimately making big money off the sordid scheme when High's records once more start to sell.

The project's weaknesses came to light through Townshend's mid-1993 staging of the musical play during a brief American road trip. The principal actors, Jan Ravens as Streeting and John Lanbanowski as High , are perfectly cast and entirely convincing. The overall production, however, is vaguely amateurish. Townshend errantly tapped his old pal Richard Barnes to direct, and Barnes delivers several awkward vignettes whereby Pete can be seen just out of the spotlight, laughing, making remarks to the actors, even blowing on a snorkel in one absurd scene.

Another major flaw is Pete's virtual-reality aspect, dusting off his old *Lifehouse* 'experience suits' to push the utopian ideology of the ultimate rock concert that will propagate peace, love, and world harmony. Pete seems determined to resurrect his beloved work, but although the message has merit, in this framework it is an intrusion that just doesn't fit.

In a 1993 interview while he was putting the finishing touches on the project Townshend made the startling revelation that the character of Ray High was, in fact, a dual representation of both Pete Townshend and Roger Daltrey. 'Whenever the press addressed the relationship I had with Roger, it always returns to that same old context, our version of the Glimmer Twins. You know, one is the good old boy who gets out there and sings, and one is the oddball who sits in the background and really fucks things up. And the stereotype of those two figures is really what I'm addressing. It's the story of two guys from a band, both in their mid-fifties, struggling with their dreams and vision for the future and to some extent with their perversity as a result of having been stars.'

Unfortunately, the play doesn't let its audience in on this vital insight. Even ardent Who fans would be hard pressed to make the connection without being told outright.

Pete does concede his characters are but 'comic book' figures and that the play is 'not supposed to be something deep,' merely dialogue to string together the songs. In fact, he contends the essence of the work is summed up simply in its title.

The disc booklet designed by Frank Gargiulo depicts a stark, eerie, out-of-focus Townshend staring out from behind the scribbled words *Pete Townshend PsychoDerelict* like a long-term patient behind the bars of the local mental ward.

Predicted by many critics to be an enormous success, *Psycho-Derelict* fell flat with the public. The album sold fewer copies than any previous Townshend offering and had him hinting it might be his final album. 'I sell records in much smaller numbers, but to a much more exclusive crowd, but that's the apology of a dying act,' he was forced to admit. 'Some of the things I write about in middle age and will probably continue to write about in late middle age are not quite so palatable as some of the slightly more raunchy, more distasteful problems of being adolescent.'

Here Pete put his finger squarely on the problem. *PsychoDerelict* may well be his best recorded work since *Quadrophenia*, yet its sophistication and intellect weeded out those good-time Who fans. Addressing that issue, he recently said, 'I want people who like what I do now, like the albums I've done in the past and loved the Who to actually feel they are the continuum. What my life is about and what my duty is as a songwriter is to serve them. And what they see is me failing in that duty because I'm not doing what Guns n Roses are doing or not doing what the Who did in the early days. The duty I took on to begin with has become deeper and more demanding.'

While Pete was hitting a low ebb commercially, things weren't exactly booming for his former mates. John Entwistle has woven his way unobtrusively through a series of generic bands, most recently touring with Ringo Starr during 1995. As for Roger Daltrey, he's enjoyed some success on the acting front, but his music career has sputtered with a brief resurgence via his collaboration with the Chieftains, an Irish folk band that earned him a Grammy Award in 1992 for Best Folk Album. He followed that up, however, with a failed summer tour of 1994 billed as 'Daltrey Sings Townshend.' Roger once feared that going out on a stage without Pete was like 'being without my right arm,' and regrettably it has played out. As *Toronto Star* critic Peter Howell observed, '[It was] a sad feeling of a man desperately trying to rekindle a dead fire.'

It was even conjectured that Daltrey, a man of nearly fifty at the time, lobbied his partner to give him the lead in *Tommy*. Absurd as it sounds, Townshend didn't deny the rumor. 'The difficult area for Roger was to let go of the piece,' was all Pete would say.

By all accounts Daltrey still has Who visions dancing in his head. Not long ago this author ran into the stocky blond front man walking down a street in London's Soho. 'When's the Who getting back together?' I prompted. 'Well, I want to, but Pete doesn't,' he glumly responded.

That prospect doesn't seem likely. True, for the past decade Townshend has spoken of the magic and chemistry of their alliance and has aired hopes of finding a joint project with his old mate. In a Toronto interview in November 1994 he voiced aspirations to write a collection of songs that addressed Daltrey's interests. 'It was a great partnership and I hope it has another chapter,' he stated.

But on the other hand, when Pete speaks of the future – an animated version of *Iron Man*; reviving *Quadrophenia* for the stage; a musical version of Arthur Miller's life; a top-secret Las Vegas project in collaboration with Tim Rice – Daltrey's role seems conspicuously absent.

Currently Townshend is tied up launching *Tommy* internationally. He oversaw the Toronto production in the spring of 1995, and additional companies were slated for Germany and Australia. Back home he began a ferry service on the Thames and still retains a position at Faber and Faber.

At fifty he seems to have gotten over the hump of his disillusion with rock, discovering rejuvenation and hope in, of all things, rap music. 'Its steep, jazzy shuffle and offensive, repetitive nature of sampling is meant to be irritating like the electric guitar was meant to be irritating,' he points out. 'It's meant to be in your face, like the Who were.'

His gigs to support *PsychoDerelict* were specifically 'to prove to myself that having a show on Broadway didn't mean I still wasn't a rock star.'

Yet it has the fading ring of nostalgia for the purity of those early days. Townshend poignantly described rock 'n' roll as 'that moment when you decide that you're alone. That moment when you let go of your parents. The loneliness of that moment, the poignancy of that moment, has been undermined by the fact that in rock 'n' roll in the sixties we felt that we had an alternative family to sustain us. . . . The music held people together and made us feel like we were part of a community that didn't necessarily need Mom and Dad. Mom and Dad were there if you wanted them, but you could survive without them.'

It's a very different age now for burgeoning rockers, Townshend contends, controlled by a big-business industry and a pervasive nihilism far from the innocence and endless possibilities of rock's heyday. As Ray High ponders, 'What happened to the truth, the dream, to all that lovely hippie shit?'

As if to underscore the point, Pete recently bit the very hand that fed him. 'Rock stars are overpaid spoiled brats. Being famous through pop music is very insubstantial. It's an annoyance, an irritant. In twenty years I'm sure that sewage is going to be our main problem, and then the guy takes away our rubbish and gives us a clean glass of water, he's going to be the greatest hero of your time. Pop music is a service industry, and when you get famous it's monumentally boring. I wouldn't go through it again.'

But are we to believe him? And does Townshend really believe it himself? Or are these outbursts simply the flip side of the same coin that is Pete Townshend, who roars, 'I'm still angry!', who admonishes Mick Jagger for giving up his dream, and who recently renewed an old vow: 'I live and work no farther than a hundred yards from the house in which I was born, and I still regard my brief as writing for those six guys and one girl who came up to me at the Goldhawk Club who'd heard "Can't Explain" for the first time and said, "That's what we want to hear more of."'

Within the contrary, complex folds of an artist who has crammed so much life into his first half century, Kathy perceives a jagged, wandering soul still very much unfulfilled. 'He seems lost; I don't think the man really ever found himself. He is blinded by the past.' She points to his recurrent themes of adolescence and isolation and a thirty-year mourning for the long-ago glow of the sixties. As Ray High nostalgically muses, 'I had a dream once, it was a good dream.'

Or perhaps the roots lie deeper. Townshend has said, 'I feel at odds with everyone in the human race most of the time. I think you're all fools, and I am one of those misfits.'

An article he penned for the *Observer* is revealing: 'Only last week my Karen looked at my face and said, "You look like someone who should let yourself be sad." And so I tried it and I was sad, sad enough to wonder what had caused such a condition. I sat down and began to write notes in a deliberately cathartic way. I had spent my life up to that moment longing for an abstract someone and trying to make abstract people long for me. My mind emptied suddenly, and I was left with one little boy in a Fair Isle jumper. He had a very serious frown on his face. It was a gift of enormous value to realize that I had simply been sad about having neglected to remember an important part of my childhood. . . . If Karen hadn't suggested I let myself feel sad, I don't suppose it would have occurred to me. We creative people have no imagination, you know.'

For Peter Dennis Blanford Townshend, his life, his incredible career, his spiritual quest is still very much a work in progress. Whether he calls himself Tommy, Jimmy, or Ray, they're all the same lost little boy reflected in Townshend's ever present mirror. Yet this self-dubbed misfit so out of step with the world is the one we identify with. For all the while he was searching for his true self he allowed the rest of us to see ourselves, with all our broken dreams, private fears, and shining hopes reflected in the same glass. Right there beside his own.

Appendices

A Diary of Events 1894–1995

Compiled by Brenda Giuliano

1894

Sunday, February 25

Merwan Sheriar Irani, known to the world as Meher Baba, is born in Poona, India, to a Persian family at 5:15 a.m. Many years later, Pete Townshend will pen dozens of songs inspired by the great spiritual master.

1944

Wednesday, March 1

Roger Harry Daltrey is born in the working-class Shepherd's Bush district of London.

Monday, October 9

John Alec Entwistle is born in Chiswick, London.

1945

Saturday, May 19

Peter Dennis Blanford Townshend is born to parents Cliff and Betty in Chiswick, London.

1947

Saturday, August 23

Keith John Moon is born in Wembley, Middlesex, London.

1959

John Entwistle invites schoolmate Pete Townshend to join his trad jazz group, the Confederates.

1961

Townshend attends Ealing Art College.

1962

John Entwistle joins Roger Daltrey's popular West End group, the Detours, featuring Roger on lead guitar, John bass, Colin Dawson lead vocals and Doug Sandom on drums. Later, at the suggestion of Entwistle, Pete Townshend comes aboard.

September 1

The Detours play the Acton Town Hall.

1963

Friday, January 11

The Detours play the Fox & Goose Hotel, Hanger Lane, Ealing W5. Admission is a mere four shillings.

1964

February

The Detours become the Who at the suggestion of Townshend's close mate and longtime co-conspirator, Richard Barnes.

Townshend accidentally demolishes his very first guitar at Harrow's premier teen spot, the Railway Tavern. When the audience goes wild he realizes that here is a gimmick that could serve to ignite the smoldering passions of the fans. It quickly becomes a permanent part of the act.

Pete Meaden becomes the group's new manager. One of his first official acts is to change their name to the High Numbers.

April

Wild man Keith Moon debuts with the group.

July

Meaden involuntarily resigns as the group's manager only to be replaced by Chris Stamp and the flamboyant Kit Lambert.

Friday, July 3

Fontana Records releases the group's first single, 'I'm the Face,' backed by 'Zoot Suit'. The number is written by mod manager Pete Meaden.

Sunday, August 23

The High Numbers play the Hippodrome, Brighton, supporting Dusty Springfield.

Thursday, October 22

The High Numbers are turned down after an audition by EMI Records Ltd. A&R manager John Burgess writes to Lambert, 'I have listened again and again to the High Numbers white labels taken from our test session, and still cannot decide whether or not they have anything to offer. You may, of course, in the meantime, have signed with another company, in which case, I wish you all the luck in the world. If you have not, I will be very interested to hear any other tapes you may have featuring the group.'

Tuesday, November 24

Once again called the Who, the group becomes the house band at London's famous Marquee Club at 90 Wardour Street, Soho. They are booked for a record-breaking sixteen weeks.

1965

January

The Who enter Pie Studios, London, to record 'I Can't Explain.'
The Who appear on the popular BBC2 television show *The Beat Room*, performing 'I Can't Explain.'
Kit Lambert and Chris Stamp produce a promotional film of 'I Can't Explain.'

Friday, January 15

Brunswick Records releases 'I Can't Explain,' produced by Shel Talmy. The record struggles to number eight in the charts.

Tuesday, January 26

The Who make the first of many appearances on the popular ITV television staple *Ready Steady Go!*

February

The Who appear on the British TV show *That's for Me*.
The Who appear on *Ready Steady Go!* performing 'I Can't Explain.'

March

The Who appear on BBC1's *Top of the Pops* performing 'I Can't Explain.'

Monday, March 15

The Who perform 'I Can't Explain' on the BBC's *Gadzooks*.

Spring

The Who appear on *Disc A Go Go* on British TV.

Friday, April 2

The group is featured on *The Joe Loss Pop Show* on BBC radio.

Sunday, April 4

The Who play Newbury Plaza.

Monday, April 5

The Who play Hendon Lakeside.

Wednesday, April 7

The Who play Hemel Hempstead Dacorum College.

Thursday, April 8

The Who play the Reading Olympia.

Friday, April 9

The Who play the Altrancham, Stamford Hall.

Saturday, April 10

The Who play London's Cavern Club.

Wednesday, April 14

The Who play the Leicester Al Rondo.

Saturday, April 17

The Who play the Brighton, Florida.

Sunday, April 18

The Who play Crawley Civic.

Monday, April 19

The Who play Hayes Botwell House.

Thursday, April 22

The Who play the Southampton Waterfront Club.

Friday, April 23

The Who play the Manchester Oasis.

Saturday, April 24

The Who play the Boreham Wood Lynx Club.

Wednesday, April 28

The Who play Bromley Bromel.

Friday, April 30

The Who play the Trowbridge Town Hall.

Tuesday, May 18

The Who appear on ITV's *Scene At 6.30.*

Friday, May 21

Brunswick releases 'Anyway, Anyhow, Anywhere.'
The gutsy pop rocker climbs to number ten in the charts.
The Who appear on *Ready Steady Go!* performing 'Anyway, Anyhow, Anywhere.'

May

The Who appear on *Top of the Pops* performing 'Anyway, Anyhow, Anywhere.'

Saturday, May 29

The Who perform 'Anyway, Anyhow, Anywhere' on *Thank Your Lucky Stars* for ITV.

Wednesday, June 2

The Who play their first gig abroad in Paris.

The Who appear on *Ready Steady Go!* via a clip they filmed in Paris.

Thursday, June 3

The Who appear on French television.

August

The Who play four weekend shows at Great Yarmouth, opening for popular Scottish folkster, Donovan.

Friday, August 6

The Who appear at the Richmond Jazz Festival, which is filmed for television.

Saturday, August 28

Melody Maker reports that Townshend has amassed nine guitars while living on the dole.

September

The Who begin their first European tour.
The Who appear on a Dutch TV special.

Saturday, September 4

The Who appear on *Ready Steady Go!*

October

The Who appear on *Ready Steady Go!* performing 'My Generation.'
The Who appear on *Top of the Pops*, performing 'My Generation.'

Monday, November 8

It is reported in *Topteen Music Parade* magazine that Pete and the band spend one hundred pounds a week each on clothes.

Saturday, November 20

Melody Maker carries the headline THE WHO SPLIT MYSTERY. The story goes on to outline Daltrey's ousting from the band by the other three. He is, however, back within a week.

Saturday, November 27

'My Generation' becomes the second most popular record in Great Britain.

December

The Who Sings My Generation, the group's first album, is issued.

Friday, December 3

The Who appear on *Ready Steady Go!*

Friday, December 31

The Who appear on *Ready Steady Go!*

1966

Early 1966

The Who are filmed at the Serpentine, Hyde Park, London, performing 'The Kids Are Alright.'
Sufism Reoriented Inc., a Meher Baba splinter group, publishes the pamphlet *God in a Pill; Meher Baba on LSD and the High Roads*, in which the Master is critical of the use of drugs as an aid to spirituality. He says, 'The experience of a semblance of freedom that these drugs may temporarily give to one is in actuality a millstone round the aspirant's neck in his efforts towards emancipation from the rounds of birth and death.'

Saturday, January 1

The Who appear on the American television show *Shindig* performing 'Daddy Rolling Stone,' 'I Can't Explain,' and 'My Generation.'

Wednesday, January 5

During an appearance on BBC Television's *A Whole Scene Going* Townshend admits to having smoked dope.

Friday, March 4

'Substitute' is issued in Great Britain, reaching number five in the charts. Shel Talmy sues the group, claiming his definitive right to produce their music. A settlement is ultimately reached granting

Talmy a royalty on all of the band's records for a five-year period.

Saturday, March 12

Pete Townshend appears on the cover of *Melody Maker* magazine.

Wednesday, March 30

The Who appear on the French television show *Music Hall De France* performing 'Substitute.'

Friday, April 1

The Who appear from Paris on *Ready Steady Go!* performing 'Substitute.'

March/April

The Who begin their first full-fledged, nationwide British tour.

May

The Who play a few select dates in Ireland.
The Who appear on the Swedish TV show *Popside* performing 'Daddy Rolling Stone' 'It's not true,' 'Bald Headed Woman,' 'The Kids Are Alright,' and 'Substitute.'

Sunday, May 1

The Who play Wembley as part of the *New Musical Express*'s Poll Winners Concert.

Monday, May 30

Townshend is involved in a car crash on the M1. He is unhurt.

Saturday, August 20

The Who again appear on *Ready Steady Go!*

Friday, August 26

The single 'I'm a Boy' is issued on Reaction Records and eventually reaches number two in England.

September

The Who do yet another French TV special performing 'I'm a Boy.'
The Who perform 'I'm a Boy' on *Beat Club,* a German television program.
The Who appear on U.S. TV performing 'I'm a Boy.'

Wednesday, September 21

Townshend is fined twenty-five pounds for so-called dangerous driving.

Thursday, September 22–October

The Who begin an extended tour of Sweden.

Friday, October 21

Ready Steady Go! mounts an ambitious Who special featuring their 'Theatre of the Absurd.' This time they play 'Circles,' 'Disguises,' 'Batman,' 'Bucket T,' and 'Barbara Ann.' The special is also seen on Swedish, German, and Swiss television.

Thursday, October 27

The same special is shown on French television.

Friday, October 28

This time the show is seen on Danish TV.

Saturday, November 12

The American NBC network films the Who in King's Road and Carnaby Street for the *Today* show.

Tuesday, November 22

Townshend appears solo on the American television program *Where the Action Is* hosted by perennial deejay Dick Clark. The brief segment was filmed in Pete's London flat.

December

A promotional film is made of the Who singing 'Happy Jack.'
The Who perform 'Heatwave' on *Beat Club*.

Saturday, December 3

The Who's second LP, *A Quick One*, is issued in Britain. American music company officials, however, find the title somewhat too suggestive and so rename the work *Happy Jack*.
Happy Jack becomes the third most popular record in the English charts.

Friday, December 23

The Who appear on *Ready Steady Go!*

1967

Sunday, January 29

The Who appear at Brian Epstein's trendy Saville Theatre on Shaftesbury Avenue in London's posh theater district.

Wednesday, February 1

The Who appear on ITV's *Scene* television show.

Friday, February 3

The Who are filmed at the Marquee, London singing 'My Generation,' 'So Sad about Us', and 'Happy Jack' for *Beat Club*.

Thursday, February 23

The Who commence a quick three-day Italian tour.

Saturday, March 25

The Who, along with Cream and several other top groups, make their American debut at the Brooklyn Fox Theater as part of a special Murray the K package. While there Eric Clapton found in possession of several large sacks of self-rising flour which he intends to use to christen the Who in their dressing room. It is a ten-day engagement.

Townshend is rushed to hospital for stitches after a guitar he has launched into the stratosphere strikes him on top of the head.

Happy Jack makes inroads on the U.S. charts, reaching number twenty-four. The Who rapidly rack up a loyal fan base stateside.

April

The Who appear on *Beat Club* performing 'Pictures of Lily.'

Tuesday, April 4

The Who appear on the American show *Coliseum*.

Saturday, April 22

'Pictures of Lily' is issued on Track Records, Lambert and Stamp's promising new label. It peaks at number three.

May

The Who begin a tour of the Netherlands.

June

The Who hit the road for their first extensive American tour.

The Who record a salute to Mick Jagger and Keith Richards, who are undergoing substantial legal problems stemming from a recent drug bust at Keith's country home, Redlands. In a so-called special announcement in the *New Music Express* manager Lambert placed an ad for the single 'The Last Time,' backed by 'Under My Thumb,' stating, 'The Who consider that Mick Jagger and Keith Richards have been treated as scapegoats for the drug problem and as a protest against the savage sentences imposed on them at Chichester yesterday, the Who are issuing today the first of a series of Jagger/Richards songs to keep their work before the public until they are again free to record themselves.'

Friday, June 16

The Who play their first gig at Bill Graham's famous Fillmore West in San Francisco.

Sunday, June 18

At Monterey, Townshend accuses Jimi Hendrix of stealing the Who's act. No word on Jimi's reaction.

July–August

The Who appear on a triple bill with Herman's Hermits and the Blues Magoos. Tickets are $1.75, $2.50, $3.50, and $4.50.

Wednesday, August 23

The Who are forever banned from Holiday Inns as a result of conduct unbecoming. It is, of course, great publicity.

September

The Who perform 'I Can See for Miles' and 'My Generation' on the popular American TV show *The Smothers Brothers Comedy Hour*. The Who appear on *Top of the Pops* performing 'I Can See for Miles.'

October

The Who tour Britain along with the Herd, the Tremeloes, Marmalade, and Traffic.

Saturday, October 14

'I can See for Miles' is issued in Great Britain and ultimately reaches number ten. In America it does only a bit better, bowing out at nine.

November

The Who do a quick stint of the United States. The group's third album, *The Who Sell Out*, is released.

1968

Saturday, January 20

The Who begin a nine-day tour of Australia and New Zealand along with the Small Faces. It will be their one and only visit.

Monday, January 29

Pete vows never again to return to New Zealand after the shoddy treatment the band receives from promoters while there.

February

The Who top the bill for the first time in the United States.

Wednesday, February 21

The Who appear at the San Jose Civic Auditorium; ticket prices have now risen slightly to $2.75, $3.75, and $4.75.

Sunday, March 31

The Who play the Daughters of the American Revolution Constitution Hall, Washington, D.C. The *Washington Post* in a review dated April 1 writes, 'The Who had already established through their playing the abrasive nihilism that is the key to electronic rock. . . . The Who's approach is a paradigm of the drug-state, distorted music that dominates pop music today. This approach is tearing down the old linear concept of music.'

Friday, April 5 and Saturday, April 6

The Who play the Fillmore East in New York with Buddy Guy and Free Spirits with lights by Joshua.

Monday, May 20

Pete marries aspiring model Karen Astley.

Spring

Townshend becomes a disciple of silent master Meher Baba, who claims to be the incarnation of God for this age. His enlightened, finely tuned teachings emphasize developing a love of God from within; he tells his followers, 'I have come not to teach, but to awaken. Understand therefore that I lay down no precepts.

'Through eternity I have laid down principles and precepts, but mankind has ignored them. Man's inability to live God's words makes the Avatar's teaching a mockery. Instead of practicing the compassion He taught, man has waged crusades in His name. Instead of living the humanity, purity and truth of His words, man has given way to hatred, greed and violence.

'Because man has been deaf to the principles and precepts laid down by God in the past, in this present Avataric form I observe silence. You have asked for and been given enough words, it is now time to live them.'

June

The Who release the nothing single 'Dogs,' which predictably does nothing.

Thursday, June 27

Townshend pays £16,500 for a lovely brick Georgian home at number 3, The Embankment, Twickenham. He will live there with his family until the late seventies.

Friday, June 28 and Saturday, June 29

The Who play the Shrine Auditorium in Los Angeles backed by Fleetwood Mac.

Sunday, July 14

The Who play the Musicarnival, Cleveland. The show is reviewed by *Billboard* on July 27. The review says, 'The concert had everything from early pandemonium and an unexpected intermission to a road manager singing along with drummer Keith Moon.'

June–August

The Who tour the United States. Townshend begins work on his musical masterwork, *Tommy*.

August

The Who are filmed riding through London on a specially decorated bus to promote the single 'Magic Bus.'

Friday, August 2

The Who top the bill at New York's Singer Bowl, supported by the Doors.

September

The Who perform 'Magic Bus' on *Beat Club*.
The film *The Monterey Pop Festival* is released with the Who performing 'My Generation.'

Wednesday, November 20

The Who play two shows at the Empire Theatre, Liverpool, along with guest stars the Crazy World of Arthur Brown, the Small Faces, Joe Cocker and the Grease Band, and the Mindbinders.

Thursday, December 12

The Who join the Rolling Stones, Eric Clapton, John Lennon, Yoko Ono, Mitch Mitchell, Taj Mahal, Marianne Faithfull, black super-model Lvna, and Jethro Tull among others for the infamous, as of yet unreleased *Rock 'n' Roll Circus*, which is shot at Intertel Studios, Wembley. The Who perform 'A Quick One.'

1969

January

Sessions for *Tommy* begin at IBC Studios London.

Friday, January 31

In India Avatar Meher Baba drops his body at twelve noon without ostensibly breaking his monumental silence. Pete Townshend is reportedly both touched and deeply distressed. Unlike many who then fall away from the master after his promised 'word of words' apparently remains unspoken, Townshend stays fiercely loyal to his mentor.

Friday, March 7

The Who's classic 'Pinball Wizard' is issued, reaching number four in Britain and five in the States.

April

The Who appear on *Top of the Pops* performing 'Pinball Wizard.' The Who appear on ITV's *This Is Tom Jones* performing 'Pinball Wizard.'

May

The Who play the Grande Ballroom, Detroit. Sharing the bill is Joe Cocker.
The Who appear on *Beat Club* performing 'Overture'; 'Tommy Can You Hear Me'; 'Tommy's Holiday Camp'; 'Pinball Wizard'; 'We're Not Gonna Take It'; 'See Me, Feel Me'; 'Smash the Mirror'; 'Sally Simpson'; and 'I'm Free.'

Friday, May 2

The Who preview *Tommy* for the British press at Ronnie Scott's on Dean Street, Soho. Although loved by the public it took the British press a while to warm up to a story about an innocent boy who becomes the victim of sexual assault, drugs, and other abuses. Headlines screamed, IS THIS MAN SICK, PINBALL WIZARD STORM BACK PAGE, WHO'S PETE, SICK OR TRUTHFUL? Under a short review entitled WHO'S SICK OPERA a reviewer wrote, 'I really was looking forward to the "pop opera" which has occupied Pete Townshend's mind for so long. Really, I was. But what a disappointment, even though I tip it for the NME LP charts.

'Admittedly, the idea's original, even though other groups seem to be jumping on the bandwagon now, but it doesn't come off. Running for over an hour, it goes on and on and isn't totally representative of the Who: Maybe it's time for a change in style, but if this is it, I long for a return to the old days.'

Sunday, May 9

The Who appear on America's favorite variety program, *The Ed Sullivan Show*, performing 'Pinball Wizard.'
The Who perform 'I Can See for Miles' on *Top Of the Pops*.

Monday, May 18

Daltrey and Townshend are charged with assaulting a police officer after he leaped on stage at the Fillmore in New York. Patrolman Daniel Mulhearn sought to inform the audience of a fire next door, but was prevented from doing so by the pair. The case was scheduled for disposition in a Manhattan court.

Friday, May 23

The two-record *Tommy* album is issued, eventually climbing to number two in the United Kingdom and four in the United States.

Sunday, May 25

The Who play Merriweather Post Pavilion in the District of Columbia. This gig sees some thirty thousand fans in attendance with a net gate of $6,750. The *Washington Post* writes, 'Pete Townshend is a writer of such talent that might only be overshadowed by his luxurious excellence on the guitar.'

Thursday, May 29

The Who play the Kinetic Playground, Chicago. Some days later the *Chicago Tribune* say, 'Everything about their performance was remarkable. Peter Townshend . . . had better control of his guitar than almost any other performer we've seen. . . . They had remarkable control. And remarkable knowledge of what they were doing at every second.'

Friday, May 9 to Thursday, June 19

The Who tour America with *Tommy*. Pete Townshend reportedly makes his first million.

June

'Something in the Air,' the debut single from Thunderclap Newman, reaches the top spot in the English charts. The record is produced by old chum Pete. Also in the group are drummer and sometime Townshend driver Speedy Keen and boy wonder guitarist Jimmy McCulloch.

Friday, June 13

The Who headline a date at the Hollywood Palladium supported by Poco and the brilliant Bonzo Dog Doo Dah Band.

Saturday, June 21

Townshend is fined thirty pounds in New York after being found guilty of harassing a policeman. The charge against Roger Daltrey is dismissed.

Wednesday, July 2

Rolling Stone Brian Jones is found dead in his swimming pool late in the evening. Townshend, a close friend of Jones for sometime, subsequently writes a song entitled 'A Normal Day for Brian (The Man Who Died Everyday).'

Saturday, July 5

The Who play the Royal Albert Hall, London.

Tuesday, August 12

The Who play with B. B. King and Jefferson Airplane at the Tanglewood, Lenox, Massachusetts. Twenty thousand attend the show, which is reviewed by *Billboard*, which says, 'The Who built excitement as they got into the *Tommy* selections. By the time they reached the single 'Pinball Wizard,' they were devastating in effect. Townshend's guitar playing, as usual, was topnotch and joined with Roger Daltrey in the effective lyrics.'

Sunday, August 17

The Who play the Woodstock festival in Bethel, New York. During their set, political activist Abbie Hoffman jumps on stage and is summarily trounced by Townshend's guitar.

Sunday, August 31

The Who play the Isle of Wight Festival.

October

The Who perform several riveting shows in the States.

Monday, October 19 to Sunday, October 26

The Who perform *Tommy* at the Fillmore East. The show was ecstatically reviewed by *Billboard*. 'Rock had one of its greatest nights. . . . The Who again showed themselves one of a kind by sustaining the excitement for so lengthy a continuous program.'

Tuesday, November 11 and Wednesday, November 12

The Who appear at the Boston Tea Party with generic singer Tony Williams.

Sunday, December 14

The Who play the London Coliseum performing *Tommy*.

1970

February

The Who perform 'The Seeker' on *Top of the Pops*.

March

On *Beat Club* the Who perform 'The Seeker.'

Sunday, March 1

Townshend writes a long editorial in the *Sunday Telegraph* enumerating his fairly well defined anti-drug stance, emphasizing Meher Baba's views on the subject.

Saturday, March 21

The spiritual rocker 'The Seeker' is released in Great Britain. Perhaps blessed by God, it is not particularly so by the record-buying public, climbing only as high as number nineteen.

Monday, April 20

Townshend is cut by a flying bottle during a Who show at Leicester University. The Hell's Angels are blamed.

May

The Who's *Live at Leeds* is issued, reaching number three in England and number four in America.

Sunday, June 7

The Who perform *Tommy* at the Metropolitan Opera House, New York. CBS television reports the event as some kind of counterculture joke. The tuned-in audience, however, is on its feet throughout.

Wednesday, June 24

Townshend is hauled off a plane in Memphis after commenting to one of the Who's entourage that their latest record was 'going a bomb.' More than a hundred passengers are immediately ordered off the plane while police search through every piece of luggage. Townshend, meanwhile, is in the clutches of the FBI, who take some five hours to be convinced that it is only an innocent English expression.

Summer

The Who once again successfully tour the United States.

July

The Who appear on *Top of the Pops* performing 'Summertime Blues' and 'Heaven and Hell.'

Saturday, July 25

The Who play Civic Hall, Dunstable. Latter-day Who fanatic Chris Charlesworth writes in *Melody Maker*, 'The Who are unique in the excitement they manage to create, and this is almost entirely due to Pete Townshend's leaping and jumping as he treats guitar and amps with little or no respect.'

Thursday, August 20

The premier date of Townshend's monthly column in *Melody Maker*, entitled 'Pete's Page.'

Saturday, August 29

The Who appear at the final Isle of Wight Festival. Author Geoffrey Giuliano sees them for the first time.

September

The Who commence an extended tour of Europe.

October

The Who play a brief, thirteen-stop British tour.

Thursday, October 8

The Who play the Orchid Ballroom, Purley. Caroline Boucher of *Disc and Music Echo* reports, 'Townshend's freeform guitar work did tend to go off rather too much at a tangent at times. . . . They're exciting visually, exciting musically and don't quit as soon as forty-five minutes are up. The Who play for nearly an hour and half.'

Thursday, November 26

Meher Baba makes the cover of *Rolling Stone* in an uplifting article penned by Townshend.

Sunday, December 20

The Who perform *Tommy* at the Roundhouse, London. *Disc and Music Echo* raves about the show, saying, 'Proof positive that they're the best band in the land, it was a pretty memorable, if a somewhat sweaty implosion. . . . We've reviewed them a million times before until the superlatives are running dry. Suffice it to say they're the guv'nors.'

1971

February

The Who play London's Young Vic Theater. Townshend begins serious work on the never realized *Lifehouse* pop opera.

Monday, April 12

A mixing session at Olympic Studios sees work done on 'Bargain,' 'Too Much of Anything,' and 'Time Is Passing.' The engineer is Glyn Johns. These tapes are presumably used for mastering purposes.

Friday, April 23

A mixing session at Olympic Studios for 'I'm in Tune [Getting in Tune]' and 'Behind Blue Eyes.' Kit Lambert produces and J. Adams engineers.

May

The Who play several surprise gigs throughout Britain.

Saturday, June 5

A mixing session at Olympic for 'Bargain' (six takes). Glyn Johns produces.

Monday, June 7

Another mixing session at Olympic for 'Getting in Tune,' 'Naked Eye,' 'Time Waits for No Man [When I Was a Boy].' Glyn Johns produces.

Friday, June 18

Mixing session for 'The Song Is Over' and 'Bargain' at Olympic Studios. The engineer is Glyn Johns.

Sunday, June 20

The Who join Glyn Johns for a mixing session at Olympic at which 'Let's See Action' is remixed several times.

Friday, June 25

'Won't Get Fooled Again' hits the streets, reaching number nine in England and ten in America. The original demo was recorded at the Beatles' basement Apple Studios at 3 Savile Row.

July

Who's Next is issued, becoming the number-one record in Britain. The critically acclaimed work only climbs to number four in the United States.

Sunday, July 4

The Who play De Montfort Hall, Leicester. In a review dated July 10 *Melody Maker* remarks, 'Despite wild applause and cheering for ten minutes, they didn't of course return for an encore. The audience was told the equipment had broken down, which sounds very much like an excuse. "They're back . . . just as dynamic and exciting as ever . . . what a night it was . . . all at their very best."'

Wednesday, July 12

A version of 'Love Reign o'er Me' is recorded at Olympic Studios. It is unclear, however, whether it was performed by the Who or another artist for the Lou Reizner *Tommy* project.

Thursday, July 29

The Who play Forest Hills Tennis Stadium, New York.

Late Summer

The Who mount a massive U.S. tour in support of *Who's Next*.

Sunday, August 8

Townshend is interviewed on a Cleveland radio station. During the course of the interview he says this about the hoopla surrounding *Tommy*: 'The kind of hump that we were dealing with *Tommy* for example was what we felt was a musical limitation. The fact that a rock song was limited by its very nature and the rock audience somehow they were stuck in the mud too. They felt that anything that wasn't two minutes fifteen or three minutes long was not a rock song. If it wasn't something you could laugh at and jive to, it wasn't a rock song. If it took itself seriously it wasn't a rock song. About the time of *Tommy* we felt the reverse happening as well, that something that was an hour long was good because it was long, because it wasn't three minutes long. And so we felt a new form of rock had to be defined, whatever it was going to do, and also the musical limitations had to be exploded. That's really why we did *Tommy*. I think it did that pretty effectively but it didn't really give a direction. Whether or not the Who are really capable of doing that, I really don't know. We've always been other groups' contemporaries, if you like. We've always been contemporaries of the Stones, rather than the Stones. We've always been doing what other groups failed to do but what other groups started doing, you know.'

Saturday, September 18

The Who play the Kennington Oval Cricket Ground, London.

October

The Who tour Great Britain, finishing up at London's Rainbow Theatre Club.

Saturday, October 2

The Who play Reading University.

Saturday, October 9

The Who play Surrey University.

Sunday, October 10

The Who play Kent University.

Monday, October 18

The Who play Southampton Guildhall.

Wednesday, October 20

The Who play the Birmingham Odeon.

Thursday, October 21

The Who play Glasgow's Green's Playhouse.

Friday, October 22

The Who play the Blackpool Opera House.

Saturday, October 23

The Who play Liverpool University.

Sunday, October 24

The Who play Stoke Trentham Gardens.

Thursday, October 28

The Who play the Manchester Odeon.

Friday, October 29

The Who play Hull ABC.

Saturday, October 30

The Who play the Newcastle Odeon.

Tuesday, November 9

The Who once again play Green's Playhouse, Glasgow.

November

The Who again tour the States.

Wednesday, December 8

The Who play the Sports Arena, San Diego, before an audience of fifteen thousand over-the-top fans. The *Los Angeles Times* raves, 'Believe what I say. See the Who. . . . There is a majestic splendor to the Who's instrumentation and an attitude expressed in its lyrics that speak directly to the rock generation in a way few other groups do. . . . There hasn't been too much excitement in the big rock 'n' roll tent lately. So when the greatest show on earth comes to town, I've got to get a little excited.'

1972

February

Townshend travels to Meherabad, Arangaon, India, to bow down at the hilltop tomb of his master, Meher Baba. He is warmly received by Baba's loyal mandali.

June

The Who appear on ITV's *Russell Harty Plus* performing 'Join Together.'

Saturday, June 17

'Join Together' is released as a single and eventually reaches number nine in England and seventeen in America.

August

The Who appear on Dutch television's *Pop Gala*, performing 'See Me, Feel Me'; 'Pinball Wizard'; 'Won't Get Fooled Again'; 'My Generation'; 'Magic Bus'; and 'Summertime Blues.'

Friday, August 11

The Who do a quick tour of Europe commencing in Frankfurt, Germany.

Saturday, September 9

The Who play their biggest gig ever before just under half a million fans at Fete de l'Humanite, Paris.

October

Townshend's first commercially released solo album of songs dedicated to Meher Baba, *Who Came First*, is issued. It becomes a touchstone for young people everywhere interested in Baba's teachings. A semi-classical version of *Tommy* is released with material covered by a variety of popular performers.
The Who appear on the BBC2 TV show *Old Grey Whistle Test* performing 'Relay' and 'Long Live Rock.'

December

The Who participate in a live performance of *Tommy* produced by Lou Reizner at the Rainbow Theatre.

Saturday, December 23

'Relay' is issued; it will reach number twenty-one in England and only a sorry thirty-nine in the States.

1973

January

Townshend helps Eric Clapton overcome a shattering addiction to heroin.

Spring

The Who commence recording of their second groundbreaking rock opera, *Quadrophenia*.

September

'5.15' is issued and begins climbing to number twenty in the UK charts.

October

The Who begin a ten-show British tour introducing the musically and emotionally enthralled audiences to *Quadrophenia*. The Who appear on *Top of the Pops* performing '5.15.' Pete Townshend gives an interview for the American film *Rock City*.

November

The brilliant *Quadrophenia* is released worldwide. In support of the album the Who tour the United States yet again.

Tuesday, November 20

The Who appear at the Cow Palace, San Francisco, presented by Bill Graham. During the concert Keith collapses and Pete invites audience member Scott Halpin to sit in on drums. By all reports he does a pretty fair job.

Thursday, November 29

The Who play the International Amphitheater, Chicago, Illinois. Longtime *Chicago Tribune* critic Lynn Van Matre writes, 'When it comes to rock theatre, the Who must be the masters. No Alice Cooper theatrics needed, no props other than the voices and the charge the group self-generates. With them, it's all energy, transcending the music, transcending the scene. Harness 'em up, and they could probably transcend the energy crisis as well. . . . *Tommy* and *Quadrophenia* may have marked the Who as rock intellectuals, but their appeal and stage presence are far less complex. They are, in the final analysis, pure, raw energy, which is, after all, what rock 'n' roll's always been about.'

December

Townshend and other members of the Who and their entourage are arrested and jailed after demolishing a luxury hotel suite in Montreal.

Tuesday, December 18 to Sunday, December 23

The Who play four shows in London at the Edmonton Sundown.

1974

February

The Who begin a seven-date tour of France.

March

Townshend plays on and produces two tunes for the *Tommy* soundtrack, 'Eyesight to the Blind' and 'Sally Simpson,' at Ramport Studios, Battersea, London. Eric Clapton also joins in on the sessions.

April

The film version of *Tommy* begins principle photography directed by the capable and ever controversial Ken Russell.

Sunday, April 14

Townshend appears solo at London's Roundhouse.

Saturday, May 18

The Who play the Charlton Football Ground.

Monday, June 10 to Friday, June 14

The Who play four shows at Madison Square Garden in New York.

September

Odds and Sods, the Who's album of previously unreleased gems, is released. Townshend pens the record's copious and amusing liner notes.

1975

March

The film *Tommy*, starring Roger Daltrey, the Who, Eric Clapton, Tina Turner, Jack Nicholson, Oliver Reed, and Ann-Margret, premiers.

May

The Who appear on the BBC2's *Second House* performing 'Young Man Blues'; 'Baba O'Riley'; 'Substitute'; 'Drowned'; 'Bell Boy'; 'See Me, Feel Me'; 'Naked Eye'; 'My Generation'; 'Blues'; and 'Let's See Action.'

August

Townshend and his family spend a month at the Meher Center in Myrtle Beach, South Carolina, after which they move on to Walnut Creek, California, for a month spent under the tutelage of Murshida Ivy O. Duce, the leader of Meher Baba's Sufism Reoriented. Townshend later writes about the experience in *Rolling Stone* in an article entitled 'The Punk Meets the Godmother.'

Saturday, October 18

The Who by Numbers, with a catchy cartoon cover by John Entwistle, is released. Included is the catchy 'Slip Kid.'

Monday, October 3 to Friday, October 24

The group begins an eleven-date British tour, going on to play eight shows in Europe. Townshend's equipment is listed in the official tour program as: 4 Hiwatt 4 × 12" speaker cabinets; 2 Hiwatt 100-watt amplifiers; 1 Superfuzz fuzz box; Gibson Les Paul guitars; Gibson guitar strings; and Mannys guitar picks.

Tuesday, October 21

The Who play the Empire Poole, Wembley. Ticket prices are £2.75.

November

The Who commence an American concert tour.

Thursday, November 6 and Friday, November 7

The Who play Berthalle, Ludwigshafen, West Germany with special guest Steve Gibbons.

Thursday, November 20

The Who play the Summit in Houston, Texas.

Sunday, November 23

The Who play Mid-South Coliseum, Memphis, Tennessee. Walter Dawson in the *Commercial Appeal* had this to say: 'The only bad part of the show was the volume. It was extremely loud as is fitting to the Who's intensity, but at times, as when Townshend took a guitar solo, it was bearable only to those whose eardrums have been bored out by many a rock show.'

Tuesday, November 25

The Who play MTSU Centre, Murfreesboro. Eve Zibart writes in the *Tennessean*, 'The very forcefulness of their music is nearly blinding. . . . A Who performance lifts and tosses the audience on the waves rushing out from the stage. It was enough to buffet, mesmerize and completely exhaust 11,000 fans. . . . A description of a Who concert is like a beginner's exercise in phenomenology. . . . They can out do any band on the block.'

Friday, November 28

The Who play the Coliseum in Greensboro. The *Winston-Salem* (North Carolina) *Journal* writes, 'Never in the performance did the band falter. . . . If their Greensboro concert was a typical performance, it would seem that they, rather than the Rolling Stones, are now the world's greatest rock group. Compared to the antics and power of Roger Daltrey, Mick Jagger comes off like a jaded, tired old man.'

Tuesday, December 2

The Who play Veterans Memorial Coliseum, Des Moines, Iowa. The *Des Moines Register* says, 'The granddaddy of full-bore, wild rhino, thunder rock left a full house stunned. . . . It was a show with class. . . . It will be recalled, no doubt as *the* rock event for some time to come.'

Thursday, December 4

The Who appear at Chicago Stadium.

Tuesday, December 9

The Who appear at the Cleveland Coliseum. The film version *Tommy* is released in Britain.

Sunday, December 21 to Tuesday, December 23

The Who perform three shows at the Hammersmith Odeon, London.

1976

The Who are voted Best Band of the Year by *Rolling Stone* magazine. The prize? A pair of flashy red suspenders for each of the band.

Saturday, January 24

'Squeeze Box' is issued; eventually it makes it to number ten in both Britain and the United States.

Saturday, January 31

Townshend once again visits Meher Baba's tomb in India. This time he is filmed performing for a group of Baba lovers. The clip is later included in the video documentary *God Man*, produced by an Australian Baba group.

Wednesday, February 25

Pete Townshend writes Geoffrey Giuliano for the first time inviting him to travel to England as Pete's guest for the opening of Meher Baba Oceanic that July.

Friday, February 27

The Who begin a quick and dirty four-date European concert tour.

Saturday, February 28

The Who play the Olympiahalle in Munich, West Germany, supported by Steve Gibbons.

February–April

Townshend plays guitar on an unreleased Eric Clapton track, 'The Path,' recorded at Shangria-La Studios, Malibu, California.

March

The Who commence a fourteen-show American tour.

Tuesday, March 9

The Who play a concert at Boston Garden Arena during which drummer Moon faints and the show is abruptly stopped.

Monday, May 31

The Who play the Charlton Football Ground yet again.

Saturday, June 5

The Who play the Celtic Park Football Ground, Glasgow. The *Scottish Sunday Express* writes, 'All went wild as the Who exploded on the special £7,000 stage and launched into the mind-bending medley of rock 'n' roll. The highlight of the £65,000 happening came when the Who illuminated the night sky above Parkhead by switching on laser gun light-equipment.'

Wednesday, July 8 to Saturday, July 10

The grand opening of Meher Baba Oceanic on Ranleigh Drive, Richmond, attended by guest of honor Sri Adi K. Irani, Meher Baba's longtime personal secretary.

August

The Who begin a brief stadium tour of the United States.

October

The Who begin another short tour of the United States and Canada.

Saturday, October 9 and Sunday, October 10

The Who play the Oakland Stadium, Oakland, along with the Grateful Dead.

1977

February

Townshend records his *Rough Mix* album with Ronnie Lane at Olympic Sound Studios, Barnes, and Eel Pie. Also participating on the sessions are Eric Clapton, Billy Nichols, John Entwistle, Rabbit Bundrick, and Henry Spinetti.

September

Pete Townshend and Ronnie Lane release *Rough Mix* to critical acclaim.

Wednesday, December 15

The Who perform at the Kilburn State Theatre, London. The *New Musical Express* writes, 'Townshend looks thinner and meaner, wasted even, as he glares angrily at the young pups playfully woofing and yelping at the grand old master and his band, the Who. . . . The energy, the music and the atmosphere have the makings of a classic Who gig.'

1978

Monday, February 27

The London *Sun* carries a story concerning Townshend's affiliation with Meher Baba entitled HOW WILD MAN PETE WAS SAVED BY SILENCE.

May

The Who rehearse 'Barbara Ann' and 'I Saw Her Standing There' at Shepperton Film Studios.

Thursday, May 25

Keith Moon plays his final gig with the Who at Shepperton.

Friday, July 14

Who Are You is issued. The album will make it to number eighteen in Britain and fourteen in America.
It is reported that Townshend is working on a one-hour musical for ITV's *South Bank Show*. Presenter Melvyn Bragg apparently gave him the idea based on Townshend's first brush with violence many years ago back in Shepherd's Bush.

August

Who Are You is released worldwide.

Tuesday, August 15

Pete Meaden, the Who's early manager, dies.

Friday, September 8

Keith Moon dies of an accidental overdose of heminevrin, a prescription medicine he has been taking to help combat his chronic alcoholism. Townshend and the rest of the group are crushed but are determined to carry on.

1979

January

Former Faces drummer Kenney Jones becomes the Who's new drummer. Others interested in the job are Phil Collins and Ginger Baker.

Tuesday, January 16

Townshend hints that the Who might once again go back on the road.

Monday, February 12

It is reported that Townshend intends to form his own record company called Propeller Records to help launch unknown artists. Townshend then signs three groups – Straight 8, Misty, and Roots and the Movies – sinking forty-five thousand pounds into the project. 'We've been giving free studio time to a lot of bands to give them a chance to make some tapes. I want bands who are a bit weird, they have to be new and weird.'

Wednesday, May 2

The 'new' Who play London's Rainbow Theatre.

Sunday, June 24

The Kids Are Alright film documentary is released along with a stirring sound track.

Thursday, August 16

Quadrophenia, the movie, starring newcomer Sting, is released.

Saturday, August 18

The Who play Wembley Stadium.

Saturday, September 1

The Who play Nuremberg, Germany, supported by Cheap Trick, AC/DC, Miriam Makeba, the Scorpions, Steve Gibbons, and Zanki & Band.

Thursday, September 13 to Tuesday, September 18

The Who play five exceptional evenings at Madison Square Garden.

December

The Who begin a new U.S. tour.

Saturday, December 1

The Who are featured on the cover of *Time* magazine in America.

Monday, December 3

The Who play Riverfront Stadium, Cincinnati, during which eleven fans are trampled to death during a mad rush when the doors are opened. Townshend, for one, is legitimately and permanently scared.

Saturday, December 8

The Who appear at Chicago Auditorium.

Wednesday, December 12

The Who appear at London Hammersmith Odeon.

Friday, December 28

The Who play the Hammersmith Odeon as part of the Concerts for the People of Kampuchea.

Sunday, December 30

A Who documentary appears on ITV's *W.G.F.A.*

1980

March

The Who commence a European tour.

April

Empty Glass reaches stores. It will climb to number eleven in Britain and five in the States.
'Let My Love Open the Door' by Townshend is a top ten hit in America.

Monday, April 21

Townshend gives an interview to a London paper voicing his opinions on the current state of English youth.

'Britain's kids seem to be desperately into uniforms and tribalism,' Pete begun. 'It's producing fantastic music but also violent, almost fascist, elements. Those people who say a spell in the army could stop street violence may well be right. The kids seem to want uniforms. And they want a license to kick one another in the head. I'm still very tender about the adolescent scene. I'm fascinated and captivated by it. I think now I've got a real picture of what's going on in the street. In the sixties I was mesmerized by it.'
It is reported in the press that director Nicolas Roeg is interested in making a movie of Townshend's long-stalled pop opera *Lifehouse*.

April–July

The Who tour the United States.

Thursday, June 26

Rolling Stone carries a cover story on Townshend.

Wednesday, July 9

Townshend comes up with the idea of publishing a book of erotic short stories. Says Pete, 'It started when I kept a detailed journal of my dreams for a few months and I discovered that I don't have the sort of dreams most people have. I turned several of the images into stories and then I went on and did a series of erotic stories as well. My wife was shocked when she discovered them. She said she didn't know I had it in me.'

1981

January–March

The Who tour Great Britain.

February

'You Better You Bet' is released and eventually makes it to number nine in England and ten in America.

February 4–5

The Who appear at the Rainbow Theatre, London. During one of the shows Pete reportedly downs four pints of brandy while on stage and subsequently picks a fight with Roger.

March

The album *Face Dances* by the Who is issued.

Thursday, March 5

The Who appear on *Top of the Pops* performing 'You Better You Bet.'

Saturday, March 28

The Who appear on *The Old Grey Whistle Test*.

March

The Who appear in a promo film performing 'You Better You Bet,' 'Another Tricky Day,' and 'Don't Let Go the Coat.'

Tuesday, April 7

Kit Lambert is killed when he falls down the stairs of his mother's London home. Townshend tells reporters that without Lambert the Who might never have been.

1982

June

All the Best Cowboys Have Chinese Eyes, Townshend's third solo offering, is released.

Friday, September 10 and Saturday, September 11

The Who play Birmingham's National Exhibition Centre. It will be their last 'official' British show for a full seven years.

September

It's Hard, the Who's final studio album, is issued.

Thursday, October 21

The Who appear on BBC2's *Newsnight* in a documentary report. The Who appear on City TV's (Canada) *The New Music* in a documentary report.

Friday, December 17

The Who appear at Maple Leaf Gardens, Toronto.

December

The Who appear on MTV's *Farewell Tour Special*.

1983

March

Scoop, an album of engaging Townshend demos, is issued. Pete proudly dubs it his 'official bootleg.'

Thursday, July 7

Townshend holds a press conference to announce his new position as an acquisitions editor for Faber and Faber publishers in London.

Sunday, September 11

Townshend reviews the novel *Nostromo* for the *Mail on Sunday*.

Friday, October 5

It is reported that Townshend aspires to open a twenty-bed drug cure clinic in London.

'If I wasn't dead by now, I'd certainly be in a lot of trouble if I hadn't had the treatment,' comments Pete. 'I was ashamed to go to Dr. Patterson at first, because I was on a fund-raising committee with other notables while I was taking drugs.

'I find all that absolutely disgusting. Particularly after having been on show for three years with a drug problem myself. It's quite incredible to realize that everybody's waiting gleefully, hoping for you to drop dead in full view.'

The clinic, which will never actually open, is to be named after Townshend.

Friday, November 4

The Who appear on *Nightflight Tribute* in a documentary report.

Friday, December 16

Pete Townshend officially leaves the Who.

1984

Tuesday, January 3

The London *Sun* reports that Townshend is in the studio producing an album and a single for his brother, Simon. Says Pete, 'We hardly knew each other before we went into the studio; there's a sixteen-year age gap between us.'

Tuesday, May 1

It is reported that Townshend has purchased an eighty-two-year-old Dutch barge formerly used to carry eels up and down the River Thames. After spending £150,000 on the project, he will admit, 'It's a folly.'

Thursday, May 10

Townshend is reportedly hard at work editing an autobiography of Eric Burdon and the Animals.

Summer

Mick Jagger records at Townshend's private studio, the Boathouse, formerly Meher Baba Oceanic.

June

Townshend attends the Prince's Rock Gala at the Royal Albert Hall.

October 9

Townshend addresses a meeting of the Young Conservatives at a Tory Party press conference in London and rails against the dangers of heroin. Says Pete, 'It's not a problem you can separate from other problems. In this society oblivion is one of the only ways you can find balance because everything seems so frantic, so dangerous. With a right-wing government everything also seems so uncaring. People tend to become absorbed in their own emotional and physical feelings. Most people go to the pub and get wrecked and that's what I did until my liver more or less gave out. I needed these moments of oblivion and when that stopped working I needed to find something else.'

Friday, December 7

Townshend admits to damaging an eighteenth-century bridge in Henley-on-Thames in a barge collision the previous year. He is subsequently billed four thousand pounds for repairs.

1985

Monday, February 11

Townshend presents Sade with the Album of the Year award at the prestigious British Phonographic Awards at London's Grovesnor House Hotel.

Thursday, April 11

Townshend urges the British government to 'grasp the snake by the neck' in reference to the rampant heroin addiction prevalent among young people in Britain. 'The government should assist large American private clinics to set up over here, and must enroll more National Health Service doctors who specialize in drug problems.'
Townshend appears at a anti-heroin benefit concert at St. James's Church, London. Also on the bill is Siouxsie and the Banshees.

Friday, April 12

Townshend comes under fire for seemingly promoting teenage burglary in a statement made during the launch of his much publicized antiheroin campaign. 'What I meant to say was that if a teenager breaks into a house or gets pregnant, society knows how to cope. But if a teenager confesses to being a heroin addict we don't know what to do.'

Sunday, April 14

Townshend writes an article for the *Mail on Sunday* advancing the theory that Britain needs more rehab centers to combat the country's savage drug problem.

Friday, April 26

Townshend personally sells T-shirts at a series of Bruce Springsteen concerts in Britain. Proceeds for the 'Stay Alive in '85' shirts will go to Pete's personal anti-heroin campaign. 'I was very lucky,' says Townshend, 'my family took me back when I kicked the habit. Now I feel obliged to help other people with drug problems.'

Monday, May 27

Townshend's first book, *Horse's Neck*, is published in Great Britain.

June

Townshend appears on the American television program *Nightline* with host Ted Koppel.

Monday, June 10

Townshend donates money to the Greenwich Theater Group so that they can mount a production of *King Arthur*.

July

Townshend joins Dire Straits on stage in London for a brief appearance.

Saturday, July 13

The Who play a short set at Live Aid at Wembley Stadium.

Friday, August 9

The British press reports that Pete Townshend is working with Prince Charles on editing a volume of his collected speeches to be published by Faber and Faber.

October

Townshend appears with his band, Deep End, on *The Tube*, a popular British television program.

November

White City, from Townshend is released as both an album and a long-form video. Neither does well.

Sunday, November 3

Townshend is profiled on the British television program *The South Bank Show*.

Monday, November 11

Townshend travels to New York to promote his recent *White City* album and *Horse's Neck*, his gloomy book of short stories.

November

Townshend attends a release party in New York for one of Bob Dylan's albums.

Sunday, December 22

Pete and Karen Townshend preside over the Snowball Revue in aid of the Chiswick Family Rescue. The venue at London's Dominion Theatre, on Tottenham Court Road, saw appearances by Pete Townshend, Bill Wyman, Emma Townshend and the Dallas Quartet, Michael Palin, Andy Summers, and several others.

1986

February

Pete and Emma Townshend perform a synthesizer duet at a benefit targeting Columbian Relief at the Royal Albert Hall.

Spring

Townshend donates a box of broken guitar parts to a charity auction in aid of the Samaritans.

October

The album *Deep End Live!* by Pete Townshend is issued.

1987

March

Another Scoop, a double LP offering of demos from Townshend, is released.

Saturday June 20

Townshend forgets his manners during a presentation at the Mayfair Hotel at which Paul Newman's daughter, Nell, gives Townshend a check for ten thousand pounds to benefit his Double O Charity. Storming out of the posh hotel after several press photographers turn up, Townshend also has a few choice words for his assistant, Sally Arnold. Newman, however, remains calm, stating, 'My father has also been known to be nervous of photographers. These things can happen.'

Tuesday, October 20

Pete Townshend's personal charity, the Double O, an organization dedicated to helping drug addicts throughout Britain, throws an upscale ball at the Mayfair Hotel. Appearing on the bill are Lorna Luft and transsexual magician, Fay Presto.

Wednesday, November 4

Emma Townshend is quoted in the British press as saying, 'I have never dabbled in drugs. Happily, my parents made sure that I am not tempted by them.'

Christmas

Townshend designs a Christmas card to benefit the Save the Children Fund.

1988

February

The Who are given a BPI Lifetime Achievement Award at the Royal Albert Hall, London.
It is reported in the British press that Karen Townshend has urged Pete to cease operation of their Double O Charity.

1989

Wednesday, January 18

Townshend finishes recording his *Iron Man* project, after which he goes on holiday in Antigua.

June

Iron Man, an album and musical based around a children's book by lauded author Ted Hughes, is released by Townshend.
The Who begin a forty-three-date U.S. tour in celebration of the group's twenty-fifth anniversary. They also play ten dates at the Royal Albert Hall.

Thursday, June 29

Townshend appears on the popular American television program *Late Night with David Letterman*.

Thursday, July 13

Townshend is a guest on the nationally syndicated American radio show *Rock Line*, where he answers questions from fans for over two hours.

Wednesday, August 16

While on tour with the Who in Tacoma, Washington, Townshend impales his hand on the whammy bar of his guitar. He is treated at a local hospital.

Saturday, September 30

Karen Townshend discovers she is pregnant on the same day she and Pete are scheduled to adopt a baby boy.

Wednesday, November 1

Townshend presides over a one hundred pound per ticket charity performance of *Tommy* at the Royal Albert Hall. He tells the audience, 'Thanks for giving us your money. What happens is: you pay us your cash. Then we give it to charity and we get the credit. Good isn't it? You pay us. Then we give the money back to your children. That's democracy.'

1990

Saturday, February 24

Townshend appears at an all-star tribute for Roy Orbison at the Universal Amphitheater, Los Angeles.

Monday, February 26

Townshend publicly backs a five hundred thousand pound appeal by independent girls' school Godolphin and Latymer in Hammersmith to fund a new science, art, and technology block.

Wednesday, May 9

Townshend invests £150,000 in a scheme to ferry commuters down the river Thames, thereby circumventing London's horrendous rush-hour traffic. Along the way Pete picks up the backing of the Hounslow Council and the Port of London Authority. Boatbuilders George Sims of Eel Pie Island are retained to build a fifty-five-foot launch to be used in the venture. The service, scheduled to run between Richmond and Charing Cross, never quite comes to fruition. In an interview given at the time Pete explains the scheme. 'I am hoping this venture will be a money-making proposition.

'I have always lived by the river, and traffic has worsened into London, it can take up to two hours by car.

'Now the sixty-minute journey by water is starting to seem more reasonable.

'I have planned the scheme as a pilot project to test the viability of commuter transport in the upper river.

'The building costs at the moment have been about one hundred thousand pounds and I expect that figure to rise to one hundred and fifty thousand pounds by the time it is finished.

'I will be calling the boat *Zephyr* and I hope it will make me a few bob as well as ease my run into work!'

Tuesday, June 5

Townshend declines a £2 million offer from Coca-Cola to feature several of his songs in television commercials.

Thursday, October 18 and Friday, October 19

Townshend appears on German and Danish television performing selections from his *Iron Man* album.

Monday, October 22 and Sunday, October 28

Townshend appears on a television program hosted by Herbie Hancock on the Showtime cable network in America.

Monday, October 29

Townshend appears on the British television show *Saturday Matters* along with Eric Clapton.

1991

Friday, September 6

It is reported that Townshend's Goring-on-Thames riverfront cottage is up for sale. Standing on 1.5 acres, Temple Cottage features a functioning private recording studio on the grounds.

Tuesday, September 25

The *Daily Mirror* runs a story entitled WHO STAR BREAKS HIS ARM. 'The guitar wizard suffered a bad break to his right arm when he pitched over the handlebars as he cycled round an island owned by Prince Charles,' they write.

'Townshend, 44, and his family were staying at Tresco in the Isles of Scilly, 30 miles off Land's End. Cars are not allowed there because there are no proper roads.

'The break was so nasty that Townshend was flown by helicopter to the accident department at Truro City Hospital.

'Yesterday the star, back home at his thatched manor house on Cornwall's Helford river, refused to comment. He answered the door in jeans and a T-shirt, his right arm in plaster from fingers to elbow.

'Townshend sailed into the islands on a 60-foot yacht and stayed at a cottage on the Tresco Estate.'

Friday, December 20

The *Daily Mail* reports that Pete Townshend's Thames-side mansion, the Anchorage, is up for sale at £595,000. Built in 1690, the white stone house has four bedrooms and a recording studio.

1992

Summer

One of Townshend's old raincoats is auctioned at Sotheby's, with the proceeds going to charity.

1993

March

Tommy opens on Broadway in New York with Townshend acting as musical director. The production goes on to win five Tony Awards.

April

Townshend records with the Ramones, performing vocals on a rowdy cover of 'Substitute.'

June

PsychoDerelict by Pete Townshend is issued.
Townshend begins his first solo American tour.

Friday, October 15

Townshend oversees auditions at the Young Vic for his theatrical adaptation of *Iron Man*.

Friday, November 26

Iron Man opens at the Young Vic, London.

Monday, December 13

Once again Townshend's up-and-down marriage makes headlines. In a story entitled PETE TOWNSHEND FIGHTS TO SAVE HIS MARRIAGE, he is quoted as saying, 'It's been a nightmare but I will sort this problem out.'

1994

May

The Who: Thirty Years of Maximum R&B, a deluxe box set of Who classics and rarities, is issued in conjunction with an excellent video of the same name.

1995

February

Tommy opens in Toronto produced by Canadian businessman 'Honest' Ed Mirvish. Townshend attends both auditions and rehearsals.

1996

August

Behind Blue Eyes: The Life of Pete Townshend, the first biography of the Who's philosophical powerhouse, is published worldwide.

Note: The above is not intended to be a definitive day-by-day diary of the busy, eventful life of Pete Townshend, but rather, simply, an extended sampling of some of the more noteworthy and/or representative days in the life of the artist.

The Who

Radio City Music Hall
April 24, 1989

Question: Will there be a live album of this latest tour?

Roger Daltrey: No.

Pete Townshend: I don't think there's room for one really.

Question: Is this a farewell tour?

Roger: No, we did our farewell tour.

Pete: It's not a fuckin' joke, we did our farewell tour. We said goodbye. We haven't been on the road. We haven't worked together for almost seven years. We're not a group as such anymore. We've come together especially for a twenty-fifth birthday party. That's what this tour represents. We're coming back to the USA to do the majority of the work. We're doing a short tour at the end of all this in the UK. We're coming back to the States because it's where the Who were properly born and certainly where they grew. I mean, when we did our farewell tour we said we might be back. I remember saying it, I remember everybody in the band saying it over and over, that we reserve the right to do whatever we like. Particularly if it was a special occasion or a charity event that made it worthwhile. Had we not decided to tour at length, we would have almost certainly done the concert at RKO for Nordolf Robbins.

Question: If inducted into the Rock 'n' Roll Hall of Fame do you anticipate Mick Jagger introducing you as you introduced the Stones last year?

Pete: Nobody could be as witty as I am.

Question: If you'll look back to when you first started performing together, what's happened in the last twenty-five years, and particularly what's happened in the seven years you've not been together?

323

John Entwistle: Do you have to ask me the hard questions? Can't you ask me an easy one?

Roger: It's great to be normal, to be honest. To live a normal life and not be involved in all that rock 'n' roll lunacy. I've actually *almost* gone out to work to a real job and it's been a process finding that bit of me I'd lost. It is only rock 'n' roll in the end, but when you're right in the middle of it like we are, or *were*, it becomes a bit overblown and it's very easy to lose sight of yourself.

Question: What did you learn from the '82 shows, which, from what I've heard, wasn't the happiest of tours, that you can bring to this tour to make it more enjoyable for everyone from a personal and musical standpoint?

Roger: Well, I was happy on the last tour. . . .

Pete: I don't think it was a particularly unhappy tour at all, but rather, fairly detached. I think we were emotionally detached.

Roger: Semi-detached.

Pete: We were doing our job and by the time we got to the end of the tour there were wonderful musical moments and experiences. But obviously I was the one who first decided not to work again. Somewhere throughout that tour I felt that the end had come for that kind of work, but it wasn't an unhappy experience. In a way it was quite a good moment. I was unhappy the very last show we did in Toronto (which was the one that was filmed) didn't come across properly, because it was frozen as a rough kind of inept performance. But that's the strokes, isn't it? It happens that way. We learned a hell of a lot from it, but then you learn a hell of a lot from everything you do.

Question: John, have you given any thought to the actual song selection, or will that wait for rehearsals in May?

John: We've got an A list, a B list and a C list, we're just working our way through them. We'll make a final decision toward the end of rehearsals. Obviously there are songs we have to play. There's a few of the nice old ones I think we've got to try and work in. Novelty songs.

Question: What did you do with Kenney Jones and why did you pick Simon Phillips over Kenney?

Pete: Kenney got fed with waiting for us to get together. He was issuing mild ultimatums like, 'Why don't we do something?' for three or four years. He just got fed up waiting and started work in a band with Paul Rogers and I was vacillating so much on whether or not I was going to do anything, even up to last February. This February I had a whole tour sketched, a smallish tour which I felt was acceptable and as I was leaving the States I decided I couldn't do it so he lost patience and is now working somewhere else. We're not unhappy about that because we feel in a sense, we can't change this particular relationship. This is the electric one, the one which always begs the presence of Keith Moon, so it puts the emphasis on the drummer. What is really nice, is that presence is always there when we three gather. You know, when the three of us gather *in his name*, he is here. A lot is expected of the drummer and it's just nice to have another try with somebody else. I used Simon Phillips when I worked solo. I discovered him almost by accident on an album I was working on with Kenney in fact, my first solo album. He's a great drummer, but I don't think he's anything like Moon. There are a lot of good drummers out there. I've been sent something like six hundred tapes from young drummers who feel they could do the job Keith does and the standard is astonishing. I mean, there's some great drummers out there, but I wasn't about to start auditioning. I'm happy with Simon, so I suggested him to John and Roger and they didn't object, so he's in.

Question: I suppose it should be brought up that you're the band that sang, 'Hope I die before I get old.' Can you talk about rock 'n' roll and middle age?

Pete: Who would you like to answer that? The youngest or the oldest?

Question: You're the youngest, so go ahead.

Pete: I don't hide the fact that I am absolutely obsessed with age and it affects everything I do. I think the passing of time is the only important thing in life. If you can stay with it as it passes you're living in the present, which is the best possible thing you can do, and if you miss it, you're missing life. It's the only thing that takes us toward death (which is the only inevitable), and to deny it's happening is a very American trait. I don't do it. *I get old* and the only thing now is looking back at those words, 'Hope I die before I get old.' In a lot of ways, it has already started, that process. Certainly bits of me that were operating extremely well when I wrote those lines don't function quite so adequately today.

Roger: Which bits are those?

Question: What could you convey in memory of Keith Moon on behalf of this reunion tour?

Pete: I don't think you have to say much. Every time we get together, particularly if we tell stories or remember things about him, he's very much present. I wouldn't like to think of him kind of locked into Who history the way we're locked into Who history. I'd like to think of him as free and released, because not all of his life was happy. What we're most conscious of is trying to recapture some of his levity.

Question: Did you miss playing with each other and do you enjoy playing together on tape?

Roger: I did, yeah.

Pete: We've done it a bit.

John: We've done it for a long time.

Pete: On my solo album John and Roger both contributed to a couple of tracks. I must say I was surprised at how fresh it felt. I expected it to be like jigsaw pieces fitting into place, but it felt new and fresh, it was different. Everybody's changed.

Question: After not playing together for so long and with the new drummer, will it be hard for you guys to get it all together on stage?

John: Well, it will take a couple of days.

Roger: We did an awards ceremony in England about a year ago. We rehearsed for a week and the old chemistry is still there. What we're trying to do on this tour is to keep a lot of what we had before, but gain something else. I mean, this is going to be much more of a musical experience for us. You kind of fall into a trap when you're constantly doing it, playing for the applause. And the Who got some great applause, I'll tell you. But the trouble is the next number's got to beat that one and the one after that has got to beat that one, so you get more and more applause. We're not trying to do that one this time, we're trying to really enjoy the music. And whether that gets loads of applause we don't really give a shit.

Pete: My theory, in answer to that question is, and this isn't just a cheap gag, it really doesn't matter. It doesn't matter how good the music is or how bad the music is. If you're in an eight-thousand-seat stadium, it's not the most important thing. The music isn't the most important thing necessarily, it's the way you approach the music, it's *why* you play the music. It's why you present it to people. The most important thing is that we're here and that the audience will be there and that we're hoping to have some fun. What Roger just said is an indication of how we lost that process. For a long time

I didn't ever want to play in a big stadium. I thought, 'That's not about music.' That's something that has just happened to rock, it's not something we created. But you just have to make the best of it. Get out there and try to bring back some of the vigor, enjoyment, and spontaneity. When you think about the early Who shows in New York, and scanning the faces here, I know some of you guys were there. One in four was a great show. The rest were absolutely awful, but those awful shows were important too. Because it was with those bad shows we all knew we were experimenting, growing, breaking new ground. You can't break new ground unless you make mistakes, so we're expecting this tour to include a lot of danger and this time, hopefully, when we make mistakes we'll laugh about it rather than, you know, fight.

Question: Tell us about the special charity show you're doing here at Radio City Music Hall.

Pete: The audience we're inviting are principals in fund-raising across the board and they're paying a lot of money for their seats. What we're also trying to do is capture their commitment to the charity. This is just one concert. This work goes on for years and we're hoping that somewhere in that crowd will be somebody who is moved by what we do to the extent of helping in the future. I don't think that kind of thing is appropriate somewhere like Madison Square Garden because it's the ballpark where we take risks. We're willing to take risks in our own career and with our bank account, but not with charities, so we just felt we wanted the best possible place. This is a fantastic place. I've never been here before. It's an extraordinary place, I'm glad it's still here.

Roger: We tried to get the Met, but they wouldn't have us back.

Pete: That's not true. They wanted us back.

Roger: Oh, did they?

Pete: We wouldn't have them back!

Question: I heard rumors you're looking for a second guitarist, is that true?

Pete: Yeah, this is kind of weird for me. The real reason I haven't performed live even on my own for a long time is that I've got very severe hearing damage and it's manifested itself as tinnitus or ringing in the ears at the kind of frequencies I play. I found the only treatment which helps is homeopathy, not drinking coffee, and not taking anything with mint in it. It sounds a bit cosmic, but it works very well for me. If I expose myself to loud electric guitar, particularly my own loud electric guitar, my hearing suffers and I have to take about two or three weeks away from any loud noises. So it's very difficult for me to work at music. I've taken two years for me to make a record for myself which should have taken about a year. A lot of that has been that I've had to give myself long rests. I don't want to make too big a thing out of this because in the format of the Who we've got the luxury to do things the way we need to and it won't be a problem. But the reason it's worth bringing up is a lot of kids out there with Marshall stacks and earphones who drink a bottle of whiskey and then play guitar all night (like I used to do [should know]) and I've shot my hearing. It's painful and frustrating when little children talk to you and you can't hear them. It's going to be quite difficult, so I've decided I'm going to play a different style of guitar on stage with the Who. I'm going to play a bit like John Denver. What I've been looking for is a guy who can not so much copy what I did, but rather try and capture the spirit of it. I'm working with a guitarist at the moment who I think is very good. As soon as I know he's happy and capable of doing it I'll announce his name.

Pete Townshend on *Tommy*

Toronto, Canada
January 1995

PETE TOWNSHEND: The role of Tommy is most difficult to cast. We're seeing people this afternoon and as the immensely cynical Roger Waters once said, 'We're hoping to get what God wants.' We've really no control. Either God is going to send us a really fabulous Canadian for the role or we're going to have to use somebody from somewhere else.

It's very, very difficult. The qualities are almost definable by one's inability to define them. We're looking for someone who has a certain androgyny, a certain delicacy, a certain youthfulness, a childlike quality, but at the same time in the later stages of the play is able to convey some of the existential suffering that someone like that had been through. What a kid who has been through this bizarrely, surreally negative and abusive family would feel. Also, the actor has to move in and out of fantasy, as I said earlier. One of the things we've tried to do is make this a real play so when you look on stage and see real people you accept they're real people and that this is a real family. That this is a real story we've plucked out of the reality of the sixties. We look back at it and we think it was all nonsense but it was real!

I was there, I had a real mum and dad, real friends, and we took real drugs and did all that stuff! It's difficult casting Tommy, it really is. The Acid Queen is a difficult role to cast. Uncle Ernie is a difficult role to cast. It's partly because they suggest stereotypes which give you problems. You tend to find when people come in to perform they fall into what they *think* you want. Then we have to say, 'No, hold on a minute, just try to *be* this person. Try to be Tommy. Try to be Uncle Ernie. Imagine you were this middle-aged man with this inanimate child in your care and you had a propensity to abuse him.' You know, that kind of thing to help actors feel the consequence of the role rather than see the whole thing as a huge comic book.

You know famous rock stars, and I can speak from experience, are overpaid, spoiled brats and so many of the people from Hollywood wouldn't do this kind of thing. They're not lining up to do it. It's eight shows a week. It's a tough job and it's not the most highly paid gig you can get if you're the kind of name that would attract people to the theater. In any case, we want someone who can really do a good job and primarily for this production we would love to have somebody Canadian. A good, new Canadian discovery would be worth any number of Hollywood stars, I think.

I'm trying my hardest to come up with something new. This is very tough because I think what *Tommy* has done for me today in musical theater it did for me in the Who twenty-five years ago. It begs questions about what will happen next.

I think it's a quirky piece in some ways. Most of all Tommy's deaf, dumb, blindness is a metaphor for the spiritual veils we carry. We quite properly live out our lives on a daily basis and leave the spiritual stuff for God to work out. . . . It might be that one could find a Greek myth that could much more satisfactorily provide a vehicle for a bunch of songs. I could reel off a few. . . . What was important for Tommy in its early days though is that it made people think about who they were. . . .

I feel as though my life today is really worth living and that's really quite a tall order. I want to know that there is some point in being alive. And I think that when I sit down to write I have to try and come down off that cloud and say, 'Come on, Pete, fucking entertain! Write something people will enjoy.' I've always been a pretentious bastard. I think *Tommy* somehow worked for me in that role. . . . I'm very involved. [We've done three] shows in the past, [California], Broadway, and now the tour.

*   *   *

Pete: Twenty-five years age my main job was trying to get hits for the Who, but that's not my job today. My job is to try and tell stories which engage the general mass of people out there that want entertainment.

I was reminded the other day by our surviving manager about Kit Lambert, who was the most important part of our creative team at the time. He actually produced the record of *Tommy*. He was, if you like, the Svengali to my Trilby, to put it pompously. He used to listen to my work, pull it apart and nurture my writing. Chris Stamp, my partner, reminded me that I resisted making a film of *Tommy* then. They were film makers, these two guys. I think they only ended up managing the Who because they were looking to make a *Quadrophenia*-type film about the swinging sixties and wound up managing a rock band. They desperately wanted to make a movie of *Tommy* and I fought it, fought it, fought it! I remember I said, 'Cinema isn't big enough to contain rock 'n' roll!' That's how I used to think. I used to feel that rock was a huge spiritual thing that only happened in concert and occasionally on records when you were in an internal world. [It was] part of that very intimate engagement between writer and listener where I would sit writing songs in my little bedroom and you, the teenybopper, would hopefully be at home in your bedroom with earphones [which] would be a very, very pure line.

*   *   *

Question: You seem to be very possessive of *Tommy*. Is there any input from the other members of the band?
Pete: Nope. I have been possessive. I have actually blocked input from other members of the band. They had their say. . . . It's not about control. In a way you're not giving me due credit to my understanding of the creative process. What I actually had to do was give up control to Des McAnuff.

I couldn't deliver to him something I didn't own. I could only deliver what I was prepared to give up, which was my possessiveness of *Tommy*. I couldn't give up Roger Daltrey's possessiveness of *Tommy* or anybody else. I couldn't guarantee to Des, for example, what Who fans would feel about what he and I did to the story on Broadway. . . . You know I've been, not the creative director of the Who for many years, but I've certainly won that hat. I've been the director of a band called the Who for a long time with a number of very difficult players to deal with, including myself. I've always worn two hats. . . . I was a difficult guy to work with. A difficult artist to work with. Difficult to second

331

guess . . . I could sit and say, 'What the Who needs for its next album is this kind of song.' [I'd] sit down and write it and then get up on stage and find myself swearing and going nuts because I didn't have what I needed on that particular occasion to do the job I needed to. But what gets me really possessive about the piece is that around about the time I was working with Des on it I discovered how much it was the story of my life. And I resent the way it's been screwed around with by the other people in the band, including Kit Lambert and anybody else.

* * *

Pete: I'm glad to see [*Tommy*] feels like a real story. The [*Tommy*] film was very much surreal fantasy, an extension of the inner world. Somebody said something to me the other day (a guy who writes for radio) and we were talking about writing for radio. It's unheard of in North America, but in the UK we still have radio plays and he said the difference between writing for radio and film is with radio you have to write a story that is an experience from within rather than an externalized story. So the big transition for me, and what I'm so happy about today, is seeing the musical properly externalized. Seeing a real family, real people on stage and seeing ideas that were very much internal become real. . . .

My creative partnership with Roger has been one of the most exciting things in my life. He and I suddenly realized it still has possibilities. . . . I was the backroom boy and he was the front man and got, if not the critical glory, the glory of being the guy on stage who fronted everything. I think he probably felt straitjacketed (and probably still does) by the fact that suddenly, when the Who was over he was left as a voice, but without new songs to sing. What's interesting about our relationship is that my writing tended to be about human frailty which he delivered in a particularly passionate and visceral way. That was part of the extraordinary chemistry of the Who and that's something we're thinking about looking at again. Not under the Who banner, but certainly looking at trying to write a collection of songs for him that might say something he would like to say. It was a great partnership and I hope it's got another chapter, but who knows?

Pete Townshend Discography 1964–1995

Compiled by Sesa Giuliano

Catalog Number	Title	Labels

1964

British Releases

480 July 3	'I'm the Face'/'Zoot Suit' (the High Numbers)	Fontana

1965

British Releases

05926 January 15	'I Can't Explain'/'Bald Headed Woman'	Brunswick
05935 May 21	'Anyway, Anyhow, Anywhere'/'Daddy Rolling Stone'	Brunswick
05944 November 5	'My Generation'/'Shout and Shimmy'	Brunswick
LAT 8616 December 25	*My Generation* (Album)	Brunswick

American Releases

31725 February 13	'I Can't Explain'/'Bald Headed Woman'	Decca

31801 June 5	'Anyway, Anyhow, Anywhere'/'Anytime You Want Me'	Decca
31877 November 20	'My Generation'/'Out in the Street'	Decca

1966

British Releases

591001 March 4	'Substitute'/'Circles'	Reaction
591001 March 4	'Substitute'/'Instant Party'	Reaction
05956 March 11	'A Legal Matter'/'Instant Party'	Brunswick
591001 March 15	'Substitute'/'Waltz for a Pig'	Reaction
05965 August 12	'The Kids Are Alright'/'The Ox'	Brunswick
591004 August 26	'I'm a Boy'/'In the City'	Reaction
592001 November 11	*Ready Steady Who!* (Extended Play)	Reaction
05968 November 11	'La La La Lies'/'The Good's Gone'	Brunswick
591010 December 3	'Happy Jack'/'I've Been Away'	Reaction
593002 December 3	*A Quick One* (Album)	Reaction

American Releases

45-6409 April 2	'Substitute'/'Waltz for a Pig'	ATCO
DL 4664mono DL 74664stereo April	*The Who Sings My Generation* (Album)	Decca
31988 July	'The Kids Are Alright'/'A Legal Matter'	Decca
32058 December 10	'I'm a Boy'/'In the City'	Decca

1967

British Releases

604 002 April 22	'Pictures of Lily'/'Doctor, Doctor'	Track

604 006 June 30	'The Last Time'/'Under My Thumb'	Track
604 011 October 14	'I Can See for Miles'/'Someone's Coming'	Track
612 002mono 613 002stereo December 16	*The Who Sell Out* (Album)	Track

American Releases

32114 March 18	'Happy Jack'/'Whiskey Man'	Decca
DL 4892mono DL 74892stereo May	*Happy Jack* (Album)	Decca
32156 June 24	'Pictures of Lily'/'Doctor, Doctor'	Decca
45-6509 August	'Substitute'/'Waltz for a Pig'	ATCO
32206 October 14	'I Can See for Miles'/'Mary Anne with the Shaky Hand'	Decca

1968

British Releases

604 023 June 15	'Dogs'/'Call Me Lightning'	Track
604 024 September 18	'Magic Bus'/'Dr Jekyll & Mr Hyde'	Track
612(613) 006 October 12	*Direct Hits* (Album)	Track

American Releases

DL 4950mono DL 74950stereo January 6	*The Who Sell Out* (Album)	Decca
32288 March 16	'Call Me Lightning'/'Dr Jekyll & Mr Hyde'	Decca
32362 July 27	'Magic Bus'/'Someone's Coming'	Decca
5064mono 75064stereo September	*Magic Bus – The Who on Tour* (Album)	Decca

1969

British Releases

604 027 March 7	'Pinball Wizard'/'Dogs Part II'	Track
613 013/4 May 23	*Tommy* (Album)	Track
613 016	*The House That Track Built* (The Who plus various artists) (Album)	Track

American Releases

732465 March 22	'Pinball Wizard'/'Dogs Part II'	Decca
DXSW 7205 May 31	*Tommy* (Album)	Decca
732519 July 5	'I'm Free'/'We're Not Gonna Take It'	Decca

1970

British Releases

604 036 March 21	'The Seeker'/'Here for More'	Track
2406 001 May 23	*Live At Leeds* (Album)	Track
2407 001/2/3/4/5 May 23	*Backtrack 1–5* (Five sampler albums featuring the Who) (Album)	Track
2662 001 June	*Woodstock* (The Who plus various artists) (Album)	Atlantic
2094 002 July 10	'Summertime Blues'/'Heaven and Hell'	Track
2094 004 October 10	'See Me, Feel Me'/'Overture from *Tommy*'	Track
2252 001 November 7	*Tommy* (Extended Play)	Track
2407 007 November 7	*Backtrack 7 Mixed Bag* (Album)	Track
2407 008 November 7	*Backtrack 8 A Quick One* (Album)	Track

| 2407 009
November 7 | *Backtrack 9 The Who Sell Out*
(Album) | Track |

American Releases

32670 April	'The Seeker'/'Here for More'	Decca
DL 79175 May 16	*Live at Leeds* (Album)	Decca
SD 3-500 May	*Woodstock* (Album)	Cotillion
32708 July 11	'Summertime Blues'/'Heaven and Hell'	Decca
732729 August	'See Me, Feel Me'/'Overture from *Tommy*'	Decca

1971

British Releases

2094 009 June 25	'Won't Get Fooled Again'/'I Don't Even Know Myself'	Track
2408 102 August 25	*Who's Next* (Album)	Track
2094 012 October 15	'Let's See Action'/'When I Was a Boy'	Track
2406 006 December 3	*Meaty Beaty Big and Bouncy* Album	Track

American Releases

32846 July 17	'Won't Get Fooled Again'/'I Don't Even Know Myself'	Decca
79182 August 14	*Who's Next* (Album)	Decca
79184 October 30	*Meaty Beaty Big and Bouncy* (Album)	Decca
32888 November 6	'Behind Blue Eyes'/'My Wife'	Decca

1972

British Releases

| 2406 007
May 13 | *Tommy Part 1*
(Album) | Track |

2094 102 June 17	'Join Together'/'Baby Don't You Do It'	Track
2406 008 June 24	*Tommy Part 2* (Album)	Track
October	*Who Came First* (Album)	Track
2094 106 December 23	'Relay'/'Waspman'	Track

American Releases

ODE SP 99001	*Tommy/As Performed by the London Symphony Orchestra and Chamber Choir with Guest Soloists* (Album)	Ode
32983 July 8	'Join Together'/'Baby Don't You Do It'	Decca
October	*Who Came First* (Album)	Decca
33041 November 25	'The Relay'/'Waspman'	Track

1973

British Releases

2094 115 September	'5.15'/'Water'	Track
2657 013 November 16	*Quadrophenia* (Album)	Track

American Releases

40152 October 27	'Love Reign o'er Me'/'Water'	Track
10004 November 3	*Quadrophenia* (Album)	MCA2
MW 2080stereo	*Eric Clapton's Rainbow Concert* (Pete plays guitar) (Album)	RSO

1974

British Releases

2409 205 May 25	*Aniseed* (Album)	Track

2409 206 May 25	*Peppermint* (Album)	Track
2409 207 May 25	*Coconut* (Album)	Track
2409 209/10 June 1	*A Quick One/The Who Sell Out* (Album)	Track
2406 116 September 28	*Odds and Sods* (Album)	Track

American Releases

40182 January 12	'The Real Me'/'I'm One'	Track
2126 October 12	*Odds and Sods* (Album)	MCA
40330 November	'Postcard'/'Put the Money Down'	Track
2-4067 November 30	*A Quick One (Happy Jack)/The Who Sell Out* (Album)	MCA
2-4068 November 30	*My Generation/Magic Bus* (Album)	MCA

1975

British Releases

2657 014 March	*Tommy Original Sound Track* (Album)	Polydor
2490 129 October 18	*The Who by Numbers* (Album)	Polydor

American Releases

PD2-9505 February 22	*Tommy Original Sound Track* (Album)	Polydor
2161 October 25	*The Who by Numbers* (Album)	MCA
40475 November 22	'Squeezebox'/'Success Story'	MCA

1976

British Releases

2121 275 January 24	'Squeezebox'/'Success Story'	Polydor

2683 069 September	*The Story of the Who* (Album)	Polydor
003-76 July	*With Love* (Album)	Eel Pie Recording Productions Ltd.
2058 803 October 30	'Substitute'/'I'm a Boy'/'Pictures of Lily'	Polydor

American Releases

SD 36-126	*Mahoney's Last Stand* (Ron Wood and Ronnie Lane; Pete Townshend plays guitar on 'Tonight's Number' and 'Car Radio') (Album)	ATCO
40603 August 7	'Slip Kid'/'Dreaming from the Waist'	MCA

1977

British Releases

2058 944	'Street in the City'/'Annie'	Polydor

American Releases

November	'My Baby Gives It Away'/ 'Lane Track'	MCA
November	'Street in the City'/'Lane Track'	Polydor

1978

April	'Keep Me Turning'/'Lane Track'	MCA
2121 361 July 14	'Who Are You'/'Had Enough'	Polydor
2683 084 August 18 MCA P-14950	*Who Are You* (Album) *Who Are You* (Picture Disc) (Album)	Polydor MCA

American Releases

40948 August	'Who Are You'/'Had Enough'	MCA
3050 August 25	*Who Are You* (Album)	MCA

40978 December 2	'Trick of the Light'/'905'	MCA

1979

British Releases

2121 383 April 1	'Long Live Rock'/'I'm the Face'/'My Wife'	Polydor
2675 179 June	*The Kids Are Alright Soundtrack* (Album)	Polydor
2001 916 September	'5.15'/'I'm the One'	Polydor
2625 037 October 6	*Quadrophenia Soundtrack* (Album)	Polydor

American Releases

MCA2–11005 June 23	*The Kids Are Alright Soundtrack* (Album)	MCA
41053 June	'Long Live Rock'/'My Wife'	MCA
2022 September	'5.15'/'I'm the One'	Polydor
PD2-6235 October 6	*Quadrophenia Soundtrack* (Album)	Polydor

1980

British Releases

Door 4 March 4	'I'm the Face'/'Zoot Suit'	Backdoor
 April 14	*Empty Glass* (Album)	ATCO
May	'Rough Boys'/'And I Moved'	ATCO
 June	'Let My Love Open the Door' 'Classified'/'Grey Hound Girl'	ATCO
V2179 October	*My Generation* (Album)	Virgin
November	'Keep On Working'/'Jools and Jim'	ATCO

American Releases

DJ 570 March	'I'm the Face'/'Zoot Suit'	Mercury

BEHIND BLUE EYES

May 10	*Empty Glass* (Album)	ATCO
June	'Let My Love Open the Door'/ 'And I Moved'	ATCO
October	'A Little Is Enough'/ 'Cat's in the Cupboard'	ATCO
November	'Rough Boys'/'Jools and Jim'	ATCO

1981

British Releases

2002 044 February 27	'You Better You Bet'/'The Quiet One'	Polydor
2302 106 March	*Face Dances* (Album)	Polydor
K 60153 March	*Kampuchea* (various artists including The Who) (Album)	Atlantic
WHO 5 May 1	'Don't Let Go the Coat'/'You'	Polydor
2675 216 May 23	*Phases* (Box Set) (Album)	Polydor

American Releases

WBS 49698 March	'You Better You Bet'/'The Quiet One'	Warner Bros.
WB HS 3516 March	*Face Dances* (Album)	Warner Bros.
SD-2 7005 March	*Kampuchea* (Album)	Atlantic
WBS 49743	'Don't Let Go the Coat'/'You'	Warner Bros.
12001 September 11	*Hooligans* (Album)	MCA2

1982

British Releases

38-149-2	*All the Best Cowboys Have Chinese Eyes* (Album)	ATTCO

WHOD 5066 September 4	*It's Hard* (Album)	Polydor
WHO 6 September 25	'Athena'/'A Man Is a Man'	Polydor
WHOPX 6 October	'Athena'/'Won't Get Fooled Again'	Polydor

American Releases

WB 23731-1/2 September 4	*It's Hard* (Album)	Warner Bros.
WBS 7-29905 September 4	'Athena'/'It's Your Turn'	Warner Bros.
WB7-29814 December	'Eminence Front'/'One at a Time'	Warner Bros.
WB7-29731 D	'It's Hard'/'Dangerous'	Warner Bros.

1983

British Releases

March	*Scoop* (Album)	
SPELP-9 August	*Rarities Volume I 1966–1969* (Album)	Polydor
SPELP-10	*Rarities Volume II 1970–1973* (Album)	Polydor

American Releases

GWB 0412	'You Better You Bet'/ 'Don't Let Go the Coat'	Warner Bros.
5408 March	*Who's Greatest Hits* (Album)	MCA
March	*Scoop* (Album)	

1984

British Releases

WHO 1 November 10	*Who's Last* (Album)	MCA
927 November	'Twist & Shout'/'I Can't Explain'	MCA

WHOD November 17	*The Singles* (Album)	Polydor

American Releases

8018 November	*Who's Last* (Album)	MCA2

1985

British Releases

252 392-1	*White City* (Album)	ATCO
IM DP4 October	*The Who Collection* (Album)	Impression

American Releases

U8859T 258859-0	'Face the Face'/'Hiding Out' (Maxi Single)	WEA
5641 November 30	*Who's Missing* (Album)	MCA

1986

British Releases

October	*Deep End Live* (Album)

American Releases

October	*Deep End Live* (Album)

1987

British Releases

March	*Another Scoop* (Album)

American Releases

March	*Another Scoop* (Album)

5712 April 11	*Who's Missing* (Album)	MCA

1988

835 389-1/2 March 18	*Who's Better, Who's Best*	Polydor
887 352-1/2 March	*This is My Generation by the Who* (Extended Play)	Polydor
887 576-7 May	'Won't Get Fooled Again'/'Boney Moronie'	Polydor
887 576-1/2 May	*Won't Get Fooled Again* (Extended Play)	Polydor

American Releases

2 8031 November 26	*Who's Better, Who's Best* (Album)	MCA
MCAD-37303 September	'My Generation'/'I Can't Explain'/'Happy Jack'/ 'I Can See for Miles' (CD Series)	MCA

1989

British Releases

The Iron Man
(Album)

American Releases

The Iron Man
(Album)

1990

British Releases

VDT 102 March	*Join Together* (From the 1989 tour with live cuts) (Live Box Set) (Album)	Virgin
VS 1259 March	*Join Together/I Can See for Miles/Behind Blue Eyes* (From the 1989 tour with live tracks) (Album)	Virgin
VST/VSCDT 1259 March	*Join Together* (Album)	Virgin

BEHIND BLUE EYES

American Releases

L1989 January 17	*The Rock 'n' Roll Hall of Fame* (The Who with other inductees) (Album)	Rock 'n' Roll
MCA3-19501 March 24	*Join Together* (Includes 'Tommy' and live tracks from the 1989 tour) (Live Box Set)	MCA

1992

American Releases

R 70596 October 9	*The Monterey International Pop Festival* (CD Box Set)	Rhino

1993

American Releases

7 82494-2	*PsychoDerelict* (Album)	Atlantic
7 82535-2	*PsychoDerelict Music Only* (Album)	Atlantic
10801 March	*Tommy* (CD)	MCAD

1994

British Releases

521 751-2 May MCA	*The Who: Thirty Years of Maximum R&B* (Box Set)	Polydor
D4/C4-11020 May	*The Who: Thirty Years of Maximum R&B* (Box Set)	MCA

BOOTLEGS

Date Unknown	*The Who Vs. Bizarre Mr. Pig* (Album)	Unknown
1973	*Who's Zoo* (Picture Disc) (Album)	RSO

1974	*Closer to Queen Mary* (Album)	Trade Mark of Quality
1974	*Fillmore East* (Album)	Trade Mark of Quality
1974	*Radio London* (Album)	Trade Mark of Quality
1974	*The Genius of Peter Townshend* (Album)	Trade mark of Quality
052 Date Unknown	*Who-La-Hoop* (Recorded in Philadephia) (Album)	K&S Records
1980	*Jai Baba for Pete's Sake* (Album)	Moon Records
September 9, 1978	*Starring the Who! Live at Woodstock* (Album)	No Further Information Available
4-88001 Date Unknown	*Who's Back* (CD)	Backtrax
LLCD 010 Date Unknown	*Fillmore East* (CD)	Living Legend
0888 D008-2 Date Unknown	*Furious Prelude* (CD)	World Productions of Compact Music
1288 D014-2 1988	*Come and Drum* (CD)	World Productions of Compact Music
02CD 3211 Date Unknown	*Obscure and Oblique* (CD)	Early Years
02 CD 3212 Date Unknown	*Tommy Live* (CD)	Early Years
Date Unknown	*Live in Amsterdam* (CD)	
GDR CD 8910 1989	*Tales from the Who* (CD)	
No Further Information Available	*Shea Stadium '82* (Album)	
No Further Information Available	*Live at the Marquee Club* (Recorded June 1964) (Album)	
No Further Information Available	*BBC '65–'67* (Album and CD)	
No Further Information Available	*Monterey '67* (Recorded June 18, 1967) (Six Songs) (Cassette Tape)	
No Further Information Available	*Fillmore '68* (Recorded April 5, 1968) (Album and CD)	
No Further Information Available	*Gather Your Wits* (Recorded in Dallas, September 1969) (Two Albums)	

No Further Information Available	*Amsterdam* (Recorded at the Concertgebouw, September 29, 1969) (Album and CD)	
No Further Information Available	*Mods and Rockers* (Recorded December 6, 1973, in Largo, Maryland) (Two Albums)	
No Further Information Available	*Decidedly Belated Response* (Recorded in 1974 from *The King Biscuit Flower Hour*) (Two Albums)	
No Further Information Available	*Tales from the Who* (Recorded in 1974 from *The King Biscuit Flower Hour*) (Two Albums)	
No Further Information Available	*When the Sun Was Going Down.* (Recorded May 18, 1974, at Charlton Athletic Football Ground, London) (Two Albums)	
No Further Information Available	*Live at Swansea 1976* (Recorded in Wales on June 12, 1976) (Two Albums)	
No Further Information Available	*Long Live Rock* (Recorded in 1979 in Europe) (Two Albums)	
No Further Information Available	*Live at Madison Square Garden* (Recorded in New York on September 16, 1979) (The cover of the December 1979 *Time* magazine was used as the cover sleeve for this album) (Three Albums)	
No Further Information Available	*'79 Tour–Gonna Rape You!* (Recorded December 15, 1979 in Hartford, Connecticut) (Three Albums)	
No Further Information Available	*Live at Rockpalast* (Recorded from a simu-cast German television/ radio show, Grugahalle, Essen, March 28, 1981) (Two Albums)	
No Further Information Available	*Tommy* (Recorded from a stereo broadcast of the Radio City Music Hall, New York show on June 27, 1989) (Album)	
No Further Information Available	*Jaguar Anyone?* (Recorded from various formats) (Album)	
U.K. release	'Rough Mix'	Polydor
U.S. release	'Rough Mix'	MCA
U.K. release	'Forever's No Time At All'/ 'This Song is Green'	Track
UK release 196??	*I Am* (Meher Baba album to which Pete contributes) (Album)	
UK release 1970	*Happy Birthday* (Album)	

UK Release	*Thunderclap Newman* (By Thunderclap Newman; produced by Pete Townshend) (Album)
UK release	*Hollywood Dream* (By Thunderclap Newman, produced by Pete Townshend) (Album)

Note: The above is by no means completely accurate. It does, however, reflect the vast majority of Pete Townshend's work with the Who, other artists, and his solo career. A sampling of bootlegs has been included for the purpose of historical accuracy. While there have been literally hundreds of Who bootlegs over the past thirty years, only a very few are represented here.

A Note on Sources

Throughout the long process of researching and writing this book I have been fortunate in enlisting the participation of many of the people closest to Pete over the last fifty-plus years. Among them several asked not to be identified for reasons best known to themselves, a request I have honored without exception. For the most part, however, there was no such trepidation, and I therefore acknowledge their kindness in having confided in me their memories of not only Pete, but also the Who and the marvelously heady, bygone days that spawned them.

Bibliography

Books

Anzar, Naosherwan, *The Beloved: The Life and Work of Meher Baba.* Myrtle Beach S. C.: Sheriar Press, 1974.

Anzar, Naosherwan. *The Glass Pearl: The Untold LSD Story.* Bombay: Glow Publications, 1971.

Baba, Meher. *Discourses.* Myrtle Beach S. C.: Sheriar Press, 1987.

Barnes, Richard. *The Who: Thirty Years Maximum R&B*

Butler, Dougal, with Chris Trengove and Peter Lawrence. *Moon the Loon: The Amazing Rock and Roll Life of Keith Moon.* London: Star Books, 1981.

Coleman, Ray. *Survivor: The Authorized Biography of Eric Clapton.* London: Little, Brown, and Co. (UK), 1985.

de Villeneuve, Justin. *An Affectionate Punch.* London: Sidgwick and Jackson, 1986.

Giuliano, Geoffrey. *Blackbird: The Life and Times of Paul McCartney.* New York: Dutton, 1991.

Herman, Gary. *Rock 'n' Roll Babylon.* New York: Perigee Books, 1982.

Hopkinson, Tom, and Dorothy Hopkinson. *Much Silence: Meher Baba: His Life and Work.* New York: Dodd, Mead, and Co.

Hotchner, A. E. *Blown Away.* New York: Fireside, 1990.

Kamin, Philip, and Peter Goddard. *The Who Farewell Tour.* Toronto: Musson, 1983.

Townshend, Peter. *Horse's Neck.* London: Faber and Faber, 1985.

Tremlett, George. *The Who.* London: Futura, 1975.

White, Timothy. *Rock Lives.* New York: Henry Holt, 1990.

Periodicals

The Who: Thirty Years Maximum R&B, CD booklet. London: Trinifold
   Management, 1994.
Billboard, magazine.
Elle, magazine.
Guitar Player, magazine.
Life, magazine.
Melody Maker, magazine.
Music Echo, magazine.
Musician, magazine.
Newsday, magazine.
Newsweek, magazine.
Oui, magazine.
Penthouse, magazine.
People, magazine.
Phonograph Record, magazine.
Pop Scene, magazine.
Q, magazine.
Relay, magazine.
Rolling Stone, magazine.
Spin, magazine.
Ten Years of Rolling Stone, magazine.
Time, magazine.
TV Times, magazine.
Boston Herald, newspaper.
Chicago Tribune, newspaper.
Evening Standard, newspaper.
London Observer, newspaper.
New Music Express, newspaper.
New York *Daily News,* newspaper.
New York Post, newspaper.
New York Times, newspaper.
Observer, newspaper.
Philadelphia Inquirer, newspaper.
Sun, newspaper.
Sunday Times, newspaper.
Toronto Star, newspaper.
Wall Street Journal, newspaper.
Washington Post, newspaper.

Interviews

Ginger Baker
Pete Bennett
Peter Brown
Jack Bruce
Kitty Davey
Steve Holly
'Kathy Browning'
Denny Laine
Jo Jo Laine
Fred Seaman
Tony Secunda
Vivian Stanshall
'Terri'

Press Conferences

Tommy Press Conference, Toronto, 1995.

Videography

Pete Townshend Live. Polygram Video, 1993
The Kids Are Alright.
The Who Thirty Years of Maximum R&B.
The Who's Tommy; *The Amazing Journey.* Buena Vista Home Video,
    1995.

Acknowledgements

Researcher: Brenda Giuliano
Photo Researcher: Sesa Nichole Giuliano
Intern: Devin Giuliano

The author would like to thank the following for their kindness and selfless hard work in helping realize this book.

Jagannatha Dasa Adikari
Dr. Mirza Beg
Deborah Lynn Black
Stefano Castino
Vrinda Rani Devi Dasi
Robin Scott Giuliano
Avalon and India Giuliano
His Divine Grace B. H. Maçalniloy Maharaja Goswami
Jasper Humprhies
ISKCON
Myrna Juliana
Larry Khan
Dr. Michael Klapper
Allan Lang
Donald Lehr
Andrew Lownie
Mark Studios, Clarence, New York
David Lloyd McIntyre
His Divine Grace A. C. Bhativedanta Swami Prabhupada
Scala Films
Self Realization Institute of America (SRI)
Wendell and Joan Smith

BEHIND BLUE EYES

Edward Veltman
Robert Wallace
Dr. Ronald Zucker

And, of course, Pete.

Photo Credits

Index